R Programming and Its Applications in Financial Mathematics

R Programming and Its Applications in Financial Mathematics

Shuichi Ohsaki

Chief Japan Rates Strategist, American Investment Bank, Tokyo, Japan

Jori Ruppert-Felsot

Equity Derivatives Trader, Tokyo, Japan

Daisuke Yoshikawa

Hokkai-Gakuen University, Sapporo, Hokkaido, Japan

CRC Press

Taylor & Francis Group

Boca Raton London New York

CRC Press is an imprint of the
Taylor & Francis Group, an **informa** business

A SCIENCE PUBLISHERS BOOK

CRC Press
Taylor & Francis Group
6000 Broken Sound Parkway NW, Suite 300
Boca Raton, FL 33487-2742

First issued in paperback 2020

© 2018 by Taylor & Francis Group, LLC
CRC Press is an imprint of Taylor & Francis Group, an Informa business

No claim to original U.S. Government works

ISBN-13: 978-1-4987-6609-8 (hbk)
ISBN-13: 978-0-367-78147-7 (pbk)

Visit the Taylor & Francis Web site at
http://www.taylorandfrancis.com

and the CRC Press Web site at
http://www.crcpress.com

Preface

The importance of having basic knowledge of computational methods continues to increase for those working in the financial services industry. Computational finance theory has developed along with advancements in computing technology. The objective of this book is therefore to present an introduction to the various computing methods used in the financial service industry, via the R programming language. This book is intended for graduate students who are interested in computational finance, junior bankers, economists and traders working in the finance industry.

We have several reasons why R has been used, rather than other available languages; e.g., C++, C#, Java, Python, EXCEL VBA, and MatLab, etc. First, R is available free and is an open source programming language. As such it is easily extensible through the addition of packages and has a large and active community of R users. And as a high-level scripting language, it is very easy to set up and to use. Second, R was developed for statistical computation and thus comes equipped with various packages which enable us to do regression analysis and statistical tests, etc. This reduces the time and effort required for implementation of many statistical methods and allows us to execute numerical experiments easily. Third, R comes equipped with a graphic capability to visualize large sets of data and the results of analysis. This is an attractive feature, particularly if we want to produce high-quality graphics for publication. Further, the basics that we learn here with R, are easily applicable to other languages, because many languages, like C# and Python have similar coding logic, albeit different syntax.

We expect readers to write and execute the sample code introduced in this book. Following the sample code will help the readers' understanding of the theory and improve their facility with R. Of course, incomplete understanding of theory may lead to codes which do not work well. However, the process of correcting an incomplete code is an important step in understanding the theory and improving one's coding technique.

We focus on two major aspects of computational finance theory: (1) statistical analysis of financial data, and (2) the valuation of financial instruments. We have divided the book into some parts. Section I of this book is devoted to statistical and time-series analysis, Section II covers the finance theory for the valuation of financial instruments and we focus on numerical methods for derivative pricing in Section III.

This book was first published in Japanese, derived from sets of lectures given by the authors Ohsaki and Yoshikawa at the Graduate School of Management, Kyoto University in the Spring terms of 2008, 2009 and 2010. The lectures formed the basis of Section II and III, while Chapter 1 and Section I were written for the publication of the Japanese version of the book. Section 3.4.3 and Appendix B were added for the current English version of the book.

We would like to thank the publishers, especially, the editor Vijay Primlani for his understanding and patience and Tetsuya Ishii who is the editor of the Japanese version for his understanding regarding the publication of the English version. We also thank Toshifumi Ikemori, Hideki Iwaki, Yoshihiko Uchida, and Zensho Yoshida for their helpful advice and support in completing this manuscript.

Shuichi Ohsaki
Jori Ruppert-Felsot
Daisuke Yoshikawa

Contents

Chapter 1

Introduction to R Programming

CONTENTS

The objective of this book is to learn the theory of finance using the R language, which is a programming language developed specifically for numerical calculation. Before the introduction of finance theory, we need to build the cases for using R. Thus, the first chapter is devoted to introducing R, its installation, and the basic usage of R. Readers already familiar with R programming can skip this chapter.

1.1 Installation of R

Let us start with the installation of R.[1] We can get the basic files for installation and packages from the website of the CRAN project (see Figure 1.1)

`http://www.r-project.org/index.html`

To get an exe file for installation of R, click `download R` (as of July 2017). Then, the screen transits to the following one like Figure 1.2. Choose a mirror site close to your location. Thus, for Japan we choose `https://cran.ism.ac.jp/`.

Then the screen transits to that like Figure 1.3. For Windows users, click "Download R for Windows" on the screen "The Comprehensive R Archive Network". If you are not a Windows user, then choose the appropriate option.

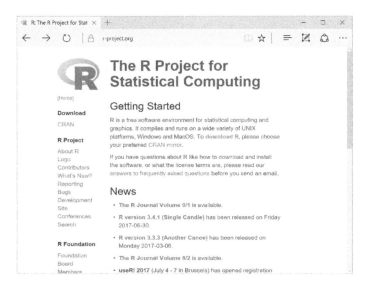

Figure 1.1: Click "download R" on the page "The R Project for Statistical Computing"

---

[1]This section covers the installation of R from a windows-based executable file. For installation on Mac choose "Download R for (Mac) OS X", and on Linux choose "Download R for Linux" (Figure 1.3). Compilation from source code depends on the operation system. Here, we just show the example based on windows-based executable file.

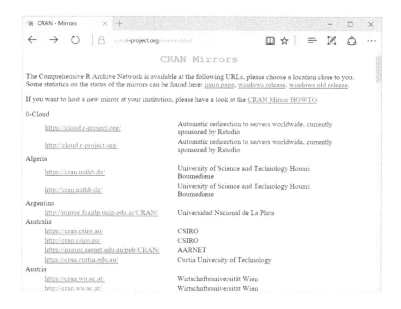

Figure 1.2: Choose a mirror site

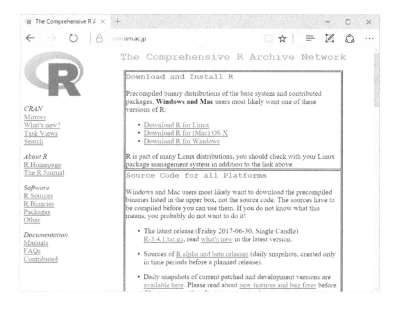

Figure 1.3: Click "Download R for Windows" on the screen "The Comprehensive R Archive Network"

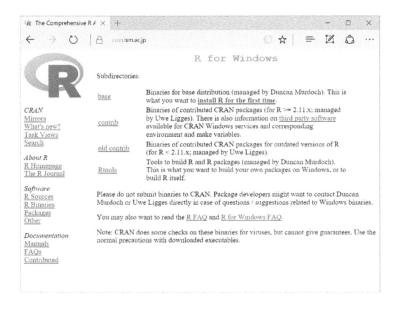

Figure 1.4: Click "base" or "install R for the first time"

Then, the screen like 1.4 appears. Click "base" or "install R for the first time".

On the next screen Figure 1.5, by clicking "Download R 3.4.1 for Windows", we can get "R-3.4.1-win.exe" (3.4.1 is the version name).

You can skip this procedure and go directly to the following site, if you use Windows.

https://cran.ism.ac.jp/bin/windows/base/

The last step is just to expand the exe file so that you can easily install R.

Now let's start R. You should be able to start R from the shortcut on your desktop or via the start menu. If your installation was successful, you should see the R console appear like Figure 1.6.

You can close the window and exit R by running the command q() from the console view (Figure 1.7). You can also quit R by selecting "Exit" in the "File" menu.

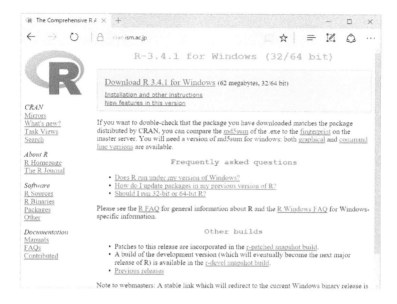

Figure 1.5: On the screen "R-3.4.1 for Windows (32/64 bit)", click "Download R 3.4.1 for Windows". Then, we can get "R-3.4.1-win.exe"

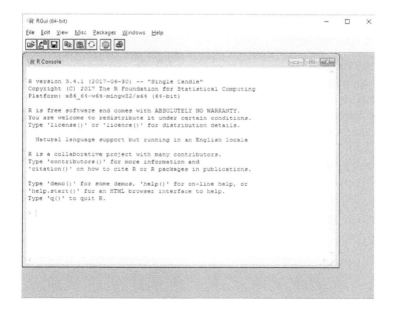

Figure 1.6: Start screen of R

Figure 1.7: Screen for quitting R

Now let's start to learn R programming by example. First, note a few things about R:

- It may be better to specify explicitly the directory to read data or scripts or write results to files in the designated directory. Later, we introduce how to read and write files in the directory. To specify the directory, click "Change directory" from the "File" menu, and choose the directory you like.

- Comment statement: Any line that starts with the # character is interpreted as a comment statement, not regarded as the programming statement. If we put # in the middle of the line, any following text is regarded as a comment.

1.2 Operators

Firstly we introduce important operators of R, i.e., arithmetic, comparative and logical operators.

The arithmetic operators includes + for addition of two scalars or vectors, − for subtraction of second scalar or vector from the first ones, * for multiplication, both scalars or vectors, / for division of the first scalar or vector by the second ones, %% for the reminder of the division, %/% for the quotient of the first scalar or vector by the second one and ^ for the exponent.

```
> 1+2
[1] 3
> 3-5
[1] -2
> 3*2
[1] 6
> 5/2
[1] 2.5
> 5%%2
[1] 1
```

```
> 5%/%2
[1] 2
> 2^3
[1] 8
```

R is also equipped with comparative operators. To test whether variables are equal to each other, we use the comparative operator ==. To test if it is not equal, we use the operator !=. For comparisons of magnitude (inequalities), we use >, >=, <, or <=.

Further, R has logical operators like && for "AND" and || for "OR". Comparative and logical operators are often used in the conditional statement described in section 1.5.1.

In addition to these operators, the most basic operator is assignment operators; e.g., <-, <<- and =.

1.3 Data structure

R is equipped with the following types of variables:

- numeric

- complex

- logical

- character

In other programming languages, e.g., C, we need to declare the type of variable like integer or double. However, in R we can declare a variable by name only without explicitly declaring a type. In general, we should avoid giving variable names, which conflict with variables, constants, or functions defined in R by default, such as pi, sin, log.

R has several useful functions that we can use to interrogate the type of variables and data.

```
> x <- 1
> is.numeric(x) # check whether the data x is numeric
[1] TRUE
> mode(x) # output the type of x
[1] "numeric"
> x <- "foo"
> is.numeric(x)
[1] FALSE
```

```
> # since it is not numeric but character, the output is FALSE
> mode(x)
[1] "character" # we can confirm it is character
> # by using the function mode()
> x <- 2+4i
> is.complex(x) # check whether x is complex number or not
[1] TRUE
> is.numeric(x)
[1] FALSE
> mode(x)
[1] "complex"
> x <- c(T,F) # generate a vector of logical values
> mode(x)
[1] "logical"
> # generate a vector of characters and numeric values,
> x <- c("foo",3)
> mode(x) # and to check the type
[1] "character"
```

The above example shows the priority of type assignment to variables in R. The assignment hierarchy is given as follows:

```
character > complex > numeric > logical
```

Let's check this order of priority.

```
> # generate a vector of a complex number and a character
> x <- c(3+4i,"foo")
> mode(x) # check the type of x
[1] "character"
> # generate a vector of a complex number and numeric number
> x <- c(3+4i,3)
> mode(x) # check the type of x again
[1] "complex"
> # generate a vector of a numeric number and logical number
> x <- c(3.0,TRUE)
> mode(x) # check the type of x again
[1] "numeric"
```

This hierarchy gives a criterion for R to decide data type. Indeed, if TRUE is substituted into a variable, it is regarded as logical. However, if the same "TRUE" has quotation signs, it is regarded as character. Similarly, "3+4i" is substituted into a variable, it is regarded as character, although it is regarded as complex without quotation.

For types of variables stated above, R is equipped with the following data structure.

■ scalar

■ vector

■ matrix

■ list

■ data frame

■ factor

1.3.1 Scalar

Scalars in R can be of the following types: numeric number, complex number, characters, and logical values. We do not need to be concerned with the difference between them. Let us describe the following in console view and assign the number 4 to the variable x:

```
>x <- 4
>x # display the value of the variable x
[1] 4
```

We can also use the operator = for variable assignment. However, the common usage in R is the operator <- which we follow in this book.

Basic arithmetic calculations such as addition, subtraction, multiplication and division are straightforward in R.

```
>y <- -3.2 # substitute -3.2 into y
>x+y # sum x and y
[1] 0.8

>x^10 # calculate the tenth power of x
[1] 1048576
> x^100
[1] 1.606938e+60
> x^1000
[1] Inf
```

Inf means infinity. This implies that the result exceeds the limit of the order that R can calculate.

To specify a complex number, we add the suffix i.

```
> 1i
[1] 0+1i
> 0i
[1] 0+0i
> i
Error: object 'i' not found
> 1+2i
[1] 1+2i
> (1+2i)*(2+1i)
[1] 0+5i
```

The above error message implies that i by itself is not interpreted as a complex number.

Characters between single quotation mark' or double quotation marks" are interpreted as a character sequence.

```
> # substitute the character sequence "character" into y
> y <- "character"
> y
[1] "character"
> # substitute the character sequence "pasted" into z
> z <- "pasted"
> y+z
Error in y + z : non-numeric argument to binary operator
```

The addition operator is not defined for two character sequences. To combine (concatenate) character sequences, we use the function paste().

```
> paste(y,z)
[1] "character pasted"
> paste(z,y)
[1] "pasted character"
```

If you do not want a blank space between the two character sequences, you need to specify a third input as follows:

```
> paste(y,z,sep="")
[1] "characterpasted"
```

Here, `sep` means the character separator between the input strings, which is a blank character by default. If we denote the inside of `sep=","`, it works as follows:

```
> paste(y,z,sep=",")
[1] "character,pasted"
```

We can use logical numbers. Logical numbers consists of the value of True and False. The logical value true, is denoted in R by T, or TRUE, and the logical value false by F or FALSE. These are case sensitive in R.

```
> T
[1] TRUE
> FALSE
[1] FALSE
> false
Error: object 'false' not found
> TRUE
[1] TRUE
```

Let's try the following simple calculations.

Exercise

1. $(3 \times 4 + 3.5)/3.3$

2. $(1 + 3i) \times (3 + 3i)$

3. 'My'+'name'+'is'+'(Daisuke)'

1.3.2 Vector

Vectors consist of a set of scalars and can be generated by the function `c()`.

```
> x <- c(0,1,2,3,4)
> x
[1] 0 1 2 3 4
> y <- c("tokyo","kyoto")
> y
[1] "tokyo" "kyoto"
> x[2] # extract second element of the vector
[1] 1
> y[1] # extract first element of the vector
[1] "tokyo"
> x[c(1,3,5)] # extract 1st, 3rd and 5th elements together
[1] 0 2 4
```

The multiplication of vectors is defined as an element-wise product, rather than as an inner product of vectors.

```
> x <- c(1,2,3)
> y <- c(3,4,1)
> x*y
[1] 3 8 3
```

The example below is an artificial calculation to derive an error; to multiply vectors which are defined as different dimensions.

```
> y <- c(3,4,1,1)
> x*y
[1]  0  4  2  3 12
Warning message:
In x * y : longer object length is not a multiple of shorter
object length
```

This example shows us that we need to make sure that the dimensions of vectors are equal.

```
> y <- c(3,4,1) # redefine y as 3-dimensional vector
> x*y
[1] 3 8 3
```

To calculate the inner product of two vectors, we use %*%. Alternatively, we can use sum(x*y) which returns the same result.

```
> x%*%y
      [,1]
[1,]   14
```

The function seq() allows us to generate a vector with a sequence of numbers.

```
> # generate a sequence from 0 to 3 by increments of 0.5
> x <- seq(0,3,by=0.5)
> x
[1] 0.0 0.5 1.0 1.5 2.0 2.5 3.0
> # generate a sequence from 0 to 3 with length (the number
> # of elements) 5
> y <- seq(0,3,length=5)
> y
[1] 0.00 0.75 1.50 2.25 3.00
```

```
> z <- 1:10 # generate a sequence from 1 to 10
by increments of 1
> z
 [1]  1  2  3  4  5  6  7  8  9 10
> z <- 10:1 # generate a sequence from 10 to 1
by decrements of 1
> z
 [1] 10  9  8  7  6  5  4  3  2  1
> z[3:8]# extract the 3rd to the 8th elements of z
 [1] 8 7 6 5 4 3
```

The function rep() generates a repeated sequence as follows:

```
> z <- rep(1,8) # repeat the scalar value 1, 8 times
> z
[1] 1 1 1 1 1 1 1 1
> y <- rep(c(1,2,3),3) # repeat the vector (1,2,3), 3 times
> y
[1] 1 2 3 1 2 3 1 2 3
> # repeat each element in (1,2,3) by 3 times
> z <- rep(c(1,2,3),each=3)
> z
[1] 1 1 1 2 2 2 3 3 3
```

We make some more manipulations of vectors

```
> # generate a sequence from 0 to 2 by the increment 0.3
> x <- seq(0,2,by=0.3)
> x
[1] 0.0 0.3 0.6 0.9 1.2 1.5 1.8
> length(x) # the length (number of dimension) of vector x
[1] 7
> y <- 2:5 # a sequence of integer from 2 to 5
> y
[1] 2 3 4 5
> z <- c(x,y)# combine vectors x and y
> z
 [1] 0.0 0.3 0.6 0.9 1.2 1.5 1.8 2.0 3.0 4.0 5.0
> rev(z) # the reverse vector
 [1] 5.0 4.0 3.0 2.0 1.8 1.5 1.2 0.9 0.6 0.3 0.0
> str(z) # structure of the vector
 num [1:11] 0 0.3 0.6 0.9 1.2 1.5 1.8 2 3 4 ...
```

The authors consider functions rep(), seq() and length() are very convenient and are often used.

1.3.3 Matrix

There are two methods to generate a matrix in R. One is to use the function matrix(). The other is to combine several vectors or several matrix.

Let us generate a matrix from arbitrary elements by using the function matrix().

```
> # generate a sequence x from 1 to 8.
> x <- 1:8
> x
[1] 1 2 3 4 5 6 7 8
> y <- matrix(x,2,4) # generate a (2,4)-matrix
> # from the element x
> y
     [,1] [,2] [,3] [,4]
[1,]    1    3    5    7
[2,]    2    4    6    8
> y <- matrix(x,4,2) # generate a (4,2)-matrix
> # from the element x
> y
     [,1] [,2]
[1,]    1    5
[2,]    2    6
[3,]    3    7
[4,]    4    8
> # example where the number of rows and columns
> # are not consistent with the number
> # of elements in x
> y <- matrix(x,3,2)
Warning message:
In matrix(x, 3, 2) :
  data length [8] is not a sub-multiple or multiple
  of the number of rows [3]
> y <- matrix(x,2,5)
Warning message:
In matrix(x, 2, 5) :
  data length [8] is not a sub-multiple or multiple
  of the number of columns [5]
```

The above example shows that we need to define the number of rows and columns to be consistent with the number of elements: The number of rows multiplied by the number of columns should be the number of elements.

Next, we combine vectors to generate a matrix.

```
> x <- 1:4
> y <- 5:8
> cbind(x,y) # combine column vectors
     x y
[1,] 1 5
[2,] 2 6
[3,] 3 7
[4,] 4 8
> rbind(x,y) # combine row vectors
  [,1] [,2] [,3] [,4]
x    1    2    3    4
y    5    6    7    8
> rbind(x,y,x) # combine 3 row vectors
  [,1] [,2] [,3] [,4]
x    1    2    3    4
y    5    6    7    8
x    1    2    3    4
>
> cbind(matrix(x,2,2),matrix(y,2,2)) # combine two matrices
     [,1] [,2] [,3] [,4]
[1,]    1    3    5    7
[2,]    2    4    6    8
> rbind(matrix(x,2,2),matrix(y,2,2))
     [,1] [,2]
[1,]    1    3
[2,]    2    4
[3,]    5    7
[4,]    6    8
```

We can generate a diagonal matrix by using the function `diag()`.

```
> diag(c(1,2,3)) # generate a diagonal matrix
     [,1] [,2] [,3]
[1,]    1    0    0
[2,]    0    2    0
[3,]    0    0    3
> diag(rep(1,3)) # generate the identity matrix
     [,1] [,2] [,3]
[1,]    1    0    0
[2,]    0    1    0
[3,]    0    0    1
```

Next, we extract elements, rows and columns from the matrix and check the number of rows and columns of the matrix.

```
> x <- matrix(seq(1,15,by=2),2,4)
> x
     [,1] [,2] [,3] [,4]
[1,]    1    5    9   13
[2,]    3    7   11   15
> x[2,3] # output the element from the 2nd row and 3rd column
[1] 11
> x[2,] # output the 2nd row
[1]  3  7 11 15
> x[,3] # output the 3rd column
[1]  9 11
> dim(x) # output the number of rows and columns
> # of the matrix
[1] 2 4
> nrow(x) # output the number of rows
[1] 2
> ncol(x) # output the number of columns
[1] 4
```

We can also perform multiplication of matrices and vectors.

```
> # generate a 3-by-3 matrix
> mat <- rbind(c(1,0.2,0.3),c(0.2,1,0.5),c(0.3,0.5,1))
> mat
     [,1] [,2] [,3]
[1,]  1.0  0.2  0.3
[2,]  0.2  1.0  0.5
[3,]  0.3  0.5  1.0

> x <- c(1,0.4,0.3) # generate 1-by-3 vector
> x
[1] 1.0 0.4 0.3
```

In the following example, we apply the operator ∗ which can be used for multiplication of matrices and vectors such as we have above. However, this operator does not generate the inner product as follows:

```
> # calculate the product of the elements in each row
> # of the matrix with each column of the vector
> mat*x
     [,1] [,2] [,3]
[1,] 1.00 0.20  0.3
[2,] 0.08 0.40  0.2
[3,] 0.09 0.15  0.3
```

To calculate the inner product, we need to use the operator %*%.

```
> mat %*% x # calculate the inner product
     [,1]
[1,] 1.17
[2,] 0.75
[3,] 0.80
```

```
> # generate two vectors y and z.
> # note that ; separates calculations on a line.
> y <- c(2,0.5,1.3);z<-c(1,5,0.2)
> # combine the vectors (x,y,z) as columns of a new matrix.
> # note that using rbind(x,y,z) would combine the vectors
> # as rows of a new matrix
> xyz<-cbind(x,y,z)
> xyz
       x   y   z
[1,] 1.0 2.0 1.0
[2,] 0.4 0.5 5.0
[3,] 0.3 1.3 0.2
> # calculate the inner product of the matrix 'mat' and 'xyz'
> mat%*%xyz
        x    y    z
[1,] 1.17 2.49 2.06
[2,] 0.75 1.55 5.30
[3,] 0.80 2.15 3.00
```

1.3.4 List

A list is a set of vectors or matrices combined in a single object. We can generate a list in R by using the function list(). It is not necessary to specify the types of the factors in a list; a list can simultaneously include different data types (i.e. numeric and characters) and items of different lengths and sizes.

```
> # generate a list including month,price,brand
> equity <- list(month=c(1,2,3),price=c(100,300,240),
+ brand="muji")
> equity # display the contents of equity
$month
[1] 1 2 3

$price
[1] 100 300 240

$brand
[1] "muji"

> # the structure of the equity object in more compact format
> str(equity)
List of 3
 $ month: num [1:3] 1 2 3
 $ price: num [1:3] 100 300 240
 $ brand: chr "muji"

> equity$month # extract month from equity
[1] 1 2 3
> equity$price # extract price from equity
[1] 100 300 240
> equity$price[3] # extract the 3rd item of price from equity
[1] 240
> equity[[3]] # extract 3rd item of equity
[1] "muji"
> equity[[2]] # to extract 2nd item of equity
[1] 100 300 240
```

We can redefine the name of items included in a list.

```
> # generate a list
> equity <- list(c(1,2,3),c(300,200,400),"muji")
> equity
[[1]]
[1] 1 2 3

[[2]]
[1] 300 200 400

[[3]]
[1] "muji"
```

```
> # give names to the items in the list
> names(equity) <- c("month","price","brand")
> equity
$month
[1] 1 2 3

$price
[1] 300 200 400

$brand
[1] "muji"

> # output names of items in equity using the
> # function names()
> names(equity)
[1] "month" "price" "brand"
> # change the name of the 3rd item to "firm"
> names(equity)[3] <- "firm"
> names(equity)
[1] "month" "price" "firm"
> equity
$month
[1] 1 2 3

$price
[1] 300 200 400

$firm
[1] "muji"
> equity$month # extract the items in month, using $
[1] 1 2 3
> # we can multiply items extracted from a list by a scalar
> equity$month*3
[1] 3 6 9
> # or multiply by a vector
> equity$month*c(3,2,3)
[1] 3 4 9
> equity$month%*%c(3,2,3) # calculate an inner product
[1] 16
> # multiplication of a single extracted item
> equity$month[3]*c(3,2,3)
[1] 9 6 9
```

1.3.5 Data frame

A data frame is a kind of list. More precisely, a data frame is a list of items with the same structure; e.g., all vectors or matrices included in a data frame have the same dimensions (i.e., number of rows and columns). We can create a data frame from a list containing variables of the same dimension as follows.

```
> equity <- list(month=c(1,2,3),price=c(430,400,100),
deal=c(1,4,10))
> equity
$month
[1] 1 2 3

$price
[1] 430 400 100

$deal
[1]  1  4 10

> market <- data.frame(equity)
> market # notice that the output format is different
> # from a list
  month price deal
1     1   430    1
2     2   400    4
3     3   100   10
> market$price # extract items of price
[1] 430 400 100
> market[2,] # extract 2nd row of market
  month price deal
2     2   400    4
```

Just as with a list, we can rename rows and columns of a data frame.

```
> rownames(market) # extract names of each row
[1] "1" "2" "3"
> rownames(market) <- c("Jan","Feb","Mar") # rename each row
> rownames(market)
[1] "Jan" "Feb" "Mar"
> colnames(market) # to extract names of each row
[1] "month" "price" "deal"
```

```
> # renaming each column
> colnames(market) <- c("tsuki","kakaku","torihiki")
> market # output the data frame with the renamed
> # rows and columns
   tsuki kakaku torihiki
Jan    1   430        1
Feb    2   400        4
Mar    3   100       10
```

1.3.6 Factor

Factor is a type used for categorizing elements. Indeed, once a variable is given as a factor, we can deal with not only the elements of the variable, but also with the category of the elements which is alphabetically sorted.

For instance, a set $\{b, c, c, aa, ab, b\}$ has six elements. As a factor, it has four categories aa, ab, b, c. Further, the alphabetical order of the categories is applied to numerics, such that $1, 2, 3, 41, 14$ is regarded as the levels of $1, 14, 2, 3, 41$.

Let us make a variable of the factor type. For generating a variable of factor type, we use the function factor()

```
> tmp_factor<-c("b","c","c","aa","ab","b",12,2,1,0,"aa")
> tmp_factor<-factor(tmp_factor)
> tmp_factor
 [1] b   c   c   aa ab b   12 2   1   0   aa
Levels: 0 1 12 2 aa ab b c
```

As the above example shows, Levels gives categories of a factor. Note that the category is sorted by the alphabetically. Indeed, "12" is prior to "2".

The structure of the factor is shown more clearly by using the function attributes()

```
> attributes(tmp_factor)
$levels
[1] "0"   "1"   "12" "2"   "aa" "ab" "b"   "c"

$class
[1] "factor"
```

This clearly shows that the type of factor is not the usual types of vector, such that factor includes levels and class. Levels gives orders of categories $0, 1, 12, 2, aa, ab, b, c$. Class shows tmp_factor is not an usual vector, but the factor type.

Note that the data extracted from csv file (the usage of reading data is given in section 1.7) is automatically regarded as factor type. For avoiding the extraction of data as a factor type, we should denote `strings As Factors=FALSE` as an argument of the function `read.csv()`.

1.3.7   Investigation of types and structures of data

R has several useful functions that we can use to interrogate the structure of data, that is, we can interrogate whether the data is a vector, matrix, list, data frame, or factor.

```
> x <- 1
> is.vector(x)
[1] TRUE
> # a scalar is regarded as a 1 dimensional vector in R
> x <- c(4,2,1)
> is.vector(x)
[1] TRUE
> x <- matrix(x,1,3)
> is.matrix(x)
[1] TRUE
> is.vector(x)
[1] FALSE
> x <- list(c(34,3,19),c("foo",'kaa'))
> is.list(x)
[1] TRUE
> is.data.frame(x)
[1] FALSE
> x <- data.frame(c(1,2,3),c(10,8,9))
> is.data.frame(x)
[1] TRUE
> tmp_factor<-c("b","c","c","aa","ab","b",12,2,1,0,"aa")
> tmp_factor<-factor(tmp_factor)
> is.factor(tmp_factor)
[1] TRUE
```

1.4   Functions

We introduce functions to do more complicated programming. A function can be defined in R using `function()`. The structure is simple such that we use the usage `"the name of the function"<-function(){}`, state the arguments within the parenthesis () and state the calculation methods within the curly braces {}. The example below shows us the usage.

```
> # define a function to calculate the circumference
> # of a circle of radius r
> circle <- function(r){
+   s <- 2*pi*r # calculate the circumference and
+ # substitute it into s
+   return(s) # return from the function the result s
+ }
> circle(1) # to calculate the circle length with radius 1
[1] 6.283185
>
> # the function can also take a vector as its argument
> circle(c(1,3,2))
[1]  6.283185 18.849556 12.566371
>
> # as well as a matrix
> circle(matrix(c(3,1,3,2),2,2))

          [,1]      [,2]
[1,] 18.849556 18.84956
[2,]  6.283185 12.56637
> circle(3+3i) # we can apply this function to a
> # complex number
[1] 18.84956+18.84956i
> # The logical value TRUE is interpreted as
> # the numeric value 1, and FALSE as 0
> circle(TRUE)
[1] 6.283185
> circle(FALSE)
[1] 0
> circle("foo")
Error in 2 * pi * r : non-numeric argument to binary operator
```

The last example returns an error because we cannot use the * operator with non-numeric arguments. The last example for character type does not imply that function() in R cannot be applied for the type of character in general. By defining the calculation corresponding to type of character, we can make functions that take characters as arguments.

```
> moji <- function(x){
+ y <- paste(x,"goo")
+ return(y)
+ }
> moji("ha")
[1] "ha goo"
> moji(3)
[1] "3 goo"
```

We can define multivariate functions.

```
> multi <- function(x,y){
+ z=x^2+y
+ return(z)
+ }
> multi(1,2)
[1] 3
> multi(c(1,1),c(2,1)) # give vectors as arguments
[1] 3 2
> a <- matrix(c(3,2,1,0),2,2)
> b <- matrix(c(5,1,4,1),2,2)
> multi(a,b) # give matrices as arguments
      [,1] [,2]
[1,]   14    5
[2,]    5    1
```

Exercise

Make a function to calculate the area of a circle.

Example of solution

```
> area <- function(r){
+   return(pi*r^2)
+ }
> area(3) # calculate the area of a circle with radius 3
[1] 28.27433
```

1.5   Control statements

We can make more sophisticated codes by using conditional statements; "if", "for", and "while".

1.5.1 *if-statement*

We often use if-statement in scripting and in the definition of functions. The if-statement allows us to execute one block of code if the result of the if-statement is true and an alternative block of code if the result of the if-statement is false.

The following are formats of the if statement.

- if(conditionals) statement 1

- if(conditionals) statement 1 else statement 2

- if(conditionals) statement 1 else if(conditionals) statement 2

- if(conditionals) statement 1 else if(conditionals) statement 2 else statement 3, ⋯

Especially in the case of conditional statements, it is better to write repeatedly the programming by ourselves to understand the structure of conditional statement.

Let's write a script to calculate the circumference of a circle with radius 3 if the variable x is equal to the character string `radius`.

```
> r<-3 # define the radius
> # substitute the character sequence 'radius' into x
> x<-"radius"
> # test the conditionality of whether x is equal to
> # the character
> # string 'radius',
> if(x=="radius")
+ {
+   z<-2*pi*r # substitute radius into z
+ }
> z # check the results
[1] 18.84956
```

Next, we write a script to calculate the length of a circle if the variable x is the "radius" and calculate the circle area if x is not "radius".

```
> x<-"area" # substitute 'area' into x
> if(x=="radius")
+ {
+   z<-2*pi*r
+ }else{ # if x is not 'radius'
+ z<- pi*r^2 # calculate the area of the circle
+ }
>
> z
[1] 28.27433
```

Further, we write the script to calculate the circumference of a circle if the variable x is "radius", the area of the circle if x is "area", the volume and surface area if x is neither "radius" nor "area".

```
> x<-"ball" # substitute the character sequence 'ball'
> if(x=="radius")
+ {
+   z<-2*pi*r
+ }else if(z=="area")
+ {
+ z<- pi*r^2
+ }else{
+   z<-c(4/3*pi*r^3,4*pi*r^2)
+ }
>
> z
[1] 113.0973 113.0973
```

Although it is a little tedious, we can do the same calculations by using logical operators.

```
> if(x!="radius" && x!= "area")
+ {
+   z<-c(4/3*pi*r^3,4*pi*r^2)
+ }else if(z=="radius" || z!="area")
+ {
+   z<-2*pi*r
+ }else{
+   z<- pi*r^2
+ }
>
> z
[1] 113.0973 113.0973
```

Now we use the if-statement within a function to test whether the input number is odd or not. Note that %% is the operator to calculate the modulus.

```
> is.odd <- function(n){ # assign the function to is.odd
+ if(n%%2==1){
+ return(TRUE)
+ }else{
+ return(FALSE)
+ }
```

```
+ }
>
> is.odd(4)
[1] FALSE
> is.odd(5)
[1] TRUE
```

1.5.2   *Iterative processing: for-statement, while-statement*

If we need to perform repeatedly similar calculations it is convenient to use the for-statement (for-loop) or the while-statement. The following is a function to calculate a product of integers from 1 to n, i.e., n factorial.

```
> acc <- function(n){
+   tmp <- 1
+   # iterate the calculation described below within
+   # the curly brackets {} in case i is between 1 and n.
+   for(i in 1:n){ # 1:n is a vector from 1 to n,
+   # incremented by 1
+     tmp <- tmp*i
+   }
+   return(tmp)
+ }
>
> acc(3)
[1] 6
> acc(0)
[1] 0
```

In the above example, we calculate the product of integers from 1 to n; i.e., the function is to calculate $n!$. However, the function acc() above does not correctly calculate $0! = 1$. In this sense, the function acc() does not precisely correspond to $n!$ (of course, it is sufficient for the case n is larger than or equal to 1). We can use a while-statement to correct our function. A while-statement differs from the for-statement in the method to describe the condition of repetition. Consider the following example:

```
> acc <- function(n){
+ tmp <- 1
+ i <- 1
+ # repeat the following calculation within the {} until i is
+ # greater than n
+ while(i<=n){
```

```
+ tmp <- tmp*i
+ i <- i+1 # without incrementing i, the condition
+ # would never be met and the calculation would
+ # repeat infinitely
+ }
+ return(tmp)
+ }
>
> acc(3) # product from 1 to 3, that is, 3!
[1] 6
> acc(0) # to calculate 0!
[1] 1
```

We can also use an if-statement to correct our function to calculate $n!$.

```
> acc <- function(n){
+ if(n==0){
+ return(1)
+ }else{
+ tmp <- 1
+ for(i in 1:n){
+ tmp <- tmp*i
+ }
+ return(tmp)
+ }
+ }
> acc(3)
[1] 6
> acc(0)
[1] 1
```

Exercise

Make two functions to calculate the summation from 1 to n; (1) using a for-statement, and (2) using a while-statement.

Example of solution

```
> # calculate the summation from 1 to n using a for-statement
> sum_1 <- function(n){
+   tmp <- 0
+   for(i in 1:n){
+     tmp <- tmp+i
+   }
+   return(tmp)
```

```
+ }
>
> # calculate the summation from 1 to n using a
> # while-statement
> sum_2 <- function(n){
+   tmp <- 0
+   i <- 1
+   while(i<=n){
+     tmp <- tmp+i
+     i <- i+1
+   }
+   return(tmp)
+ }
> sum_1(10)
[1] 55
> sum_2(10)
[1] 55
```

1.6   Graphics

Figures depicting numerical results are useful for visualizing large sets of data and often give better insight or new perspectives on the analysis. Especially, it is important for the TEX user to depict the good looking eps files. Fortunately, R comes equipped with built-in functions that make visualization easy. The function plot() can be used to generate graphics. Let us try a few examples (see left panel of Figure 1.8).

```
> # generate random numbers from a standard
> # normal distribution
> x <- rnorm(10)
> x
 [1] -0.24031720  2.21984392 -0.16325784  0.58818735
-1.60562434
 [8] 0.37173777 -1.28146059 -0.06356494 -1.22452429
0.05484006
> plot(x) # display the above numbers on a plot
```

Next, we generate another random number y and plot x which is generated above on the horizontal axis versus y on the vertical axis (see right panel of Figure 1.8).

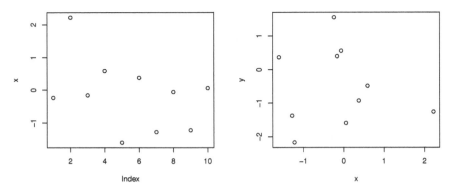

Figure 1.8: Random numbers x, versus index number (left), and (x,y) (right)

```
> y <- rnorm(10)
> y
 [1]  1.5564341 -1.2587830  0.3978732 -0.4926095  0.3683764
 [8] -0.9308361 -1.3766497  0.5590627 -2.1707921 -1.5921009
> plot(x,y)
```

Let us plot a quadratic function (Figure 1.9).

```
> # generate a sequence from 0 to 5 by the increment of 0.2.
> x <- seq(0,5,by=0.2)
> # generate a quadratic function from the above sequence.
> y <- 2*x^2-5*x
> # plot a solid curve of quadratic function letting x be
> # horizontal axis and y be vertical axis
> plot(x,y,type="l")
> plot(x,y,type="p") # plot points curve of
> # quadratic function
```

We can also plot the values of a function, letting the function name, like 'sin', 'log' and so on, be the argument of plot() (Figure 1.10).

```
> # plot values of logarithmic function with domain
> # from 0 to 10.
> plot(log,0,10)
```

Other than the function log(), R is equipped with standard mathematical functions, like the exponential function exp(), and trigonometric functions sin(), cos(), etc.

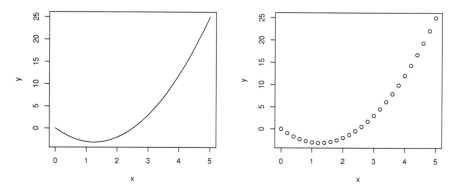

Figure 1.9: A solid curve (left) and points (right) of quadratic function $y = 2x^2 - 5x$

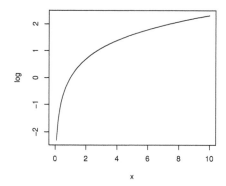

Figure 1.10: Values of logarithmic function $y = \ln x$ in domain $[0, 10]$

We can add values of functions to a figure and change the colour of points and lines (Figure 1.11).

```
> x <- seq(-2,2,by=0.2)
> plot(x,x^3,type="l")
> points(x,x^2) # add points of f(x)=x^2
> lines(x,x^2) # add a solid curve of the above function
> # change the colour by specifying the argument col
> lines(x,x^2,col="red")
```

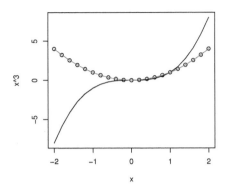

Figure 1.11: After plotting, $y = x^3$, add points and solid curves of $y = x^2$

We can make 3D plots in R using, the function `persp()`, instead of `plot()` (left panel of Figure 1.12).

```
> x <- seq(-3,3,length=50) # set the domain of x-axis
> y <- seq(-3,3,length=50) # set the domain of y-axis
> # dnorm() is standard normal density function
> gauss3d <- function(x,y){dnorm(x)*dnorm(y)}
> # the values of gauss3d with arguments x, y is substituted
> # into z
> z <- outer(x,y,gauss3d)
> # the function persp() generates cubic figure of (x,y,z)
> persp(x,y,z)


> # rotate the preceding cubic figure by 30 degree to left,
> # 20 degree to upward and scale it to 0.5 size of
> # its height
> persp(x,y,z,theta=30,phi=-20,expand=0.5)
```

Similar to `plot()`, we can change the line colour by specifying the argument `col` in `persp()`. We show the example of script as follows to change the colour of the cubic figure to light blue (right panel of Figure 1.12).

```
> # to change the colour
> persp(x,y,z,theta=30,phi=30,expand=0.5,col="lightblue")
```

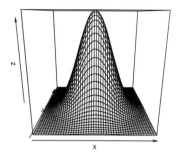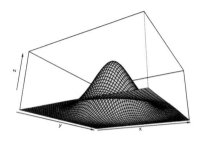

Figure 1.12: Left panel is the 3D plot generated by persp(x,y,z), where $z = \left(\frac{1}{\sqrt{2\pi}}e^{-\frac{1}{2}x^2}\right)\left(\frac{1}{\sqrt{2\pi}}e^{-\frac{1}{2}y^2}\right)$ and the right panel show the rotation of the cubic figure of left panel by 30 degree to left, 20 degree to upward and to scale it to 0.5 size of height.

To open several figures simultaneously, we use the following command to make windows in which the figures are contained.

```
> windows()
```

As TEX users, the authors prefer to store graphics as eps files (options exist to store in other formats, such as pdf). Next, let us output the figure as an eps file. We need to set the file name to be written in the current folder, as follows,

```
> dev.copy2eps(file="fig.eps")
```

We can also export the graphics by right-clicking on the figure and choosing 'save as postscript.', to save an eps file with the name specified. We can export graphics to a pdf file via the command line with the following.

```
> # opens a pdf file entitled "bar.pdf" for writing
> pdf(file="bar.pdf")
> # generate some plots which get written into
> # the pdf file bar.pdf
> plot(1:10,rep(5,10),xlab="x",ylab="y")
> plot(1:10,20:11,xlab="x",ylab="y")
> plot(1:10,exp(1:10),xlab="x",ylab="y")
> dev.off() # close the file
```

The resulting pdf file, bar.pdf, includes the 3 plots.

1.7 Reading and writing data

We can store the results of calculations to a file with the built-in R functions. Let us now write results of calculations on a file and read the data on the written file. To write data to a file, we can use the functions `write.table()` or `write.csv()`. To read data from a file, we can use the functions `read.table()` or `read.csv()`.

```
> mat<-rbind(c(1,0.2,0.3),c(0.2,1,0.5),c(0.3,0.5,1))
> mat
     [,1] [,2] [,3]
[1,]  1.0  0.2  0.3
[2,]  0.2  1.0  0.5
[3,]  0.3  0.5  1.0
> write.table(mat,"matrix.txt")
> write.csv(mat,"matrix.csv")
```

The two files that result from the above will be saved to the current folder with names of "matrix.txt" and "matrix.csv". We can read these files back into the R workspace as follows.

```
> Rmatrix1<-read.table("matrix.txt")
> Rmatrix1
   V1  V2  V3
1 1.0 0.2 0.3
2 0.2 1.0 0.5
3 0.3 0.5 1.0
> Rmatrix2<-read.csv("matrix.csv")
> Rmatrix2
  X  V1  V2  V3
1 1 1.0 0.2 0.3
2 2 0.2 1.0 0.5
3 3 0.3 0.5 1.0
```

1.8 Reading program

For simple programming, a short script using the console will be sufficient. However, we often write long scripts and run it many times repeatedly. We also may want to make small corrections to our program. In this case, it is not sufficient to keep a script only in the R console, or rewrite it each time. Fortunately, R allows us to save the script as a file and read it repeatedly.

We can start a new script file from the command "New Script" in the "File" menu, then the screen like Figure 1.13 appears.

Let us write the following programming.

```
x <- seq(-pi,pi,by=0.1)
y <- sin(x)
plot(x,y,type="l")
```

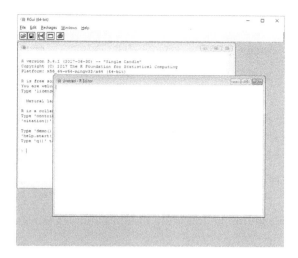

Figure 1.13: Script window

We save this script as a file named "program.r". R script files are denoted with the .r file extension. We can save the script file by choosing "Save" or "Save as....(alternative name)" from the "File" menu. When we want to use this program, we can call this by choosing "Open script..." from the "File" menu and edit it.

We can run the script from the console window by the function source(), as below.

```
> source("program.r")
```

The other way to run a script is to choose "Open script" from the "File" menu, and then selecting "Run all" from "Edit" menu once the script "program.r" appears.

Note that when we write a program in a script file, we need to pay attention to the starting point of a new line. Consider the script used to calculate '3+4' which contains the following lines

```
a<-3
+4
```

R interprets this program as 3 should be substituted into the variable a and the line is ended. Then, +4 on the next line is interpreted as the value +4 being just given to show or being commanded to calculate 0+4. Indeed, running this script, R returns the following result.

```
> a<-3
> +4
```

```
[1] 4
```

Let us call the variable a on the console view.

```
> a
[1] 3
```

We can see that only 3 has been substituted into the variable a. If we make new line before a calculation has clearly ended, R will search where the operation will be ended. Let us write the following program on the script.

```
a<-3+ # it is unclear what should be added to 3
4 # here, R interprets that 4 should be added to 3
```

Indeed, we can confirm the following result by running the above script.

```
> a<-3+
+ 4
```

Let us call a on console view.

```
> a
[1] 7
```

Indeed, we can confirm "3+4 = 7" is substituted into the variable a. Although the above discussion looks trivial, it is important to write programs with a clear set of operations on each line. If the description on one line is too long and you want to start a new line, you should start the new line such that R can understand that the calculation is not ended in the end of the current line.

1.9　Packages

Although R itself is equipped with various built-in functions, additional packages are available which extend the capability of R to do more complicated operations and calculations. There are two methods of installing new packages in R: One is to access the website of CRAN project and download packages via a web browser. This is similar to the method of installing R. The second is to do it via GUI of R. Since the latter method is easier and we have already used GUI, we show the method using the R GUI.

1. In the R GUI, select the "Packages" menu and click "Install package(s)...".

2. The window like the left panel of Figure 1.14 appears for showing available mirror sites from which to download packages. Select one of them, like the case of installation of R. Here, we choose "Japan (Tokyo) [https]", because we live there.

3. The window like the middle panel of Figure 1.14 where we can see names of packages available for download. For example, to select "tseries" package which will be used in Chapter 3, and to click "OK" and "Yes" for the successive questions, like "Would you like to use a personal library instead?" Then the download will start.

4. Before using downloaded package, we select "Load package..." from the 'Packages' menu. Then, the right panel of Figure 1.14 appears. Select "tseries" and click "OK". Then, we can use functions contained in "tseries" package. To load the specific package from the console view, we write the following;

```
> library(tseries)
```

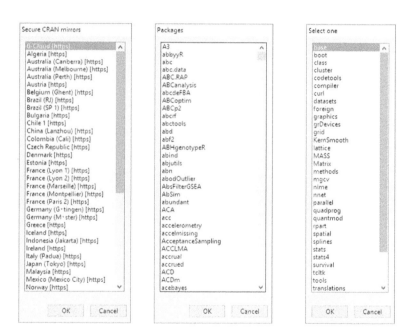

Figure 1.14: Selection of mirror cite (left panel). Selection of packages for download (middle panel). Available packages (right panel)

Many other packages are also available. The proliferation of packages is one of the attractive features of R.

So far, we have learned some of the basics of R Programming. From the next chapter, let us use R for finance.

STATISTICS IN FINANCE

Chapter 2

Statistical Analysis with R

CONTENTS

2.1 Basic statistics

The most common financial data is comprised of asset prices,[1] such as the prices of the shares of companies traded on the stock exchange.[2] These prices could be sampled quarterly, monthly or daily at the close of trading. We could even sample every stock transaction in this age of high-frequency trading, which can occur on a time-scale of less than a millisecond, resulting in a very large volume data.

---

[1] or price returns, which are the percent changes from previous prices.

[2] Of course financial data is not necessarily limited to asset prices. It can be the time series of trades volume of a given stock, or economic data such as monthly GDP or unemployment figures.

We can make some quantitative descriptive measures such as min, max, the size of the data (length of the time series). And we can visualise or plot the financial time series to make a qualitative analysis, looking for trends or patterns. But for large sets of data, we will need more powerful analytic tools.

If we have a large enough data set (more than a few hundred samples), it is helpful to use statistics to characterise the data. As we will see later, we can use statistics and assumptions regarding the statistics of the data to make predictions and to understand financial data better.

To estimate mean μ and variance σ^2 is the first and one of the most important things for statistical analysis.

The most important thing is to assume that data can be described by a probability distribution. Distributions are described in terms of moments. The mean and variance are the first two moments. The first two moments the mean and variance describe where the distribution is centered and how spread out the populations is about the mean.

This estimation assumes the existence of population which makes it possible to sample data and estimate statistics, like mean and variance.[3] In the context of finance, it might be difficult to define the population. However, we often analyze financial data, with an implicit assumption of the existence of a probability distribution.

For given dataset (observations) $x_1, x_2, \cdots, x_n$, sample mean $\bar{x}$ and sample variance $\hat{s}^2$ is calculated as follows,[4]

$$\bar{x} = \frac{1}{n}(x_1 + x_2 + \cdots + x_n) = \frac{1}{n}\sum_{i=1}^{n} x_i,$$

$$\hat{s}^2 = \frac{1}{n}\sum_{i=1}^{n}(x_i - \bar{x})^2 = \bar{x^2} - \bar{x}^2.$$

Note that the square root of variance is the standard error of the sample. Using R, we can calculate the mean and variance as follows,

```
> x <- seq(1,10) # sequence from 1 to 10
> mean(x) # average as a scalar
[1] 5.5
> ave(x) # average as a vector
 [1] 5.5 5.5 5.5 5.5 5.5 5.5 5.5 5.5 5.5 5.5
> mean((x-ave(x))^2) # to calculate sample variance
[1] 8.25
```

---

[3]The good example is TV program ratings and exit polls. They are the estimation of population distribution from sampled data.

[4]Although unbiased variance might be defined as sample variance, we call the statistic divided by n sample variance, the statistic divided by $n-1$ unbiased variance.

```
> # (average of squares of x)-(squares of average of x)
> mean(x^2)-(mean(x))^2
[1] 8.25
```

R has a built-in function to calculate the variance and standard error as `var()` and `sd()`, respectively: The unbiased variance s^2 and unbiased standard error s; is defined as

$$s^2 = \frac{1}{n-1} \sum_{i=1}^{n} (x_i - \bar{x})^2 .$$

Note that unbiased variance and unbiased standard error have in the denominator $n-1$, not n. Then, the mean of unbiased variance is same as the variance of population σ^2, although the sample variance is a little bit smaller than the variance of population.

```
> var(x) # unbiased variance
[1] 9.166667
> # sample variance is unbiased variance multiplied
> # by (n-1)/n
> var(x)*9/10
[1] 8.25
> sd(x) # unbiased standard error
[1] 3.027650
> sqrt(var(x))
[1] 3.027650
```

It is often not necessary to take care of the above point, because sample variance and unbiased variance in the context of finance are very close because of the large amount of data. With large sample sizes, variance and unbiased variance converge as $n-1$ becomes close to n. However, we should understand why we need to adopt the denominator $n-1$ to derive the unbiased variance. It is the problem of the degree of freedom. Before the discussion of the degree of freedom, we introduce the law of large numbers[5] and the central limit theorem.[6] Both of which are important theorems and the foundation of statistics.

Theorem 2.1 Law of Large Numbers

As the sample size n increases, the probability that the sample mean $\bar{x}$ is different from the population mean μ converges to zero.

---

[5]More precisely, the law of large numbers is divided into two versions; i.e., weak and strong laws of large numbers. See [CK05] who gives succinct proof for them. [Dur05] is also a good guidance.

[6]The idea of the law of large numbers goes back to Jacques Bernoulli in 17th century. The central limit theorem was demonstrated by de Moivre and Laplace in the 18th century. See [Wil91], [HH80] and [Shr04] for detailed proofs of the central limit theorem.

Theorem 2.2 Central Limit Theorem

Increasing sample size n, the distribution of standardized sample mean $\frac{\bar{x}-\mu}{\sqrt{\sigma^2/n}}$ converges in distribution to standard normal distribution, regardless of the distribution of population; i.e., for sufficiently large n, sample mean $\bar{x}$ is close to the normal distribution with mean μ and variance σ^2/n.

Note that central limit theorem assures that the distribution of the standardized sample means a sufficiently large number of data converges to the standard normal distribution, even if the population distribution is not normal. This is theoretical basis for approximating real world data by the normal distribution.

Indeed, we calculate the expected value and variance of sample mean $\bar{x}$ as follows,

$$
\begin{aligned}
\mathbb{E}(\bar{x}) &= \mathbb{E}\left[\frac{1}{n}(x_1 + x_2 + \cdots + x_n)\right] \\
&= \frac{1}{n}[\mathbb{E}(x_1) + \mathbb{E}(x_2) + \cdots + \mathbb{E}(x_n)] = \mu. \\
Var(\bar{x}) &= Var\left[\frac{1}{n}(x_1 + x_2 + \cdots + x_n)\right] \\
&= \frac{1}{n^2}[Var(x_1) + Var(x_2) + \cdots + Var(x_n)] = \frac{\sigma^2}{n},
\end{aligned}
$$

where we assumed that the sample x_i are independently and identically distributed (i.i.d.) and used facts $\mathbb{E}(x_i) = \mu, Var(x_i) = \sigma^2$.

Further, we can experimentally confirm the law of large numbers as follows,

```
> mean(rnorm(10))
[1] 0.1094647
> mean(rnorm(100))
[1] -0.0943789
> mean(rnorm(1000))
[1] -0.04676734
> mean(rnorm(10000))
[1] 0.0008186049
```

The function `rnorm()` generates random numbers from a standard normal distribution.[7] The function generates a different set of random numbers each time it is used. However, we can observe that the mean converges to zero with increasing sample size.

---

[7] If you need to generate *n* random numbers of normal distribution with mean *m* and standard error *s*, use `rnorm(n,m,s)`. That is, `rnorm(n)` = `rnorm(n,0,1)`.

For an experimental demonstration of central limit theorem in R, we define a function such that,

```
> Center <- function(n){
+ x <- rep(0,10000)
+ # calculate 10000 averages of random numbers with
+ # sample size n
+ for(i in 1:10000){
+   x[i] <- mean(rnorm(n))
+ }
+ return(var(x))
+ }
```

We calculate this function with size 10, 100, 1000, and 10000, as follows,

```
> Center(10)
[1] 0.09919644
> Center(100)
[1] 0.00991062
> Center(1000)
[1] 0.0009896516
> Center(10000)
[1] 0.0001004920
```

The above calculation shows that, with increasing sample size $n = 10 \to 100 \to 1000 \to 10000$, the order of the variance of the sample mean decreases as $1/n = 1/10 \to 1/100 \to 1/1000 \to 1/10000$. We used the normal random numbers in the above example. Of course, the same result appears with the random numbers of another distribution.

Let us return to the discussion of unbiased variance. We can confirm the expectation value of the unbiased variance is the same as the population variance σ^2 as follows,

$$\mathbb{E}\left[\sum_{i=1}^{n}(x_i - \bar{x})^2\right] = \sum_{i=1}^{n}\mathbb{E}\left[(x_i - \mu)^2\right] - n\mathbb{E}\left[(\bar{x} - \mu)^2\right]$$

$$= \sum_{i=1}^{n}Var(x_i) - nVar(\bar{x}) = n\sigma^2 - n\frac{\sigma^2}{n}$$

$$= (n-1)\sigma^2, \tag{2.1}$$

where we used the following fact,

$$\sum_{i=1}^{n} (x_i - \bar{x})^2 = \sum [(x_i - \mu) - (\bar{x} - \mu)]^2$$

$$= \sum (x_i - \mu)^2 - 2(\bar{x} - \mu) \sum (x_i - \mu) + n(\bar{x} - \mu)^2$$

$$= \sum (x_i - \mu)^2 - 2(\bar{x} - \mu)(n\bar{x} - n\mu) + n(\bar{x} - \mu)^2$$

$$= \sum (x_i - \mu)^2 - n(\bar{x} - \mu)^2.$$

(2.1) implies that the sample mean $\bar{x}$ is different from the population mean μ and the variance of the sample mean $Var(\bar{x})$ is σ^2/n. Therefore, we have to divide $\mathbb{E}\left[\sum_{i=1}^{n} (x_i - \bar{x})^2\right]$ by $n - 1$ to derive unbiased variance, not by n.

2.2 Probability distribution and random numbers

R has various functions to calculate probability density functions, cumulative distribution functions and random numbers of probability distributions. We have already used the normal distribution and random numbers taken from the normal distribution. Note that, for the name of a probability density "aaa", the R function for the probability density function is given by daaa(x), the cumulative distribution function[8] is given by paaa(x), and the random numbers generated from the distribution are given by raaa(x). For example, let us depict the probability density function and cumulative distribution function of the standard normal distribution (Figure 2.1).

```
> x <- seq(-4,4,b=0.1) # the parameter b=0.1 has same meaning
> # as by=0.1
> plot(x,dnorm(x),"l") # plot the probability density
> # function
> plot(x,pnorm(x),"l") # plot the cumulative distribution
> # function
```

---

[8]The cumulative distribution function is used for describing the probability of a random variable X, such that

$$F(x) = P(X \leq x),$$

where $F(\cdot)$ is the cumulative distribution function, $P(\cdot)$ is the probability measure.

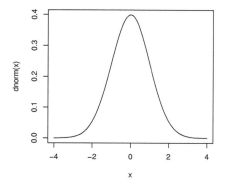 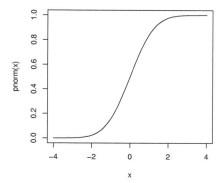

Figure 2.1: Probability density function (left) and Cumulative distribution (right) of normal distribution

R comes equipped with various probability distributions; log normal distribution (`lnorm`), Poisson distribution (`pois`), Gamma distribution (`gamma`), binomial distribution (`binorm`), t-distribution (`t`), f-distribution (`f`), Beta distribution (`beta`), and ξ^2-distribution (`chisq`).

2.3 Hypothesis testing

2.3.1 What is hypothesis testing?

Hypothesis testing is used to test statistical assumptions on a population using a sample. Consider a sample of data set which is the results of tossing a coin ten times. A "fair"coin will have an equal probability of ending up heads or tails when tossed; i.e., we will expect the heads to appear with 50% probability and tails to appear with 50% probability. However, if the heads appears 10 times out of 10 tosses, we naturally will doubt that the coin is fair. Of course, it is possible that heads can appear ten times in a row with a fair coin, but this probability is very small, $(1/2)^{10} \simeq 0.000977 = 0.0977\%$. Thus, we usually consider the coin is unfair. In this way, we first set a hypothesis like which the head and tail of a coin appear with 50% of the probability, respectively, and test the hypothesis by using observable sample. This is hypothesis testing.

Consider two outcomes of a series of coin tosses:

■ A: Heads appears 6 times out of 10 coin tosses.

■ B: Heads appears 60 times out of 100 coin tosses.

Note that in both A and B heads comes up 60% of the coin tosses. In hypothesis testing, we first assume that the coin is fair and calculate the probability of heads and tails appearing. For a fair coin, the probability of heads coming up r times out of a sample of n coin tosses is,

$$P(n,r) = \frac{\displaystyle\sum_{i=r}^{n} {}_nC_i}{2^n}.$$

Where ${}_nC_i$ is the number of the combination choosing i items from a set of n items; i.e., it is mathematically defined by ${}_nC_i := \frac{n!}{i!(n-i)!}$. We can calculate combination ${}_nC_i$ in R using the function choose(n,i). Using this, we define a function such that

```
> Prob <- function(n,r){
+ tmp <- 0
+ for(i in r:n){
+ tmp <- tmp+choose(n,i)
+ }
+ return(tmp/2^n)
+ }
```

and run this function to get results as follows,

```
> # probability of heads coming up 6 times out of 10
> # coin tosses
> Prob(10,6)
[1] 0.3769531
> # probability of heads coming up over 60 times out of
> # 100 coin tosses
> Prob(100,60)
[1] 0.02844397
```

This result shows that the probability of heads coming up over 6 times is 37.7%, while the probability of heads coming up over 60 times is only 2.8%. Thus, we might not suspect the coin to be unfair if we get heads six times out of 10. However, with more tosses, it becomes more difficult to consider that the coin is fair if we end up with heads 60 times out of 100.

This is the basic idea of hypothesis testing (see [NP33] which shows the essence of the hypothesis testing). We summarize the terminology related to hypothesis testing. The hypothesis in which the coin is fair is called the null hypothesis and we write it as $H_0 : q = 0.5$, where q is the probability of tossing heads. On the other hand, the hypothesis in which the coin is unfair is called the alternative hypothesis and we write it as $H_1 : q \neq 0.5$. In outcome A above, the probability of 6 heads out of 10 tosses is such that we cannot reject the null hypothesis. In outcome B, however, the probability of 60 heads out of 100 tosses is low, and we lean towards rejecting the null hypothesis.

The natural question is, how many times do heads have to come up out of 100 coin tosses to reject the null hypothesis? We set a threshold on the probability of times an outcome would theoretically occur and call this the "significance level". The question then is: how many times does the outcome occur before the probability falls below the significance level. We can set the significance level as something low, for example, 5% or 1%. If the probability of the outcome is lower than these values, we say that the null hypothesis H_0 is rejected with significance level 5% or 1%. Thus, for outcome B, H_0 is rejected with significance level 5%, but is not rejected with significance level 1%.

Further, we can calculate

```
> Prob(100,62)
[1] 0.01048937
> Prob(100,63)
[1] 0.006016488
```

Therefore, if we define the criteria to reject H_0 by heads appearing over 62 times, the significance level is approximately 1%. Instead of significance level, we can adopt the criteria by the probability $P(n, r)$, called the p-value.

Note that we do not positively prove the null hypothesis, but rather demonstrate that we cannot necessarily reject the null hypothesis. Thus, it is possible that the coin is unfair even in the case of heads coming up 6 times out of 10, or that the coin is fair even when heads comes up 60 times out of 100. However, defining a significance level and testing allow us to quantify the confidence with which we adopt or reject a hypothesis.

2.3.2 t-Test of population mean

Suppose that the mean of a sample is positive. Can we test whether the population mean is significantly positive or not? How large is the probability that the population mean is actually less than zero? The t-test gives one of the solutions to such a question. More precisely, the t-test is used to calculate the statistical significance, or the confidence interval, of whether a population mean dominated by the normal distribution is equal to a particular value, or whether two population means which are both described by the normal distribution, are equal to each other. In finance theory, we often use the t-test to check whether regression coefficients are significantly different from zero. Before the discussion of t-test, we need to introduce the t-distribution. The t-distribution is the basis of the t-test and is used for the estimation of the mean of normally distributed population from a small sample.[9]

---

[9]t-distribution was discovered by William Sealy Gosset who was an engineer and a statistician of Guinness Company. He used the pseudonymous Student in his academic activity. Thus, the t-distribution is well known as Student's t-distribution, instead of his original name.

Let $x_1, x_2, \cdots, x_n$ be independent random numbers, normally distributed with mean μ and variance σ^2; i.e.,

$$x_1, x_2, \cdots, x_n \sim \mathcal{N}(\mu, \sigma^2).$$

The sample mean $\bar{x}$ normalized by population mean μ and unbiased variance s^2 is called the t-statistic and is the t-distribution with $n-1$ degrees of freedom, if

$$t = \frac{\bar{x} - \mu}{s/\sqrt{n}} \sim t(n-1).$$

The distribution function of the t-distribution is described with a Gamma function $\Gamma(\cdot)$ as follows,

$$f(x) = \frac{\Gamma((v+1)/2)}{\sqrt{v\pi}\, \Gamma(v/2)} \left(1 + \frac{x^2}{v}\right)^{-(v+1)/2},$$

where $v = n - 1$ is the degree of freedom. In R, we can use the function $dt(x, v)$ to calculate the t-distribution and plot the distribution as in Figure 2.2.

```
> x <- seq(-4,4,b=0.1)
> # the density function of t-distribution with the degree
> # of freedom 100
> plot(x,dt(x,100),ylab="f(x)","l")
> # the density function of t-distribution with the degree
> # of freedom 10
> lines(x,dt(x,10),lty=2)
> # the density function of t-distribution with the degree
> # of freedom 1
> lines(x,dt(x,1),lty=3)
> # the legend
> legend(-4,0.4,legend=c("nu=100","nu=10","nu=1"),
> # lty=c(1,2,3))
```

The t-test is a statistical test, whether a statistic follows the t-distribution, or not. We test the hypothesis that the population mean of the above sample is 0; i.e., the null hypothesis is $H_0 : \mu = 0$ and the alternative hypothesis is $H_1 : \mu \neq 0$. If the population follows normal distribution, the sample mean $\bar{x}$ satisfies

$$\frac{\bar{x} - \mu}{s/\sqrt{n}} \sim t(n-1),$$

where μ is population mean and s^2 is population variance. If the null hypothesis $\mu = 0$ is correct then,

$$t = \frac{\sqrt{n}\bar{x}}{s} \sim t(n-1). \tag{2.2}$$

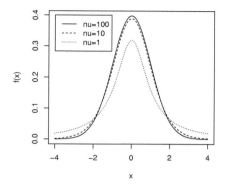

Figure 2.2: A probability density function of the t-distribution

The significance level of 5% implies that the confidence interval should be set 2.5% in each side. For calculating a confidence interval, R is equipped with the function qt(). For example, when we do two-sided test with significance level 5%, we can calculate the probability point by qt(0.025, n-1) and qt(0.975, n-1). In the case of the degree of freedom 10, use the following code,

```
> qt(0.025,10) # lower probability of 2.5%
[1] -2.228139
> qt(0.975,10) # upper probability of 2.5%
[1] 2.228139
```

From these, if t-statistic of (2.2) is in $[-2.228139, 2.228139]$, the null hypothesis is adopted with significance level 5%. Otherwise, it is rejected. Further, for a given t-statistic, the distribution function is calculated as follows,

```
> pt(-2.228139,10)   # Probability P[X < -2.228139]
> # for t=-2.228139
[1] 0.02499999
> pt(2.228139,10)   # Probability P[X< 2.228139]
> # for t=2.228139
[1] 0.975
> pt(2.228139,10,lower=F) # Probability P[X>2.228139]
[1] 0.02499999
```

R is equipped with various functions for estimation and hypothesis testing. For t-test, we can use t.test(). We show an example of t.test(). To do it, we first generate random numbers with normal distribution.

```
> # 20 normal random numbers with mean 0 and variance 1
> data0 <- rnorm(20,0,1)
> # 20 normal random numbers with mean 1 and variance 1
> data1 <- rnorm(20,1,1)
```

We test the population mean μ to be 0 and calculate confidence interval of 95% using following R script,

```
> t.test(data0,mu=0)

        One Sample t-test

data:   data0
t = 0.3717, df = 19, p-value = 0.7142
alternative hypothesis: true mean is not equal to 0
95 percent confidence interval:
 -0.3500176  0.5011681
sample estimates:
 mean of x
0.07557523
```

From the above result, we can read the t-statistic 0.3717 is in the confidence interval. df = 19 means this test is done by the t-distribution with the degree of freedom 19 (=20-1). If p-value is less than 0.05, it is considered that the population mean is significantly different from 0 and the null hypothesis is rejected. However, the above result shows the p-value = 0.7142.[10] Thus, the null hypothesis $H_0 : \mu = 0$ cannot be rejected. Further, the confidence interval of 95% is $[-0.3500176, 0.5011681]$ which includes 0. Thus, the null hypothesis $H_0 : \mu = 0$ is adopted.[11] We do the similar test for data1.

```
> t.test(data1,mu=0)

        One Sample t-test

data:   data1
t = 6.66, df = 19, p-value = 2.275e-06
alternative hypothesis: true mean is not equal to 0
95 percent confidence interval:
 0.923481 1.769931
```

---

[10]This value is the probability that t-statistic is inside of the confidence interval, i.e., pt(-0.3717,19)+pt(0.3717,19,lower=F).

[11]The confidence interval is calculated by mean(data0)+qt(0.975,19)*sd(data0)/sqrt(20).

```
sample estimates:
mean of x
 1.346706
```

The above result shows that the t-statistic is 6.66 and confidence interval is [0.923481, 1.769931]. Therefore, the null hypothesis is rejected. Further, we can read the p-value is 2.275e-06 which is significantly small. This also implies that the null hypothesis should be rejected. If we change the confidence interval to 99%, we write the following,

```
> t.test(data1,mu=0,conf.level=0.99)

        One Sample t-test

data:  data1
t = 6.66, df = 19, p-value = 2.275e-06
alternative hypothesis: true mean is not equal to 0
99 percent confidence interval:
 0.7682037 1.9252086
sample estimates:
mean of x
 1.346706
```

For the case of one-sided test, we add the script
`alternative="greater"` or `"less"` into arguments (without any specification, R do two-sided test. The specification for two-sided test is done by the script, `"two.side"`).

```
> t.test(data1,mu=0,alternative="less",conf.level=0.99)

        One Sample t-test

data:  data1
t = 6.66, df = 19, p-value = 1
alternative hypothesis: true mean is less than 0
99 percent confidence interval:
    -Inf 1.860209
sample estimates:
mean of x
 1.346706
```

Finally, we introduce the test for means of data0 and data1 to be different from each other. If we test it under the assumption that both of their variances is same, we add the script `var.equal=T` into arguments. Otherwise, we just do not write it (or write `var.equal=F`).

```
> t.test(data0,data1,var.equal=T)

        Two Sample t-test

data:  data0 and data1
t = -4.4326, df = 38, p-value = 7.671e-05
alternative hypothesis: true difference in means is not
equal to 0
95 percent confidence interval:
 -1.8516576 -0.6906043
sample estimates:
 mean of x  mean of y
0.07557523 1.34670618
```

The above result shows that the t-statistic -4.4326 is out of the confidence interval $[-1.8516576, -0.6906043]$ and p-value is less than 0.05. Thus, the null hypothesis which means data0 and data1 are the same is rejected.

2.4 Regression Analysis

Regression analysis is one of the most used methods in finance and econometrics. The essence is to estimate the relationship between explanatory variable X and explained variable Y as the linear form $Y = \sum a_i X_i + c$,[12] where coefficient a_i is sensitivity and c is a constant. The case of the single explanatory variable might be good to get intuition of regression analysis, because it is easy to depict the scattered plot of variables (X, Y). Such a single variable case is called single regression analysis, and the multi variables is called multiple regression analysis. The regression analysis is an important method in various areas including finance. Thus, many statistical softwares for regression analysis have been developed. The most familiar one might be EXCEL. Here, we discuss how we do regression analysis in R.

Suppose the rate of change of a stock price ($Y = $ Stock) and the rate of change of two economic indexes ($X_1 = $ Eco1, $X_2 = $ Eco2) are given in Table 2.1. To analyze how sensitive the stock price is to the economic indexes, we estimate the following regression equation

$$Y = a_1 X_1 + a_2 X_2 + c. \tag{2.3}$$

---

[12]For example, we can pick up stock price as an explained variable and macro economic indexes as explanatory variables. We may forecast the future stock prices, using the result of regression analysis and macro economic indexes. See [MPV12] for more details on regression analysis.

Table 2.1: The rate of change on a stock price and economic indexes

	Stock	Eco1	Eco2
Jan	4.8	0.5	0.1
Feb	−3.3	−1.8	−2.6
Mar	6.4	5.5	3.2
Apr	3	−1.7	6.5
May	−0.4	−0.9	1.9
Jun	2.6	2.9	−2.4
Jul	−8.2	−4.8	−2.6
Aug	−2.5	0.1	−1.5
Sep	6.9	0.7	5.3
Oct	−5.1	−2.6	0.9
Nov	2.7	1	−2.4
Dec	−7.9	−1.8	−0.6

That is, regression analysis is to determine the coefficient a_1, a_2 and constant c in (2.3) to be fitted most to the given data.

We proceed to the regression analysis in R. First, we need to set the data.[13] For the example of Table 2.1, we define a data frame called price, as follow,

```
> stock <- c(4.8,-3.3,6.4,3,-0.4,2.6,-8.2,-2.5,6.9,-5.1,
  +2.7,-7.9)
> eco1 <- c(0.5,-1.8,5.5,-1.7,-0.9,2.9,-4.8,0.1,0.7,
  -2.6, +1,-1.8)
> eco2 <- c(0.1,-2.6,3.2,6.5,1.9,-2.4,-2.6,-1.5,5.3,0.9,
  +2.4,-0.6)
> price <- data.frame(Stock=stock,Eco1=eco1,Eco2=eco2)
```

From them, we can calculate their means, standard errors and correlations,

```
> mean(price$Stock)
[1] -0.08333333
> sd(price$Stock)
[1] 5.287521
> cor(price$Stock,price$Eco1) # correlation between Stock
> # and Eco1
[1] 0.7679317
> cor(price$Stock,price$Eco2) # correlation between Stock
> # and Eco2
[1] 0.5322617
```

---

[13]Refer to Section 2.5, if you need to read big data from a csv file,

```
> cor(price$Eco1,price$Eco2) # correlation between Eco1
> # and Eco2
[1] 0.1751904
```

If the correlations between explanatory variables and explained variable are small, it might induce the weak explanatory power. If the correlation between explained variables is high, it might induce the multicollinearity.[14] Thus, it is important to check the basic statistics before regression analysis.

First, let us try the single regression analysis using Eco1. R has a function lm() for regression analysis. The first argument of lm() defines the form of regression model. In the case of single regression analysis, we signify Stock~Eco1 of which Stock is set as explained variable and Eco1 is set as explanatory variable. For the second argument, we specify the data for the regression analysis.

```
> plot(Stock~Eco1, data=price) # scatter plot
> reg <- lm(Stock~Eco1, data=price) # regression analysis
> abline(reg) # depiction of the regression line
> summary(reg) # the summary of analysis

Call:
lm(formula = Stock ~ Eco1, data = price)

Residuals:
   Min     1Q Median     3Q    Max
-5.466 -2.087 -1.053  1.624  5.563

Coefficients:
            Estimate Std. Error t value Pr(>|t|)
(Intercept)   0.2812     1.0299   0.273  0.79035
Eco1          1.5086     0.3979   3.791  0.00354 **
---
Signif. codes:  0 *** 0.001 ** 0.01 * 0.05 . 0.1   1

Residual standard error: 3.552 on 10 degrees of freedom
Multiple R-squared: 0.5897,    Adjusted R-squared: 0.5487
F-statistic: 14.37 on 1 and 10 DF,  p-value: 0.003536
```

---

[14] If the correlation between explanatory variables is high, one explanatory variable may be explained by another explanatory variable. Thus, using both of them as explanatory variables might induce an unstable result. This problem is called multicollinearity [GRS99]. Trial and error is necessary to choose appropriate explanatory variables.

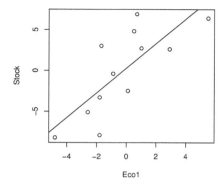

Figure 2.3: Scatter plot and regression line

Figure 2.3 depicts the result of regression analysis. The summary of regression analysis implies that the constant of regression equation is 0.2812 and coefficient is 1.5086. More precisely, the most fitted model suggested by this single regression analysis is given by the linear equation (Stock) = 1.5086 × (Eco1) + 0.2812. We explain the details of summary(reg).

- Residuals: The residual is one of the basic statistics. The residual is the difference between the data of Stock and the estimated values 1.5086×(Eco1) + 0.2812. That is, the residual is the difference between the scattered points and the regression line in Figure 2.3. The summary(reg) shows the minimum value, first quantile value, median value, third quantile value and maximum value of residuals. If you want to show only the model value, type predict(reg) and if you want to show the residual only, type residuals(reg).

- Coefficients: This is the main part of regression analysis. Estimate shows the regression coefficients which are determined to minimize the sum of squared errors between data and model values. (Intercept) shows the constant, Eco1 shows the regression coefficient of the explanatory variable Eco1. This result implies that the regression equation is given by (Stock) = 1.5086 × (Eco1) + 0.2812. Further, the results of standard error, t-statistic and p-value are shown; i.e., t-statistic is the statistic for the hypothesis of "the regression coefficient is zero" and the absolute value of t-statistic is preferable to be larger than approximately 2 which is given as a good criteria of t-statistic. That is why the small t-statistic means that the sign of the coefficient might be inverted; this implies that the credibility of the model is fragile. Further, p-value is the probability that t-statistic is inside of the confidence interval. Thus, the larger the absolute value of t-statistic, the smaller the p-value. R shows the degree of goodness of p-value as the star mark ∗. If you want to show only coefficients, write `coefficients(reg)`.

■ R-Squared: R^2 is called determinant coefficient and used to evaluate how the model fits the data. The closer the value is 1, the better the fitness of the model is. It is the standard interpretation of determinant coefficient. R shows the `Multiple R-squared` which is determinant coefficient and `Adjusted R-squared` which is adjusted determinant coefficient. Determinant coefficient R^2 is the square of the correlation R between model values and samples. Adjusted determinant coefficient is often used in the multiple regression analysis because this coefficient is adjusted according to the data size and the number of explanatory variables. Although the data size is small, if the large number of explanatory variables is used, R^2 might be extremely high. To avoid this, it is recommended that the adjusted determinant coefficient is used. Further, `F-statistic` and p-value under `Adjusted R-squared` are statistics for the test of hypothesis "All coefficients is zero".

We proceed to multiple regression analysis. In R, we can do it by specifying the first argument of `lm()` as `Stock~Eco1+Eco2`.

```
> # regression on explained variable Stock with explanatory
> # variables Eco1 and Eco2
> reg <- lm(Stock~Eco1+Eco2, data=price)
> summary(reg)

Call:
lm(formula = Stock ~ Eco1 + Eco2, data = price)

Residuals:
   Min     1Q Median     3Q    Max
-4.942 -1.661  0.300  1.371  4.132

Coefficients:
            Estimate Std. Error t value Pr(>|t|)
(Intercept) -0.08471    0.85575  -0.099  0.92332
Eco1         1.36738    0.33061   4.136  0.00254 **
Eco2         0.68653    0.28158   2.438  0.03748 *
---
Signif. codes:  0 *** 0.001 ** 0.01 * 0.05 . 0.1  1

Residual standard error: 2.906 on 9 degrees of freedom
Multiple R-squared:  0.7529,    Adjusted R-squared:  0.698
F-statistic: 13.71 on 2 and 9 DF,  p-value: 0.001853
```

The above result shows the estimation is given by (Stock) = 1.36738×(Eco1) + 0.68653×(Eco2) - 0.08471. R^2 of this case is higher than R^2 of single regression. Thus, it confirms that the addition of Eco2 increases the explanatory power. The t-statistic of Eco1 and Eco2 is larger than 2, while the t-statistic of the constant is very small. Such a case might suggest to us not to use the constant for stable analysis. If you do not want to use constant, add the argument -1 in `lm()`; i.e., write `lm(Stock~Eco1+Eco2-1,data=price)`. If you want to use all variables except for Stock, use period mark; i.e., write `lm(Stock~.,data=price)`. If you want to analyze for logarithmic variable, use the function `log()`; e.g., write `lm(log(Stock)~log(Eco1),data=price)`.

2.5 Yield curve analysis using principal component analysis

This section is devoted to describe principal component analysis which is a statistical method as often used in finance theory as regression analysis, especially focusing on yield curve analysis. Principal component analysis is a good method to extract characteristics of the data or categorize the data. In this section, we use examples of yield curve, but there are fruitful applicability for other fields of finance. Since yield curve analysis is the most important issue in almost all fields of finance, including derivative pricing, it is meaningful for us to grasp the essence of yield curve analysis.

2.5.1 Yield curve

Consider a bond. The price of the bond is given by the present value (PV) of future cash flows generated by the bond. These cash flows consist of coupon and principal amount of the bond discounted by appropriate interest rate. This appropriate interest rate is called (bond) yield. Before discussing the details, we have to define "to discount by the appropriate interest rate" and "present value". Imagine you have a bank account of 1 dollar for 5 years with 1% of interest rate. Then, you will have 1.05101 dollars (=1 dollars ×$(1+0.01)^5$). Thus, 1.05101 dollars at maturity (5 years later) and 1 dollar at present has to have the equivalent value. In other word, 1 dollar at maturity is $1/(1+0.01)^5 = 0.95147$ dollars at present. Thus, we call the present value of 1 dollar at maturity is 0.95147 discounted by 1% of interest rate. More generally, consider a bond with coupon C a year, the maturity of N years later and 100 dollars of principal amount. If the present value of this bond is given by coupons and principal amount discounted by interest rate r such that

$$PV = \sum_{i=1}^{N} \frac{C}{(1+r)^i} + \frac{100}{(1+r)^N},$$

then the r is called bond yield.[15] If the coupon $C/2$ is paid twice a year, the present value is given by

$$PV = \sum_{i=1}^{2N} \frac{C/2}{(1+r/2)^i} + \frac{100}{(1+r/2)^{2N}}.$$

The above equations imply that the low yield induces the high bond price and the high yield induces the low bond price.

Yield is different from maturity of bonds. The yield curve is given by a curve showing the relationship between the yield and the maturity (Figure 2.4 is an example). The yield of long term bond is often higher than the yield of short term bond, and this phenomenon is called forward yield.[16] Conversely, if the yield of long term bond is lower than the yield of short term bond, the yield is called inverted yield.

The shape of the yield curve changes by business cycle. This change affects the bond price. Thus, it has a important role in the analysis of bond. The change of yield curve is categorized into 3 types, and we can qualitatively and quantitatively explain the movement of yield curve by using following 3 types of change.

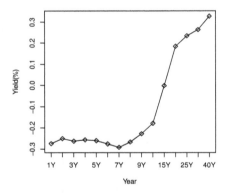

Figure 2.4: JGB yield curve on 29 July 2016

---

[15]More precisely, this yield is called compound interest rate. There are other types of yield; e.g., simple interest rate and continuous interest rate. In this section, we use the same usage for yield and interest rate, if there is no confusion.

[16]Even in the case of mortgage loan or fixed deposit, the interest rate of long term is usually higher than that of short term loan.

The typical movement of yield curve:

■ Shift: Yields for all years changes to same direction, that is, all yield moves up or down.

■ Slope: Short term yield changes oppositely to long term yield. For example, when the short term yield goes up, the long term yield goes down.

■ Curvature: The movement of short and long term yield changes in opposite direction to mid term yield. For example, short term yield and long term yield go up, whereas the mid term yield goes down.

The curve trading is the trading strategy which utilizes the yield curve movements; e.g., making position called yield spread, butterfly, brett or barbell.[17] For the quantitative analysis of yield curve, the principal component analysis gives an effective way to make decision which bonds to buy or sell and how many bonds to buy or sell.

If you need to get information on JGB, you can get it by the following homepage of Ministry of Finance Japan. In this section, we use the JGB yield.

http://www.mof.go.jp/english/jgbs/reference/interest_rate/index.htm

2.5.2 What is principal component analysis?

We often need to analyze the relationship between market or economic variables in finance. The statistical method which deals with multi variables is called multivariate analysis. The most intuitive method is multiple regression analysis which is described in Section 2.4 and is given by

$$Y = a_1 X_1 + a_2 X_2 + \cdots + c \qquad (c \text{ is constant}),$$

where Y is explained variable, X_i are explanatory variables and coefficients a_i are sensitivities. For example, if you analyze the interest rate model, you can choose Y to be 10 years interest rate and X to be economic growth, price movement and so on. Regression analysis constructs the linear relationship between explanatory and explained variables. Since it is intuitive, it is the most representative method used in many economic models.[18]

---

[17]Roughly speaking, these strategies try to make profit by buying a bond with a maturity and selling another bond with different maturity, observing the movement of yield curve. We discuss these strategies, later.

[18]Instead of simplicity, regression analysis might generate multicollinearity which makes unstable results in analysis. To avoid it, a careful selection of explanatory variables is required.

Although regression analysis enables us to explain yields for each years by various explanatory variables, yields have correlation with each other. Principal component analysis (PCA) makes it possible to extract the characteristics of the simultaneous movement of yields and categorize yields in some groups. More precisely, principal component analysis is a method to reduce the dimension of variables [JW07]. Thus, this method is often used to compress the digital data.

We introduce the essence of principal component analysis by the example of JGB data. For more details of the concrete calculation, refer to Section 2.5.4. Figure 2.5 is the scatter plot of the 5 year yield of JGB and 10 year yield of JGB. We can observe the positive correlation between them. One day, a yield of 5 year bond was 0.5% and 10 year yield was 1.2%. Then, the data (0.5,1.2) is put on the figure with horizontal axis of 5 year bond and vertical axis of 10 year bond. However, if the axes are rotated and define a new coordinate x,y in Figure 2.5, then, x-axis can explain the essential status of 5 year yield, ignoring the minor details. While, the value on y-axis means the distance from x-axis. If it is positive, 10 years yield is larger than 5 years yield; i.e., the yield curve is steep.

Principal component is the values on these rotated axes x,y. Note that, the present example shows that x has stronger explanatory power than y. The axis with the most explanatory power, x in the above example, is called first principal component (PC1), the second one, y, is called second principal component (PC2), and so on. Further, the value on each axis is called principal component score. For example, for $x = 1.5$, the principal component score is 1.5. In summary, principal component analysis defines the new coordinate for effectively explaining the relation between variables and determines the value on this rotated coordinate.

Eigenvector

To precisely understand the principal component analysis, it is necessary to deal with eigenvector, because the principal component analysis is mathematically eigendecomposition of a matrix. Since eigenvector is also vector, this indicates a direction consistent with principal components. Thus, the interpretation of the result of principal component is equivalent to the interpretation of the eigenvector. In the financial service industry, it is important to understand how to interpret the eigenvector, rather than understanding the mathematical idea of the eigenvector. Although there are several ways to interpret the eigenvector, the core point of the interpretation of eigenvector is to define the variable transformation from the observations of data (in this context, 5 years and 10 years bond) to the principal component (x,y). By the observation of eigenvector, we can get information as follows;

- the direction of new coordinates (principal component)

- the weights to derive the principal component scores from observations

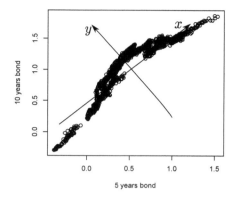

Figure 2.5: Scatter plot of 5 year yield of JGB and 10 years yield of JGB

■ the sensitivity for the principal component score of the observations; i.e., how sensitively the observations move, when the principal component scores change

In the regard with the third interpretation, we can describe the yield at each year by eigenvectors, like as factor model (see Section 4.4), that is,

$$Y_i = a_{i,1}PC1 + a_{i,2}PC2 + \cdots + c_i \qquad (c_i \text{ is constant}), \qquad (2.4)$$

where Y_i ($i = 5y, 10y$, etc.) is yield of $5, 10, \cdots$, years bond, $PC1, PC2$ are principal component scores, and sensitivity $a_{i,j}$ is the eigenvector.[19] This expression implies that the first principal component should be analyzed at first, neglecting the second principal component. The second principal component precedes all other principal component except for first principal component. Same logic continues to the last principal component. Then, the principal movements of yield curve can be effectively grasped.

Characteristics of principal component analysis:

Comparing with regression analysis, principal component analysis has the following characteristics,

■ Whereas the explanatory variables are observed values in a regression analysis, they cannot be directory observed in a PCA, as they are artificially derived variables for detecting patterns in explained variables.

---

[19]Eigenvector is usually defined as the normalized one: i.e., original covariance matrix, for which eigenvector is derived by decomposition, is adjusted by mean extraction and division by the standard error. Hence, the sensitivity is given by eigenvector multiplied by standard error of observations.

■ Principal components are somewhat more difficult to interpret than the explanatory variables of a regression analysis.

■ With PCA, the arbitrariness involved in the selection of explanatory variables for a regression analysis is eliminated.

■ Since principal components are mutually independent (orthogonal), multicollinearity is not an issue, as it is often with multiple regression analysis.

2.5.3 Example of principal component analysis using JGB

We show an example of principal component analysis with R using yield curve data.[20] Via the example, we will grasp the essence of principal component analysis. Here, we use the JGB data from 2 years bond to 30 years bond. For this analysis, we downloaded data from the homepage of Ministry of Finance Japan. By clicking "Historical Data (1974~)", the download of a csv file named "jgbcme_all.csv" starts. We read data by read.csv().

```
> # data extraction as string type
> data <- read.csv("jgbcme_all.csv",stringsAsFactors=FALSE)
```

This is very long data and includes missing values on long term bonds. Thus, we extract data as necessary. Here, we pick up the data after 6 November 2007 from where JGB includes 40 years bond.

```
> jgb.data<-list(0)
> for(i in 1:length(data[1,]))
+ {
+   # line 8691 corresponds to 6 November 2007
+   if(i==1){
+     jgb.data[[i]]<-as.Date(data[8691:length(data[,1]),i])
+   }else{
+     jgb.data[[i]]<-as.numeric(data[8691:length(data[,1]),i])
+   }
+ }
> jgb.data<-data.frame(jgb.data)
>
> # name setting of data.frame
> for(i in 1:length(jgb.data))
+ {
+   names(jgb.data)[i]<-data[1,i]
+ }
```

---

[20][LX08] also gives good examples using PCA.

Next, we see the mean and the standard error of data.

```
> # using interest rate data from 2 years bond to 30
> # years bond
> Mean <- rep(0,13)
> StDev <- rep(0,13)
> for(i in 1:13)
+ {
+   Mean[i]<-mean(jgb.data[,i+2])
+   StDev[i] <- sd(jgb.data[,i+2])
+ }
> Mean
 [1] 0.1783410 0.2296328 0.3089556 0.3809780 0.4581876
     0.5528798
 [9] 0.6742479 0.7967605 0.8972091 1.3355772 1.6516721
     1.7795122
[13] 1.8385182
> StDev
 [1] 0.2377067 0.2780413 0.3173738 0.3444768 0.3692043
     0.3825336
 [9] 0.4057912 0.4403678 0.4579533 0.5056952 0.4684131
     0.4742541
[13] 0.4651794
```

Normalizing data to be mean 0 and standard error 1, we conduct principal component analysis on the JGB data.

```
> X <- t((t(jgb.data[,3:15])-Mean)/StDev)
> # t() is a function to make transpose matrix
```

Note that R has a function scale() to calculate the normalization of data.
Principal component analysis in R can be done by the function princomp().[21]

```
> # principal component using unbiased correlation matrix
> PC <- princomp(X, cor=TRUE)
```

We can see the result of principal component analysis by using the function str().

---

[21] Since this example uses normalized data, correlation matrix generates same result with covariance matrix. If not, you have to specify cor = TRUE for the analysis using correlation matrix, or have to specify cor = FALSE for the analysis using covariance matrix for doing principal component analysis with R.

```
> str(PC)
List of 7
 $ sdev     : Named num [1:13] 3.4806 0.8519 0.3589 0.1268 0.0788 ...
  ..- attr(*, "names")= chr [1:13] "Comp.1" "Comp.2" "Comp.3" ...
 $ loadings: loadings [1:13, 1:13] -0.264 -0.269 -0.275 -0.279 ...
  ..- attr(*, "dimnames")=List of 2
  .. ..$ : chr [1:13] "2Y" "3Y" "4Y" "5Y" ...
  .. ..$ : chr [1:13] "Comp.1" "Comp.2" "Comp.3" "Comp.4" ...
 $ center   : Named num [1:13] 5.89e-17 1.56e-17 7.20e-17 1.33e-17 ...
  ..- attr(*, "names")= chr [1:13] "2Y" "3Y" "4Y" "5Y" ...
 $ scale    : Named num [1:13] 1 1 1 1 1 ...
  ..- attr(*, "names")= chr [1:13] "2Y" "3Y" "4Y" "5Y" ...
 $ n.obs    : int 2138
 $ scores   : num [1:2138, 1:13] -6.06 -6 -5.86 -5.79 -5.73 ...
  ..- attr(*, "dimnames")=List of 2
  .. ..$ : NULL
  .. ..$ : chr [1:13] "Comp.1" "Comp.2" "Comp.3" "Comp.4" ...
 $ call     : language princomp(x = X, cor = TRUE)
 - attr(*, "class")= chr "princomp"
```

Contribution ratio, cumulative contribution

We investigate the explanatory power of each principal component. To do it, see the eigenvalues which corresponds to the square of $ sdev derived above by the command str(), because contribution ratio and cumulative contribution is calculated based on eigenvalue (the more details is explained in Section 2.5.4).

```
> PC$sd^2 # eigenvalue
> PC$sd^2/sum(PC$sd^2) # contribution ratio
> cumsum(PC$sd^2/sum(PC$sd^2))# cumulative contribution
```

Figure 2.6 depicts the contribution ratio and cumulative contribution.[22]

```
> posit<-barplot(PC$sd^2/sum(PC$sd^2),ylim=c(0,1.1),col=8)
> lines(posit,cumsum(PC$sd^2/sum(PC$sd^2)))
> points(posit,cumsum(PC$sd^2/sum(PC$sd^2)),pch=5)
> legend("right", legend = c('Contribution ratio',
+ 'Cumulative contribution'),bty = "n",lty = c(1,NA),
+ pch = c(5,NA),fill = c(0,8),border = c(NA,1),
+ x.intersp=c(1.2,0.5))
```

By this result, we can see approximately 99% of the movement of yield curve can be explained by 1st, 2nd and 3rd principal components only.

---

[22] Although we can depict it using R, it is also possible to depict it using EXCEL by outputting a text file with the command: write.table(PC$sd^2,file="eigen.txt"), for example.

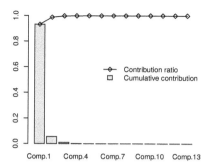

Figure 2.6: Result of principal component analysis of yield curve: Contribution ratio and cumulative contribution

Eigenvector

We check the eigenvector and principal component scores to see the meaning of each principal component.[23] We can see eigenvector by using the function loadings().

```
> unclass(loadings(PC)) # eigenvector
```

The function unclass() outputs the arguments extracted from the class information. On the analysis of interest rates, the important factors are only 1st, 2nd and 3rd principal components. Thus, the other principal components are excluded:

```
> unclass(loadings(PC)[,1:3])
         Comp.1        Comp.2        Comp.3
2Y   -0.2644728   -0.41713785    0.41602161
3Y   -0.2690465   -0.39943444    0.21792955
4Y   -0.2750215   -0.33676995    0.03337381
5Y   -0.2792171   -0.26832556   -0.09379876
6Y   -0.2837785   -0.15871381   -0.19215574
7Y   -0.2855189   -0.02340250   -0.25087538
8Y   -0.2849840    0.05567663   -0.30026467
9Y   -0.2846106    0.09324031   -0.30150581
10Y  -0.2828399    0.14391048   -0.30802425
15Y  -0.2784177    0.27062437   -0.13617938
20Y  -0.2726930    0.35749091    0.17904979
25Y  -0.2732279    0.33197337    0.34121182
30Y  -0.2706822    0.33399146    0.47611523
```

---

[23]Eigenvector shows the new coordinates. Principal component scores is the values on the coordinates; e.g., the direction of *x*-axis and *y*-axis in Figure 2.5 is eigenvector and the values on the coordinate are principal component scores.

By the following code, Figure 2.7 depicts the above result.

```
> barplot(t(pca3),beside=TRUE,col=c(8,1,0))
> legend(20,0.4,legend=c("PCA1","PCA2","PCA3"),fill=c(8,1,0))
```

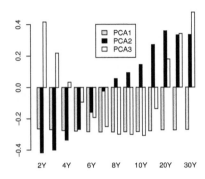

Figure 2.7: The result of principal component analysis: Eigenvector

From this result, we interpret the meaning of each principal component. The sign of eigenvectors of 1st principal component (PCA1) is negative for all years (2Y-30Y). This implies that the 1st principal component relates with movement of level of yields (in this example, the decreases of yield, since the value is negative). While the sign of eigenvectors of 2nd principal components (PCA2) corresponding to short term is negative, the sign of eigenvectors to long term is positive. This implies that the 2nd principal component relates with the change of steepness of yield curve (in this example, the decrease of short term and increases of long term yield). On signs of eigenvectors of 3rd principal components, the sign of mid term yield is opposite to the sign of short and long term yields. This implies that the 3rd principal component expresses the curvature of the yield curve.

The above example shows us the direction of 1st principal component implies the decrease of interest rate, the direction of 2nd principal component implies that yield curve is getting steeper and the direction of 3rd principal component implies the decrease of curvature which is called positive butterfly: i.e., the increase of short and long term interest rates and the decrease of mid term interest rates.[24]

---

[24]The sign of eigenvector might have a different sign to the above result, by using other dataset. However, this means just the case where the direction of coordinates are inverted.

Principal component score

In addition to the direction of each principal components, we need to check the principal component scores which show the status of yield curve. The principal component score is calculated by original data and eigenvector, as follows,

```
> # principal component score
> data.matrix(X) %*% unclass(loadings(PC))
```

If you analyze the skewness of yield curve or appropriateness of bond price, it is better for principal component scores to be standardized to have mean 0 and variance 1. Standardization makes easy for the judgement of magnitude of principal component scores. This also makes it easy for the judgement how far steepness and curvature of yield curve deviate from the average of them. To calculate the standardized principal component scores and the corresponding principal component loadings, we need to regulate values by using standard error PC$sd, that is,

```
> # standardized principal component score
> Score <- t(t(data.matrix(X) %*% unclass(
+ loadings(PC)))/PC$sd)
> # principal component loading
> Loading <- t(PC$sd * t(unclass(loadings(PC))))
```

The time series of principal component score is shown in Figure 2.8. In general, if the absolute value of principal component is over 2, it is considered to be deviated from the average. Indeed, the assumption of normal distribution implies that the probability exceeding 2 is less than 2.5%.

Note that the principal component loading is given for standardized yield data (X). To derive the sensitivity of non-standardized yield data for principal component score, that is, to derive the coefficient $a_{i,j}$ in (2.4), we use the standard error of original yield dataset such that

```
> Loading * StDev
```

For curve trading, we need to investigate the status of yield curve observing the principal component score and sensitivity (eigenvector). The example we pick up here shows that the increasing score of 1st principal component implies the decreasing level of yield curve, increasing score of 2nd principal component implies the more steepness of the yield curve, and the increasing score of 3rd principal component implies the increasing short and long term yield and decreasing mid term yield. Thus, if the score of 2nd principal component is large, we will construct the position which generates profit for flattering curve, because the score characteristics show that the curve is too steep, comparing to the fair level. This strategy is called flattener. Indeed, we can make the flattener by selling short term bond and buying long term bond. The opposite position is called steepener.

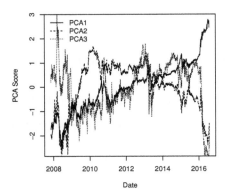

Figure 2.8: Time series of standardized principal component score

If the score of 3rd principal component deviates from the mean, we have a good opportunity to construct the position of buying (selling) the mid term bond and selling (buying) the short and long term bond, because we consider the strong curvature of the yield curve will be regulated to the mean. This strategy is called butterfly. The above status of the principal component score also shows us the opportunity to switch the bullet and barbell, where bullet is a position which invests intensely in bond of a specific term, and barbell is also a position which invests short and long term bond.

Further, constructing a fair curve using a few principal component scores and sensitivities, we will analyze the appropriateness of bond prices at specific terms by comparison with the fair curve. The logic is based on that the curve constructed only by the principal components with strong explanatory power shows the fair value. That is, this strategy is based on the idea that the error will be regulated and the value will converge to the fair value.

2.5.4 How to calculate the principal component analysis?

Although it is not the numerical problem, we show that the principal component analysis is induced to the eigenproblem of matrix. Consider a set consisting of m data of T samples; e.g., sampling m bonds for T days. We describe such a dataset as a matrix X of $T \times m$, as follows,

$$X = \begin{bmatrix} x_1^1 & \cdots & x_1^m \\ \vdots & \ddots & \vdots \\ x_T^1 & \cdots & x_T^m \end{bmatrix}.$$

The dataset X has a geometrical meaning. Indeed, we can interpret that $(x^1, \cdots, x^m)$ has a point in m dimensional space. There exist T points in this space. That is, we have scatter plot with these points. The principal component analysis is to find a new coordinate $(y^1, \cdots, y^m)$ by the orthogonal rotation of the original coordinate $(x^1, \cdots, x^m)$ such that the new coordinate $(y^1, \cdots, y^m)$ enable us to grasp the clearer characteristics of data. More precisely, we measure the explanatory power of the new axis y^1 by observing dispersion of the data on this axis; to make a perpendicular line on the axis y^1 from each point of the data and to find the direction of the axis with mostly dispersed longitudes of the perpendicular lines. We call the value of each point on y^1 as 1st principal component score. The axis y^2 corresponding to 2nd principal component is determined to maximize the dispersion of data with constraint where y^1 and y^2 are orthogonal to each other. The following axis are also determined by the same way and these axes are ordered by the explanatory power. Here, to compare each dispersions of data which might have various units, we have to standardize the data X by mean 0 and standard error 1. Further, for the dataset with strong correlation between the components of the data, like yield with several maturities, we usually pick up a few principal components, not all principal components, because they are enough to capture the essential property of the yield curve (it is called compression of data). Indeed, in the example in the previous section, we showed only 1st to 3rd principal components were good explanatory powers to express the yield curve.

Each vector of X is expressed as

$$
X = \begin{bmatrix} x_1 \\ \vdots \\ x_t \\ \vdots \\ x_T \end{bmatrix},
$$

$$
x_t = (x_t^1, \cdots, x_t^m).
$$

Let v be a m dimensional column vector with euclidean norm of 1. The length of perpendicular foot from the point x_t to the vector v is given by the inner product of them. Thus, it follows that

$$
y_t = x_t v.
$$

The 1st principal component maximizes the sum of squares of y_t. Let y be a column vector with factors y_t. Then, $y = Xv$. Our purpose is to find a vector v which maximizes

$$
\begin{aligned}
\|y\|^2 &= y'y \\
&= (Xv)'(Xv) \\
&= v'(X'X)v
\end{aligned}
\tag{2.5}
$$

with the constraint $v'v = 1$, where $X'X$ is the correlation matrix of sample X and

$'$ is the operator of transpose. Define a Lagrange function and solve the optimization problem by the Lagrange multiplier method; i.e., the Lagrange function is given by

$$L(v,\lambda) = v'(X'X)v - \lambda(v'v - 1).$$

The first order condition derived from it is as follows,

$$\frac{\partial L}{\partial v} = 2(X'X)v - 2\lambda v = 0.$$

The solution (v,λ) satisfies the above equation. However, this equation is simplified to the following eigenproblem on correlation matrix,

$$(X'X)v = \lambda v, \tag{2.6}$$

where λ and v satisfying (2.6) are called eigenvalue and eigenvector, respectively. Further, it holds,

$$y'y = v'(X'X)v = v'\lambda v = \lambda. \tag{2.7}$$

This implies that the eigenvector corresponding to maximum eigenvalue shows the direction of 1st principal component. By the order of eigenvalues, the subsequent principal components are determined. Then, we can construct the vectors which correspond to 2nd, 3rd, 4th principal components, and so on.

Arrange the eigenvectors derived by the above and define $V = (v_1, \cdots, v_m)$. Then, the principal component scores are derived as follows,

$$Y = XV.$$

From (2.7), the euclidean norm of principal component score is the eigenvalue λ. Therefore, how each principal component reflects the information of original data depends on the size of the eigenvalue. The contribution ratio of i-th principal component and cumulative contribution of i-th principal component is respectively given by

$$\frac{\lambda_i}{\lambda_1 + \cdots + \lambda_m}, \qquad \frac{\lambda_1 + \cdots + \lambda_i}{\lambda_1 + \cdots + \lambda_m}.$$

If we use the normalized dataset, it holds $\lambda_1 + \cdots + \lambda_m = m$.

Chapter 3

Time Series Analysis with R

CONTENTS

We have learned statistical analysis in the previous chapter. In this chapter, we will learn time series analysis with R. In the financial service industry, we often use various data; e.g., interest rates, stock prices, foreign currency rates and so on. It is useful to analyze how these variables evolve in time, independently as well as together with other signals. Ideally, we would like to forecast the future movement of these processes. With time series analysis we can use models to forecast financial times series.

3.1 Preparation of time series data

The package `tseries` extends the R functionality by including many useful functions for time series analysis. The package includes the function `get.hist.quote()` which can be used to obtain historical time series data for a wide range of assets.[1] For example, using this function, we get historical data of the stock price of Google from 2 March 2016 to 1 April 2016:[2]

```
> get.hist.quote(instrument="GOOGL",start="2016-3-2",
+ end="2016-4-2", quote=c("Open","High","Low","Close"),
+ provider=c("yahoo"), compression="d")
```

Then, we can see the data as follows.

```
            Open    High     Low   Close
2016-03-02 742.87  743.12  733.25  739.48
2016-03-03 739.48  741.00  729.63  731.59
2016-03-04 734.80  735.00  725.62  730.22
2016-03-07 725.15  727.21  705.14  712.80
2016-03-08 708.39  722.25  704.00  713.53
2016-03-09 715.17  726.24  712.66  725.41
2016-03-10 727.79  736.54  723.29  732.17
2016-03-11 739.95  744.90  736.70  744.87
2016-03-14 744.97  754.26  743.66  750.24
2016-03-15 746.02  753.01  742.84  750.57
2016-03-16 749.05  759.00  746.50  757.36
2016-03-17 757.65  765.34  757.36  758.48
2016-03-18 761.63  762.14  751.82  755.41
2016-03-21 753.91  763.34  751.27  762.16
2016-03-22 758.44  765.00  757.88  760.05
2016-03-23 763.35  765.39  756.03  757.56
2016-03-24 751.20  757.56  750.50  754.84
2016-03-28 756.17  758.30  752.04  753.28
2016-03-29 753.68  767.18  748.29  765.89
2016-03-30 768.21  777.31  767.58  768.34
2016-03-31 768.34  769.08  758.25  762.90
2016-04-01 757.16  770.04  755.20  769.67
```

---

[1]We use here `get.hist.quote()`, which uses US Yahoo Finance. However, note that Japanese stock data is not included in US Yahoo Finance. Since authors live in Japan, we often use the function `getSymbols.yahooj()` included in the `quantmod` package, instead of `get.hist.quote()`. We can also obtain financial data using, for example, the `yahoo.import()` function in the `fImport` package.

[2]The data is extracted by the preceding day denoted `end=` (version 3.4.1 of R). Thus, by denoting `end="2016-4-2"`, the time series ends on 1 April 2016.

The arguments of the function `get.hist.quote()` should be specified as follows:

1. `instrument`: We have to specify the quote symbol. Here, we try to download the stock price of Google with its quote symbol `GOOGL`.

2. `start` and `end`: We specify the start and end date for data to be downloaded.

3. `quote`: We specify the quote type of data. For example, if we only need close data, then it should be described as `quote="Close"`. We can specify multiple fields by using c().

4. `provider`: We specify the data provider. For stock data, we should specify `"yahoo"`.[3]

5. `compression`: The data frequency. `"d"` is daily data, `"w"` is weekly data and `"m"` is monthly data.

The function `get.hist.quote()` has other arguments of `method`, `origin`, `retclass`, `quiet` and `drop`, which you may find useful but we won't go into detail here.[4] We can use the function `get.hist.quote()` without specifying `start` and `end`. In this case, the data is downloaded as long as possible. For example, we try it by setting `compression="m"` to have monthly data.

```
> get.hist.quote(instrument="GOOGL",
+ quote=c("Open","High","Low","Close"), provider=c("yahoo"),
+ compression="m")
```

---

[3] The foreign currency rate data was available by denoting `provider=c("oanda")` on the former version of `get.hist.quote()`. However, it is not available, now.

[4] For more details on get.hist.quote(), see the following link for the package `tseries` documentation: https://cran.r-project.org/web/packages/tseries/tseries.pdf

Then, the following result will appear.

```
time series starts 2004-09-01
time series ends    2017-07-01
              Open      High      Low      Close
2004-09-01   51.401    67.578   49.520   64.86487
2004-10-01   65.465   100.075   64.515   95.41541
2004-11-01   96.872   100.901   80.736   91.08108
2004-12-01   91.066   100.040   84.319   96.49149


                        ⋮


2016-10-01 802.550    839.000  796.230  809.90002
2016-11-01 810.870    816.040  743.590  775.88000
2016-12-01 778.550    824.300  753.360  809.45001
2017-01-01 800.620    867.000  796.890  820.19000
2017-02-01 824.000    853.790  812.050  844.92999
2017-03-01 851.380    874.420  824.300  847.79999
2017-04-01 848.750    935.900  834.600  924.52002
2017-05-01 924.150    999.600  920.800  987.09003
2017-06-01 990.960   1008.610  929.600  929.67999
2017-07-01 933.220    998.680  915.310  992.19000
```

We also have to note that functions, like get.hist.quote(), depend on the provider of the data. If the policy of the provider changes, we may have to find another source of the data. We use get.hist.quote() here, since this is available as of July 2017. Further, we have to note that, when get.hist.quote() does not work well, we should update the version of R, before finding another source of the data. This is because this function often works again on the latest version of R.

Here, let us proceed to the analysis by using the dairy closing price data of stock. Thus, we again download the stock price data of Google from 8 January 2015 to 9 March 2015 as follows;

```
> google <- get.hist.quote(instrument="GOOGL",start="2015-1-8",
+ end="2015-3-9",quote="Close",provider=c("yahoo"),compression="d")
```

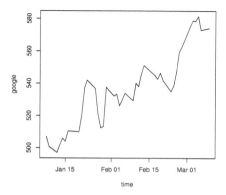

Figure 3.1: Stock price data of google

Next, we plot the data of `google` (Figure 3.1)

```
> plot(google,type="l")
```

Here, we specify the start data as 8 January 2015, although the time series data of Google starts from 19 August 2004.

That is why dataset including too old data might not be good for accurate analysis. In addition, the structure of economy might be essentially changed; e.g., the economy before the bankruptcy of Lehman Brothers might be different from the economy after this critical event. Nevertheless, it is very subtle how to specify the number of data to be used for analyzing time series. Is 30 days data appropriate? 60 days? Or only 10 days? It is sensitive problem. This might be good to decide sample size based on our experience, although there are several theories on this. Here, we do not argue this point further and use the 2 month daily data.

3.2 Before applying for models

One of purposes of time series analysis is to specify the model dominating observed data and (if possible) to estimate future values of the time series by using that model. Before specifying the model, we need to investigate the stationarity of sample. Indeed, if we apply a model with the assumption of stationarity to non-stationary data, the estimation will mislead us. Here, stationarity means that the mean and the variance of time series data are not dependent on time and the autocorrelation of time series data is dependent only on time difference. Before proceeding we should test the sample for statistical stationarity. The unit root test is often used for testing the stationarity of time series data.[5] However, by default, R is not equipped with a function for the augmented Dickey-Fuller test which is often used for the unit root test. Hence we need to introduce the package `tseries` which is equipped with `adf.test()` which is a function used for the augmented Dickey-Fuller test [DF79]. Let us run `adf.test()`.

```
> adf.test(google)

        Augmented Dickey-Fuller Test

data:   google
Dickey-Fuller = -2.7298, Lag order = 3, p-value = 0.2865
alternative hypothesis: stationary
```

The null hypothesis of unit root test is "unit root exists (data is non-stationary)". The above result shows the big p-value, 0.2865. Hence, we cannot reject the null hypothesis of the existence of unit root. That is, we cannot attain the stationary data.

However, such phenomena often happen when we deal with financial time series data. One will often find that financial time series of asset prices are non-stationary. However, the difference between successive prices is often approximately stationary. Let us calculate the difference of time series data by using the function `diff()`. First, we use `diff()` and show the result as follows:

```
> google.diff<-diff(google)
> google.diff
                 Close
2015-01-09  -6.190003
2015-01-12  -3.660003
2015-01-13   4.739990
2015-01-14   4.130005
2015-01-15  -1.919983
2015-01-16   6.449981
2015-01-20  -0.519989
2015-01-21  10.450013
2015-01-22  16.909973
2015-01-23   4.650024
2015-01-26  -5.230041
2015-01-27 -15.529969
2015-01-28  -8.760009
```

---

[5]Unit root test is to test whether the data has unit root or not. Data with a unit root is called a unit root process and are considered non-stationary, but the series of their lagged values is stationary.

⋮

```
2015-02-17   -6.149963
2015-02-18   -2.359986
2015-02-19    3.799988
2015-02-20   -4.650024
2015-02-23   -6.799988
2015-02-24    3.650024
2015-02-25    8.679993
2015-02-26   11.959961
2015-02-27    3.340027
2015-03-02   12.390015
2015-03-03    3.769958
2015-03-04   -0.459961
2015-03-05    3.099976
2015-03-06   -8.529969
2015-03-09    1.199952
```

We can confirm google.diff is the difference of google. Next let's apply the unit root test for google.diff.

```
> adf.test(google.diff)

        Augmented Dickey-Fuller Test

data:  google.diff
Dickey-Fuller = -4.2435, Lag order = 3, p-value = 0.0103
alternative hypothesis: stationary
```

Indeed, we can confirm the stationarity of data with a small p-value, 0.0103.

Other than taking the difference of time series, it is often done to calculate the difference for logarithmic values of time series data[6] to generate the stationary data; e.g., we do it as follows:

```
> diff(log(google))
```

Although the augmented Dickey-Fuller test is often used for testing stationarity of time series data, the Phillips-Perron test is also widely used [Phi87, PP88]. We use the Phillips-Perron test with the function PP.test().

```
> PP.test(google.diff)

        Phillips-Perron Unit Root Test
```

---

[6]The differences of the logarithmic values of the time series are called the log returns.

```
data:  google.diff
Dickey-Fuller = -5.3009, Truncation lag parameter = 3,
p-value = 0.01
```

The p-value is 0.01. For this value, similar to the result of the augmented Dickey-Fuller test, it seems to be good to reject the null hypothesis. Here, we finish the test of time series data as the preparation of model estimation.

3.3　The application of the AR model

Next, we investigate the model appropriate for the data in the previous section. We start by choosing the simplest model and, if the simple model is not appropriate for explaining the data, proceed to more complicated models. Hence, we start the discussion with an autoregressive model (AR model), which is the basic model in time series analysis. The AR model assumes that the current value is dependent on a linear combination of previous values and a stochastic (normally distributed) variable. Mathematically, this relationship for time series can be written as follows $\{y_t\}_{t=-\infty}^{\infty} = \{...,y_{-1},y_0,y_1,y_2,...\}$;

$$y_t = c + a_1 y_{t-1} + a_2 y_{t-2} + \cdots + a_n y_{t-n} + \varepsilon_t, \tag{3.1}$$

where $\varepsilon_t \sim N(0,\sigma^2)$; i.e., ε is normally distributed random variable with mean 0 and variance σ^2. Further, for arbitrary $s \neq t$, ε_t and ε_s are independent of each other.

Since the AR model assumes stationary data, we apply the AR model to `google.diff`, rather than `google` (recall that the stationarity of `google` was rejected).

The function `ar()` calculates parameters of AR model using given data. Here, for the calculation of model parameters, we specify the method `ols` (ordinary least squares). By using the function `ar()`, we can calculate model parameters with maximum likelihood method, Yule-Walker method and Burg method, by specifying `mle`, `yw` and `burg`, respectively. The function `ar()` takes time series objects as input, so we must transform the data in `google.diff` into time series form by using `ts()`.

```
> # recast google.diff as a time series object
> google.diff<-ts(google.diff)
> google.ar<-ar(google.diff,method="ols")
> google.ar # display the results

Call:
ar(x = google.diff, method = "ols")
```

```
Coefficients:
       1          2          3          4          5          6          7
  0.7391     0.1081    -0.2562    -0.0955     0.2391    -0.1442     0.3313
       8          9         10         11         12         13         14
  0.1085     0.3191     0.4078    -0.0227    -0.0042     0.8089    -0.1368
      15         16
 -0.2072     0.5644

Intercept: 1.212 (0.5323)

Order selected 16  sigma^2 estimated as  3.951
```

Coefficients contains the coefficients of model, i.e., $a_1, a_2, \ldots$, in (3.1) Intercept is the constant c in (3.1) and sigma^2 is the variance of ε. Note that the function ar() estimates parameters based on the relation, $y_t - \mu = \tilde{c} + a_1(y_{t-1} - \mu) + \cdots + a_n(y_{t-n} - \mu) + \varepsilon_t$. The estimated value of $\tilde{c}$ is 1.212, with a standard error of 0.5323 (in parenthesis). We can use the command google.ar\$asy.se.coef to check other coefficients' standard error. The value μ is the average of time series data and is defined by $\mu := \sum_{i=1}^{N} Y_i/N$ for sample of the time series $\{Y_i; i = 1, \cdots N\}$. This is confirmed as follows:

```
> google.ar$x.mean
     Close
1.679749
```

Hence, the constant c in (3.1) is given by $c = \tilde{c} + \mu(1 - \sum_{i=1}^{n} a_i) = 1.212 + 1.679749(1 - 0.7391 - 0.1081 - \cdots - 0.5644) = 5.847115$. Order selected 16 means that y_t is explained by $\{y_{t-1}, \cdots, y_{t-16}\}$, that is, ar() estimates the following model:

$$y_t = 5.8471 + 0.7391y_{t-1} + 0.1081y_{t-2} - 0.2562y_{t-3}$$
$$- 0.0955y_{t-4} + 0.2391y_{t-5} - 0.1442y_{t-6} + 0.3313y_{t-7}$$
$$+ 0.1085y_{t-8} + 0.3191y_{t-9} + 0.4078y_{t-10} - 0.0227y_{t-11}$$
$$- 0.0042y_{t-12} + 0.8089y_{t-13} - 0.1368y_{t-14} - 0.2072y_{t-15}$$
$$+ 0.5644y_{t-16} + \varepsilon_t. \tag{3.2}$$

Next, let's check the accuracy of this estimated model.

Intuitively, the criteria of model accuracy is how well it fits the time series. First, we check the residual between the model values and the time series by \$resid.

```
> google.ar$resid
Time Series:
Start = 1
End = 40
Frequency = 1
 [1]          NA          NA          NA          NA          NA
 [6]          NA          NA          NA          NA          NA
[11]          NA          NA          NA          NA          NA
[16]          NA  0.17892185 -2.77673899  0.44035111  1.24890528
[21] -1.36123915 -0.29251607 -1.59846218  1.78868008  0.42837244
[26] -3.72467250 -0.07598574  2.34073271 -2.08251981 -0.92633701
[31]  1.11508145  0.14500994 -1.38850160  2.89830593  2.23518718
[36]  2.57213506 -1.93007312 -3.61409037  3.47699394  0.90245956
```

Data from [1] to [16] are NA, because the model uses the first 16 samples to estimate its coefficients. These residuals are plotted in the left panel of Figure 3.2.

```
> plot(google.ar$resid,xlab="time index",ylab="residuals")
```

Further, we plot model values and sample time series in the right panel of Figure 3.2.

```
> plot(google)
> # exclude first 16 sample from google,
> # first 15 samples from google.diff and residual
> # before adding them
> points(google[-(1:16)]+ google.diff[-(1:15)]
+ -google.ar$resid[-(1:15)])
```

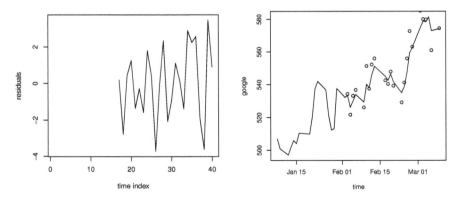

Figure 3.2: Residual of AR model (left panel) and Sample and model values (right panel)

3.3.1 Residual analysis

The right panel of Figure 3.2 intuitively shows the fitness of our model to the time series data. Let's check the fitness quantitatively with a statistical method.

If the analysis is right, that is, if the estimation by autoregressive is right, then the residual

$$\varepsilon_t = y_t - a_1 y_{t-1} - a_2 y_{t-2} - \cdots - a_n y_{t-n} - c$$

is normally distributed with mean 0 and autocorrelation 0. To test this, we will use the Jarque-Bera test, which is used to test normality of data, and the Box-Ljung (Ljung-Box, Box-Pierce) test, which is used to test autocorrelation. These tests are applied to the residual, google.ar$resid.[7] We can do Jarque-Bera test, as follows:

```
> jarque.bera.test(google.ar$resid[-(1:16)])

        Jarque Bera Test

data:  google.ar$resid[-(1:16)]
X-squared = 0.84357, df = 2, p-value = 0.6559
```

The p-value is 0.6559. The null hypothesis of Jarque-Bera test is "the distribution is normal" [JB78]. Since the p-value is not low, it is difficult to reject the null hypothesis. We also do the Box-Ljung [LB78] test, with the function Box.test().

```
> Box.test(google.ar$resid[-(1:16)],type="Ljung")

        Box-Ljung test

data:  google.ar$resid[-(1:16)]
X-squared = 0.23471, df = 1, p-value = 0.6281
```

By the Box-Ljung test, we test the null hypothesis, "there is no autocorrelation". Since the p-value 0.6281 is not small, we cannot reject the null hypothesis.[8]

---

[7]Note that the first 16 data of residuals are missing values. Hence, before testing, we exclude them.

[8]We can test the autocorrelation by the specified lag order. For example, by denoting Box.test(google.ar$resid[-(1:16)],lag=5,type="Ljung"), we test the null hypothesis by lag order 5. Here, we have 24 data of google.ar$resid. Thus, we can do the Box-Ljung test by lag order 24. However, for larger lag order, the result of p-value is decreasing. Thus, it seems to be difficult to adopt the null hypothesis. In this sense, we can check the autocorrelation.

Note that by not specifying lag order, the function Box.test() assumes lag order 1.

3.3.2   Forecasting

Once we have a model with a good fit to the time series, we can then predict what comes next in the time series. We use the function predict(), to calculate predicted values.

```
> google.pred<-predict(google.ar,n.ahead=10)
> # n.ahead specifies the length of forecasting
> google.pred
$pred
Time Series:
Start = 41
End = 50
Frequency = 1
  [1] 10.999883 12.256805 11.158278 14.665264 20.041360
      15.580047
  [7]  9.923197 15.937889 16.602206 18.533166

$se
Time Series:
Start = 41
End = 50
Frequency = 1
  [1] 1.987677 2.471603 2.792927 2.858944 2.859062 2.860384
      2.864262
  [8] 2.924782 3.110018 3.707299
```

The object google.pred consists of predicted value $pred, which is the absolute change from the previous value in the time series, and standard error $se. We want to check how the predicted values fit the real stock price data. So, we do it as follows:

```
> # calling 11 days of stock price data of google from 9 March 2015
> google.ft <- get.hist.quote(instrument="GOOGL",start="2015-3-9",
+ end="2015-3-21",quote="Close",provider=c("yahoo"),compression="d")
trying URL 'http://chart.yahoo.com/table.csv?s=GOOGL&a=2&b=09&c=2015
&d=2&e=21&f=2015&g=d&q=q&y=0&z=GOOGL&x=.csv'
Content type 'text/csv' length 200 bytes
downloaded 758 bytes

time series ends    2015-03-20
Warning message:
In download.file(url, destfile, method = method, quiet = quiet) :
  downloaded length 758 != reported length 200
> # plot of the future data of google
> plot(google.ft,type="l",ylim=c(550,700),xlab="time",
```

```
+ ylab="future values")
> # since predicted values are differences, we need to build
> # the forecasted series values
> google.pred.orig<-google.ft
> google.pred.orig[1]<-google.ft[1]
> for(i in 2:10){
+   google.pred.orig[i]<-google.pred.orig[i-1]+google.pred$pred[i-1]
+ }
> # plot of the predicted values by AR
> lines(google.pred.orig[1:10],lty="dotted")
```

Figure 3.3 plots the real market data and predicted values by AR model. Unfortunately, it shows weak accuracy on forecasting. Our AR model forecasts a monotonously increasing of stock price of Google, but the speed of increases is too steep. It does not do a good job forecasting. Thus, we need to consider the next step. We have the following candidates;

1. abandon the forecasting by time series analysis

2. try modifications of the AR model

3. try other models

Let us discuss the first option. We know that real economic variables depend on various events which include sudden governmental events, natural disasters, and so on, as well as micro-events such as a surprise earnings report. Thus, it is reasonable to assume that we cannot necessarily make a long-term forecast using time series analysis alone. Therefore, we often calculate the confidence interval of our forecast, for example, within 90%, 95%, and so on.

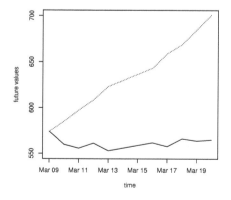

Figure 3.3: The market data (solid line) and predicted values of AR model (dotted line)

On the second option: Actually, we have already tried "accurate" forecasting in the sense of theory. Hence, we do not have any room for sophistication of AR model, in a sense. The things we can do are not sophisticated, but based on trial and error. The function `ar()` automatically calculates the optimal lag order by Akaike information criteria (AIC). The theory of statistics recommends the lag order of AR model to minimize the AIC. The above example shows the lag order 16 in (3.2). This means that lag order 16 minimizes AIC.[9] We can confirm the lag order of the AR model as follows:

```
> google.ar$order
[1] 16
```

The value of AIC is confirmed by the following:

```
> google.ar$aic
        0        1        2        3        4        5        6
75.89337 77.15111 79.39599 78.37233 79.61554 81.51611 82.33702
        7        8        9       10       11       12       13
84.42860 82.88447 80.83700 82.41760 85.60000 84.43471 83.73723
       14       15       16
84.75643 43.60518  0.00000
```

On 16th lag order, AIC takes 0, which implies that the lag order 16 actually minimizes the AIC. However, the optimal lag order shown by AIC might make the model too complicated and the accuracy of forecasting might be worse (this is called over fitting). In practice, referring to AIC, we often decrease the lag order. There is no theoretical ground on what lag order should be used. We decide it by trusting our experienced sense.[10] Note that the lag order shown by AIC is optimal in the sense of fitting to sample data. Thus, the model with shorter lag order worsens the fitting to sample data.

Here, let us reconstruct the AR model by fixing the lag order to be 2. The procedure of the estimation is almost same as one described previously, but we need to specify `order.max = 2` in the function `ar()`.

```
> # AR with lag order 2
> google.ar2 <- ar(google.diff,method="ols",order.max=2)
> # depiction of future values
> plot(google.ft,type="l",ylim=c(550,700),xlab="time",
+ ylab="future values")
> # depiction of predicted values by AR(2)
```

---

[9] AIC implies the relationship between the likelihood of model and the number of model parameters. [Aka74]

[10] Although it depends on the type of data, we feel that lag order 1 is sufficient. Whatever using larger order, 2 or 3 of the lag order will often give us the good result. In other words, we often observe that unreliable forecasting appears if higher lag order is used to construct an AR model.

```
> google.pred2<-predict(google.ar2,n.ahead=10)
> google.pred.orig2<-google.ft
> google.pred.orig2[1]<-google.ft[1]
> for(i in 2:10){
+ google.pred.orig2[i]<-
  google.pred.orig2[i-1]+
+ google.pred2$pred[i-1]
+ }
> lines(google.pred.orig2[1:10],lty="dotted")
```

Here, we do not test the residual, just check the fitting of forecasting.

Figure 3.4 shows the forecasting by AR model is improved in the sense that the predicted values is closer to the sample by fixing the lag order to be 2. However, we again note that this is found by trial-and-error, not by any theoretical underpinning. Thus, we will proceed to the discussion of models extended from the AR model to improve accuracy.

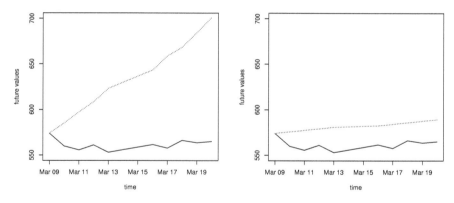

Figure 3.4: The market data (solid line) and the predicted values (dotted line) of AR(16) (left panel, plotting Figure 3.3 again) and AR(2) (right panel)

3.4   Models extended from AR

3.4.1   ARMA and ARIMA model

As discussed above, according to the result of residual analysis, the accuracy of the AR model seemed not to be bad, but the accuracy of forecasting was not good. It might be possible to improve the accuracy by decreasing the lag order. However, as there is no theoretical ground as to how much the lag order should be decreased, there is no guarantee that we can improve the accuracy of forecasting by decreasing the lag order. Thus, it might be helpful instead to extend AR model.

In this section, we consider the autoregressive moving average (ARMA) model. ARMA model is described as follows:

$$y_t = c + \sum_{i=1}^{p} a_i y_{t-i} + \sum_{j=1}^{q} b_j \varepsilon_{t-j} + \varepsilon_t.$$

We now have two lag order parameters, p and q, and we write the model as ARMA(p,q). This is same as AR model, except for third term, $\sum_{j=1}^{q} b_j \varepsilon_{t-j}$. One of the merits of ARMA is, by introducing a second lag order parameter, is to decrease the overall lag order; too many lag order is often derived in AR model. Indeed, the AR estimation discussed in the previous section shows 16 orders of lag.[11] The reason why the ARMA model has less lag order than AR model is simple. The AR model and moving average (MA) model[12] are switchable with each other. Since AR and MA are derived from each other, ARMA, which is a composite model of AR and MA, is also derived from the AR and MA models.

To construct the ARMA model in R, we use the function `arima()` which generates autoregressive integrated moving average (ARIMA) [BJRL15].

As discussed above, financial data is often non-stationary, but the differences of the data is often stationary, which are called unit root processes. Thus we apply the model to the differences of the time series, rather than to the time series itself. For such processes,[13] we apply ARIMA, instead of ARMA. For example, ARIMA of first order integrated process is described as follows:

$$\Delta y_t = c + \sum_{i=1}^{p} a_i \Delta y_{t-i} + \sum_{j=1}^{q} b_j \varepsilon_{t-j} + \varepsilon_t.$$

The difference can be taken for any order. In the case of d-th order, we denote ARIMA(p,d,q) for specifying the order of difference. Hence, ARIMA(p,0,q) is ARMA(p,q).

Unfortunately, the `tseries` package is not equipped with the function to calculate the optimal (p, q). Thus, we need to calculate AIC, successively and derive the optimal (p, q) which minimizes AIC. For example, the following code might be helpful to calculate the optimal (p, q).

---

[11]It seems unreasonable if such a result appears in the estimation using monthly data. The 16 lag order implies that the current stock price depends on data of 16 month ago, which seems too old to impact the current price.

[12]MA model is characterized as follows:

$$y_t = \mu + \sum_{j=1}^{q} b_j \varepsilon_{t-j} + \varepsilon_t,$$

where μ is constant. This is equivalent to ARMA, excluding the term $\sum_{i=1}^{p} a_i y_{t-i}$.

[13]If a series with $(d-1)$-th order of difference is not stationary, but the series with d-th order of difference is stationary, then the series is called the d-th order integrated process.

```
> opt.order<-function(data_,pMax_,qMax_){
+   aic<-0
+   opt.p<-1
+   opt.q<-1
+   for(i in 1:pMax_)
+   {
+     for(j in 1:qMax_)
+     {
+       # ARIMA(i,0,j) for data_
+       tmp <- arima(data_,order = c(i,0,j))
+       if(i==1 && j==1){
+         aic <- tmp$aic
+       }else{
+         if(aic>tmp$aic){
+           aic<-tmp$aic
+           opt.p<-i
+           opt.q<-j
+         }
+       }
+     }
+   }
+   return(c(opt.p,opt.q))
+ }
```

Using this data and the function `opt.order()`,

```
> opt.order(google.diff,5,6)
[1] 2 1
```

Hence, it seems good to choose ARIMA(2,1,1).[14] This significantly decreases the number of model parameters as we hoped. We plot the sample and the predicted values by ARIMA using the below code.

```
> google.arima <- arima(google.diff,order=c(2,0,1))
> plot(google,type="l",xlab="time",ylab="Google price")
> points(google[-(1:2)]+ google.diff[-1]-
+ google.arima$resid[-1])
```

Figure 3.5 shows that the fitting of the model does not seem bad. Residual test can be done by the same procedure discussed in the previous section. The forecasting by ARIMA is given in the following code and the result is shown in Figure 3.6.

---

[14]The function `auto.arima()` in `forecast` library automatically calculates the optimal (p,q). However, the contents of calculation is also searching the optimal (p,q) with iteration, like our example.

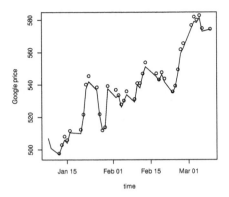

Figure 3.5: Sample (solid line) and model values by ARMA (points)

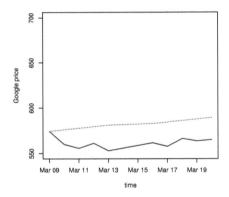

Figure 3.6: Forecasting by ARMA (dotted line)

```
> # plot the future values of google
> plot(google.ft,type="l",ylim=c(550,700),xlab="time",
+ ylab="Google price")
>
> google.pred.arima<-predict(google.arima,n.ahead=10)
> # since predicted values are differenced, we need to
> # reconstruct them to raw data style
> google.pred.orig<-google.ft
> google.pred.orig[1]<-google.ft[1]
> for(i in 2:10){
+   google.pred.orig[i]<-google.pred.orig[i-1]+
+     google.pred.arima$pred[i-1]
+ }
```

```
> # depiction of the predicted values by ARIMA
> points(google.pred.orig[1:10])
```

As we can see, ARIMA makes it possible to construct the model with less lag order. However, it does not necessarily imply that ARIMA and ARMA are better than AR. Rather, if we can use the simpler model, then it is better. AR model is clearly simpler than ARIMA and ARMA, and we should not discount it.

3.4.2   Vector autoregressive

If you construct the model including multiple stocks which seem to be relevant to each other, vector autoregressive (VAR) may be a good candidate. VAR is one of the extension of AR model and is given as the following form:

$$\mathbf{y}_t = \mathbf{c} + \Phi_1 \mathbf{y}_{t-1} + \Phi_2 \mathbf{y}_{t-2} + \cdots + \Phi_p \mathbf{y}_{t-p} + \boldsymbol{\varepsilon}_t,$$

where we consider n stocks. Coefficients, Φ_i is the $n \times n$-matrix, $\mathbf{y}_i$, $\mathbf{c}$ and $\boldsymbol{\varepsilon}_t \sim N(\mathbf{0}, \Omega)$ are n-vector. Further, we define n-vector $\mathbf{0}$, which only includes elements of zero, and Ω, which is $n \times n$ variance-covariance matrix.

R is equipped with a package, vars,[15] for VAR model, which is more recent than tseries package. However, we continuously use tseries package for the analysis of VAR. In the previous section, we did time series analysis using only Google stock price. Hereafter, we use several time series. For instance, we add Apple and Microsoft to Google stock price data. First, we call the data of Apple and Microsoft as follows:

```
> apple <- get.hist.quote(instrument="AAPL",start="2015-1-8",
+ end="2015-3-9",quote="Close",provider=c("yahoo"),
+ compression="d")

> msft <- get.hist.quote(instrument="MSFT",start="2015-1-8",
+ end="2015-3-9",quote="Close",provider=c("yahoo"),
+ compression="d")
```

Similarly in the case of Google stock price, we need to check the stationarity of data. Hence, we do Dickey-Fuller test and Phillip-Perron test:

```
> adf.test(apple) #Dickey-Fuller test for Apple
> adf.test(msft) #Dickey-Fuller test for Microsoft
```

---

[15]The vars package is convenient such that it is equipped with functions to easily calculate the confidence interval and impulse responses. Since the usage of this is similar to tseries package, it may be good to try it.

```
> pp.test(apple) #Phillip-Perron test for Apple
> pp.test(msft) #Phillip-Perron test for Microsoft
```

The result of Dickey-Fuller test for stock price data of Apple is as follows:

```
        Augmented Dickey-Fuller Test

data:  apple
Dickey-Fuller = -1.2681, Lag order = 3, p-value = 0.8614
alternative hypothesis: stationary
```

The p-value is 0.8614 which is weak to reject the null hypothesis. The other results on Apple and Microsoft was similar. Thus, the sample does not show the stationarity. We proceed to taking difference of sample and doing the stationarity test.

```
> apple.diff<-diff(apple)
> msft.diff<-diff(msft)

> adf.test(apple.diff)
> adf.test(msft.diff)
> pp.test(apple.diff)
> pp.test(msft.diff)
```

Then, we can confirm the low p-values and confirm the stationarity. We use the differenced data like as AR model.

When we construct VAR model by `tseries` package, we can do it with the same way as AR model, as follows:

```
> # VAR estimation
> stocks.data<-data.frame(google.diff,apple.diff,msft.diff)
> names(stocks.data)<-c("Google","Apple","Microsoft")
> stocks.var<-ar(ts(stocks.data),method="ols")
```

Then, we get the following result:

```
> stocks.var

Call:
ar(x = stocks.data, method = "ols")
```

```
$ar
, , 1

              Google   Apple  Microsoft
Google       0.68794  1.1961    -3.7069
Apple       -0.35092  0.1029    -1.0066
Microsoft   -0.06356  0.1314    -0.1304

, , 2

              Google    Apple  Microsoft
Google      -0.81124 -0.66261    5.42666
Apple        0.37686  0.21498   -1.32115
Microsoft    0.05258  0.09758   -0.06469

, , 3

              Google    Apple  Microsoft
Google      -0.72290 -3.1696     1.7566
Apple       -0.01380  0.8809    -1.5792
Microsoft   -0.05759 -0.1639     0.7846

, , 4

              Google    Apple  Microsoft
Google      -0.53386 -2.7130    3.98597
Apple       -0.12895 -0.3517    1.57675
Microsoft   -0.09987 -0.2891    0.08013

, , 5

               Google    Apple  Microsoft
Google      -0.194115   0.5406   -10.5666
Apple       -0.090934  -0.1692     2.2573
Microsoft   -0.007996  -0.2487     0.3063

, , 6

               Google    Apple  Microsoft
Google      -0.275710  -2.1957      7.007
Apple        0.015606   0.7418     -2.222
Microsoft   -0.001699   0.1885     -1.345
```

, , 7

	Google	Apple	Microsoft
Google	-0.34272	-1.52384	-6.2037
Apple	-0.05153	0.44964	1.0256
Microsoft	0.01709	0.03935	0.3488

, , 8

	Google	Apple	Microsoft
Google	-0.106550	-0.17890	8.353604
Apple	0.007622	-0.39895	-1.126703
Microsoft	-0.026013	-0.03341	-0.001473

, , 9

	Google	Apple	Microsoft
Google	-0.32553	-2.47374	-1.0457
Apple	-0.05996	0.93894	0.4948
Microsoft	-0.02689	0.02276	0.7610

$x.intercept

Google	Apple	Microsoft
4.3894	-0.7783	0.1549

$var.pred

	Google	Apple	Microsoft
Google	1.5028	0.6218	0.2465
Apple	0.6218	0.6676	0.3601
Microsoft	0.2465	0.3601	0.2326

Further, we see stocks.var$x.mean:

```
> stocks.var$x.mean
    Google      Apple   Microsoft
 1.6797493  0.3812500  -0.1185001
```

This implies that the estimated model has the following form:

$$
\begin{pmatrix} \Delta \text{Google}_t - 1.6797493 \\ \Delta \text{Apple}_t - 0.3812500 \\ \Delta \text{Microsoft}_t - (-0.1185001) \end{pmatrix} = \begin{pmatrix} 4.3894 \\ -0.7783 \\ 0.1549 \end{pmatrix}
$$

$$
+ \begin{pmatrix} 0.68794 & 1.1961 & -3.7069 \\ -0.35092 & 0.1029 & -1.0066 \\ -0.06356 & 0.1314 & -0.1304 \end{pmatrix} \begin{pmatrix} \Delta \text{Google}_{t-1} - 1.6797493 \\ \Delta \text{Apple}_{t-1} - 0.3812500 \\ \Delta \text{Microsoft}_{t-1} - (-0.1185001) \end{pmatrix}
$$

$$
+ \begin{pmatrix} -0.81124 & -0.66261 & 5.42666 \\ 0.37686 & 0.21498 & -1.32115 \\ 0.05258 & 0.09758 & -0.06469 \end{pmatrix} \begin{pmatrix} \Delta \text{Google}_{t-2} - 1.6797493 \\ \Delta \text{Apple}_{t-2} - 0.3812500 \\ \Delta \text{Microsoft}_{t-2} - (-0.1185001) \end{pmatrix}
$$

$$
+ \cdots + \begin{pmatrix} -0.32553 & -2.47374 & -1.0457 \\ -0.05996 & 0.93894 & 0.4948 \\ -0.02689 & 0.02276 & 0.7610 \end{pmatrix} \begin{pmatrix} \Delta \text{Google}_{t-9} - 1.6797493 \\ \Delta \text{Apple}_{t-9} - 0.3812500 \\ \Delta \text{Microsoft}_{t-9} - (-0.1185001) \end{pmatrix}
$$

$$
+ \begin{pmatrix} \varepsilon_t^1 \\ \varepsilon_t^2 \\ \varepsilon_t^3 \end{pmatrix},
$$

where $\left(\varepsilon_t^1, \varepsilon_t^2, \varepsilon_t^3\right)$ is normal random variable with mean 0 and the variance-covariance matrix given by

$$
\begin{pmatrix} 1.5028 & 0.6218 & 0.2465 \\ 0.6218 & 0.6676 & 0.3601 \\ 0.2465 & 0.3601 & 0.2326 \end{pmatrix}.
$$

Next, we plot the estimated data comparing with sample data. Since we have 3 variables, we choose Microsoft and plot it in Figure 3.7.

```
> plot(stocks.data$Microsoft,type="l")
> points(stocks.data$Microsoft + stocks.var$resid[,3])
```

Since the sample is given as the differenced form, it is difficult to intuitively judge the fitting is good or bad (Figure 3.7). Thus, we do residual test. The following result is of Jarque-Berra test:

```
> jarque.bera.test(stocks.var$resid[-(1:9),3])

        Jarque Bera Test

data:  stocks.var$resid[-(1:9), 3]
X-squared = 1.0707, df = 2, p-value = 0.5855
```

The p-value is not large and the null hypothesis, "The distribution is normal", cannot be rejected. The next result is of Box-Ljung test:

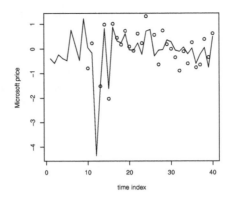

Figure 3.7: Sample (solid line) and estimated values by VAR (points)

```
> Box.test(stocks.var$resid[-(1:9),3], type="Ljung")

        Box-Ljung test

data:  stocks.var$resid[-(1:9), 3]
X-squared = 0.0031967, df = 1, p-value = 0.9549
```

It also shows the large p-value, 0.9549, and the null hypothesis, "The series does not have auto correlation", cannot be rejected. From these results, we consider the residual test is passed and proceed to forecasting.

```
> stocks.pred.var<- predict(stocks.var,n.ahead=10,se.fit=FALSE)
```

The usage is almost same as the case of AR. The only difference is that we need to specify se.fit=FALSE in the function predict(). This is because the function predict() does not correspond to the estimation of standard error in multivariate analysis. By plotting the object stocks.pred.var, we can see the predicted values of Google, Apple and Microsoft, simultaneously (Figure 3.8).

```
> plot(pred.cur.var,type="l")
```

Comparing with the real data, we can confirm that these forecasting values do not fit well. Since VAR model deals with multiple economic variables, the number of parameters to be estimated is large. Thus, it may be difficult to get a good result. But, in other words, the complexity gives us the room to improve the model; i.e., we are able to increase the accuracy of the VAR model, although it requires us to proceed by trial and error. For example, we can replace the combination of time series ("Google", "Apple", "Microsoft") to ("Google", "Yahoo", "Facebook"), can restrict a few parameters to be 0, can normalize the time series, and so on. Many of these trials are often based on our experience, not on the

stocks.pred.var

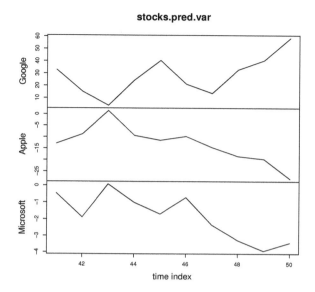

Figure 3.8: The forecasting value by VAR model

theory.[16] Nevertheless, there is a good reason that we try to use VAR, because VAR model explicitly shows us the relationships between different time series. For instance, we can numerically calculate the impact of Google stock price to the other stock prices of Apple and Microsoft.[17]

3.4.3 GARCH model

So far, we have considered various statistical methods using R assuming linearity of data. In this subsection, we consider cases in which the financial data is not necessarily linear and show methods to deal with non-linearity. Thus, we introduce GARCH model which does not assume the linearity of residuals of models.

The residuals in time series model, like AR, ARMA, ARIMA and VAR, are simply considered as mean zero and constant variance. However, the real

---

[16]Notice that we should believe our intuition. For example, we said that the order of AR model should not be too large. This is because it seems unnatural that the current stock price depends on old stock prices.

In the case of VAR model, we often try to introduce many types of data; i.e., stock price, GDP, inflation rate, etc. To use these data simultaneously, we regulate the stock price data and GDP to stock price change ratio and GDP growth rate, because the unit of data should coincides with each other. For removing unnatural features, we should do anything we can. For example, if we decide lag order 3 is acceptable level of VAR model, then we will try to estimate the model with first, second and third lag orders and choose one of them which fits the sample well.

[17]The impact of a variable on the other variables is called impulse response which is easily calculated by VAR. Indeed, the `vars` package makes it possible for us to calculate it. The readers who are interested in it, are recommended to try it.

financial data shows the residuals fluctuating. Accordingly, Engle [Eng82] suggests the model called autoregressive conditional heteroscedastic (ARCH), which is later extended as generalized autoregressive conditional heteroscedastic (GARCH) [Bol86, Tay86].

Especially dealing with financial data, ARCH and GARCH plays the crucial roles, because the financial data often shows the phenomenon called "fat-tail", as pointed out by [Man63] and [Fam65]. However, "fat-tail" cannot be explained well by AR and VAR. Here, fat-tail is the phenomenon that the probability of the extremely large change of price is larger than the probability given by normal distribution. This implies that the assumption of the normality of stock price might lead to the extremely big loss, because of the underestimate of the probability of the big loss. On the other hand, ARCH and GARCH show the consistency to the fat-tail, as explained below. Thus, it is considered that they are well suited models with real financial market (we refer to [FY05] for the following discussion).

The stochastic process y_t is called ARCH, if y_t is

$$y_t = \mu + u_t, \ u_t = \sqrt{h_t} v_t, \ t = 1, \cdots \tag{3.3}$$

$$h_t = \omega + \alpha_1 u_{t-1}^2 + \cdots + \alpha_m u_{t-m}^2, \tag{3.4}$$

where $\omega, \alpha_1, \cdots, \alpha_m$ are positive constants, $v_t \sim \mathcal{N}(0,1)$, $Var(v_t, v_s) = 0$ for $s \neq t$, and $m \geq 1$. If $\sum_{i=1}^{m} \alpha_i < 1$, then y_t has stationarity (Theorem 1 of [Bol86]).

For specifying the lag order, we write ARCH(m). Let us show the consistency of ARCH to fat-tail. Noting that the kurtosis κ_v of v_t is given by $\kappa_v = \mathbb{E}[v_t^4]/(\mathbb{E}[v_t^2])^2$, we calculate the 4-th moment of u_t;

$$\mathbb{E}[u_t^4 | u_{t-1}, \cdots, u_{t-m}] = h_t^2 \mathbb{E}[v_t^4] = \kappa_v h_t^2 (\mathbb{E}[v_t^2])^2 = \kappa_v (\mathbb{E}[u_t^2 | u_{t-1}, \cdots, u_{t-m}])^2.$$

Taking expectation of both sides and using Jensen's inequality, it holds that

$$\mathbb{E}[u_t^4] = \kappa_v \mathbb{E}[(\mathbb{E}[u_t^2 | u_{t-1}, \cdots, u_{t-m}])^2] \geq \kappa_v (\mathbb{E}[\mathbb{E}[u_t^2 | u_{t-1}, \cdots, u_{t-m}]])^2 = \kappa_v (\mathbb{E}[u_t^2])^2.$$

This implies that the kurtosis of u_t has the following property:

$$\frac{\mathbb{E}[u_t^4]}{(\mathbb{E}[u_t^2])^2} \geq \kappa_v.$$

This shows the consistency of ARCH to fat-tail.

Let us proceed to GARCH. Stochastic processes y_t are called GARCH, if it is described by

$$y_t = \mu + u_t, \ u_t = \sqrt{h_t} v_t, \tag{3.5}$$

$$h_t = \omega + \sum_{i=1}^{m} \alpha_i u_{t-i}^2 + \sum_{j=1}^{r} \beta_j h_{t-j}, \tag{3.6}$$

where $\omega, \alpha_i, \beta_j$ are positive constants, $v_t \sim \mathcal{N}(0,1)$ and $Var(v_t, v_s) = 0$ for $s \neq t$.

For specifying the lag order, we write GARCH(m, r). If $\sum_{i=1}^{m} \alpha_i + \sum_{j=1}^{r} \beta_j < 1$, GARCH also shows the stationarity. Under this condition, like as ARCH, GARCH also shows the consistency to fat-tail. Further, for small order of m, r, the stationarity of GARCH is guaranteed under relaxed condition [Nel90]. In practice, GARCH does not require the big order to show goodness of fit to real data.

Using R, we apply ARCH and GARCH for time series of the return of Google stock price. Introducing packages `tseries` and `fGarch`, we run the following script.

```
> library(tseries)
> library(fGarch)
```

We get Google stock price by

```
> google <- get.hist.quote(instrument="GOOGL",start="2014-6-9",
+ end="2017-3-1",quote="Close",provider=c("yahoo"),compression="d")
> google<-data.frame(google)
> google<-ts(google)
> google.d<-diff(log(google))
```

The data from 9 June 2014 to 28 February 2017 is used here. We try to apply ARMA(1,1)-GARCH(1,1) to this data using the function `garchFit()`;

```
> google.fit<-garchFit(formula=~arma(1,1)+garch(1,1),
+ data=google.d,include.mean=TRUE)
```

Here we designate the model by ~ `arma(1,1)+garch(1,1)`. If we set `~garch(m,0)`, ARCH(m) model is applied. We can choose whether μ is included in the model by option `include.mean`, μ is included by selecting TRUE and not included by FALSE.

We can check the summary by `summary()`;

```
> summary(google.fit)


Title:
 GARCH Modelling

Call:
 garchFit(formula = ~arma(1, 1) + garch(1, 1),
    data = google.d, include.mean = TRUE)

Mean and Variance Equation:
 data ~ arma(1, 1) + garch(1, 1)
<environment: 0x00000000066a1670>
 [data = google.d]
```

```
Conditional Distribution:
 norm

Coefficient(s):
         mu          ar1          ma1         omega       alpha1
1.1134e-04   7.9420e-01   -8.4532e-01   3.7289e-05   2.8883e-01
       beta1
5.6804e-01

Std. Errors:
 based on Hessian

Error Analysis:
          Estimate   Std. Error   t value   Pr(>|t|)
mu        1.113e-04   8.420e-05      1.322   0.18608
ar1       7.942e-01   7.550e-02     10.519   < 2e-16 ***
ma1      -8.453e-01   6.630e-02    -12.750   < 2e-16 ***
omega     3.729e-05   1.290e-05      2.890   0.00386 **
alpha1    2.888e-01   5.989e-02      4.823   1.42e-06 ***
beta1     5.680e-01   9.325e-02      6.091   1.12e-09 ***
---
Signif. codes:  0 *** 0.001 ** 0.01 * 0.05 . 0.1   1

Log Likelihood:
 1984.317     normalized:   2.89259

Description:
 Mon Mar 20 11:21:30 2017 by user: tract


Standardized Residuals Tests:
                               Statistic   p-Value
 Jarque-Bera Test   R    Chi^2  672.2663   0
 Shapiro-Wilk Test  R    W      0.9580653  4.392398e-13
 Ljung-Box Test     R    Q(10)  9.965413   0.443533
 Ljung-Box Test     R    Q(15)  12.01441   0.6779382
 Ljung-Box Test     R    Q(20)  21.57816   0.3638321
 Ljung-Box Test     R^2  Q(10)  3.827194   0.954806
 Ljung-Box Test     R^2  Q(15)  5.429521   0.9878227
 Ljung-Box Test     R^2  Q(20)  18.27255   0.5694595
 LM Arch Test       R    TR^2   4.093152   0.9816962
```

```
Information Criterion Statistics:
     AIC        BIC        SIC       HQIC
-5.767687 -5.728058 -5.767838 -5.752354
```

In Coefficient(s), mu, omega, alpha1, and beta1 correspond to μ, ω, α_1, and β_1 in GARCH model respectively. We can also check standard error, t-statistic, and p-value as well as estimated value in Error Analysis.

We can also plot 13 types of charts using plot() and select a number below;

```
> plot(google.fit)
```

```
Make a plot selection (or 0 to exit):

 1:    Time Series
 2:    Conditional SD
 3:    Series with 2 Conditional SD Superimposed
 4:    ACF of Observations
 5:    ACF of Squared Observations
 6:    Cross Correlation
 7:    Residuals
 8:    Conditional SDs
 9:    Standardized Residuals
10:    ACF of Standardized Residuals
11:    ACF of Squared Standardized Residuals
12:    Cross Correlation between r^2 and r
13:    QQ-Plot of Standardized Residuals

Selection:
Enter an item from the menu, or 0 to exit
```

Or using option which=, e.g., which=3 shows Series with 2 Conditional SD Superimposed (see Figure 3.9)

```
> plot(google.fit,which=3)
```

To extract residuals, fitted values, and formula expression from a fitted fGARCH object, we can use @residuals, @fitted, and @formula respectively. Fitted value is plotted in Figure 3.10 by

```
> plot(google.fit@fitted,type="l")
```

Series with 2 Conditional SD Superimposed

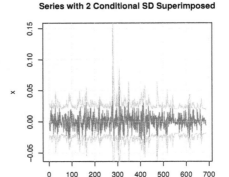

Figure 3.9: Series with 2 Conditional SD Superimposed using the application of GARCH model for Google stock prices

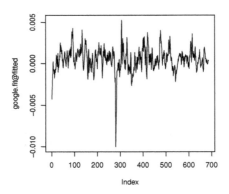

Figure 3.10: Fitted value for Google stock prices based on GARCH model

To plot predictions;

```
> predict(google.fit, n.ahead = 10, plot=TRUE, crit_val=2)
    meanForecast    meanError  standardDeviation  lowerInterval
1   0.0006541419  0.009957731       0.009957731     -0.01926132
2   0.0006308625  0.011068579       0.011056869     -0.02150629
3   0.0006123740  0.011938565       0.011918326     -0.02326476
4   0.0005976902  0.012636520       0.012609756     -0.02467535
5   0.0005860284  0.013205293       0.013173387     -0.02582456
6   0.0005767664  0.013673870       0.013637831     -0.02677097
7   0.0005694106  0.014062978       0.014023572     -0.02755655
8   0.0005635685  0.014388034       0.014345855     -0.02821250
9   0.0005589287  0.014660838       0.014616361     -0.02876275
```

10	0.0005552438 0.014890624	0.014844230	-0.02922600

```
   upperInterval
1      0.02056960
2      0.02276802
3      0.02448950
4      0.02587073
5      0.02699661
6      0.02792451
7      0.02869537
8      0.02933964
9      0.02988060
10     0.03033649
```

See Figure 3.11 as the prediction of GARCH model.

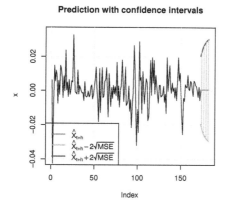

Figure 3.11: Predicted values based on GARCH model

3.4.4 Cointegration

We will finish this section with explaining cointegration [CS87, EG87]. Cointegration is itself not a model, but an important concept related to the stationarity. This also requires multiple time series, similarly to VAR. So, we take up it here.

Many time series models are constructed with the assumption of stationarity. Hence, we need to test the stationarity of time series before applying models to time series data. If the data does not pass the stationarity test, we need to process the data to have the stationarity. The most common manipulation is to take time differences of data; i.e., $\Delta y_t = y_t - y_{t-1}$. Not taking difference on time, cointegration requires to take difference between two time series. If the time difference of a time series shows the stationarity, this is called first order integrated process.

Further, if the difference between two integrated processes shows the stationarity, this is called cointegrated processes. Consider two time series, $\{y_t; t = 1, \cdots, T\}$ and $\{z_t; t = 1, \cdots, T\}$. Assume that both of them are first order integrated process. For a constant, α, we define

$$x_t = y_t - \alpha z_t. \tag{3.7}$$

If the time series $\{x_t; t = 1, \cdots, T\}$ is stationary, it is called cointegrated process.[18]

Our sample, Google, Apple, and Microsoft are all integrated processes (they are not stationary, but the time differenced data is stationary). Thus, let us test the cointegration between Google and Apple. The famous cointegration test is Phillips-Ouliaris test [PO90] and Johansen test [Joh88, Joh91]. R is equipped with both of them. However, if we do Johansen test, we need to introduce the urca package (urca is the package for unit root test and cointegration test. For cointegration test, we should call the function ca.jo()). Phillips-Ouliaris test is now available for us, because the function po.test() is included in tseries package which we have already installed. Thus, we use it, here. Let us test the cointegration between Google and Apple.

```
> po.test(data.frame(google,apple))

        Phillips-Ouliaris Cointegration Test

data:  data.frame(google, apple)
Phillips-Ouliaris demeaned = -7.2257, Truncation lag
parameter = 0, p-value = 0.15

Warning message:
In po.test(data.frame(google, apple)) :
  p-value greater than printed p-value
```

The null hypothesis of Phillips-Ouliaris test is "Time series do not have cointegration". The above test result shows the p-value 0.15. Further, warning message appears on the larger p-value. Thus, we do not reject the null hypothesis, that is, the cointegration between Google and Apple does not exist.

Unfortunately, for other combination (Google, Microsoft) and (Apple, Microsoft), we could not find the cointegration.

To show an example appearing cointegration, we use a combination of stocks from Tokyo stock exchange. One of the pair is Kozosushi which is Sushi restaurants chain of the ticker code 9973. The other one is Renesas Easton which is a semiconductor manufacture of the ticker code 9995. Since we cannot extract the

---

[18]When the process x_t defined such that $x_t = y_t - \alpha z_t - \beta$ is stationary for constants α and β, we also call y_t and z_t has cointegration.

stock price data of them by using the function `get.hist.quote()`, we use the function `getSymbols.yahooj()` which is included in quantmod package.

```
> library(quantmod)
> library(XML)

> start.date<-"2015-04-26"
> end.date<-"2015-08-17"
>
> symbol<-c('9973.T','9995.T')
> data<-list(0)
> for(i in 1:length(symbol)){
+   data[[i]]<- getSymbols.yahooj(symbol[i],src="yahooj",
+   auto.assign=FALSE,from=start.date,to=end.date)[,6]
+ }
> price<-data.frame(data)
> colnames(price)<-symbol
```

Here, we extract the stock price data from 26 April 2015 to 17 August 2015. Then, we can see the result as follows:

```
> po.test(price)

        Phillips-Ouliaris Cointegration Test

data:  price
Phillips-Ouliaris demeaned = -26.834, Truncation lag
parameter = 0, p-value = 0.01494
```

The p-value is 0.01494. Then, we can reject the null hypothesis and we finally find the cointegration between 2 stocks.

Here, we show the two time series of Kozosushi and Renesas in Figure 3.12.

The movements of these stock prices seem not to have relevance. The reader might cast doubt on that they are cointegrated processes. However, the statistic says that there are strong relationships of cointegration. Hence, we further proceed to the analysis of the time series combined with these series. More precisely, we construct the following series,

$$x_t = y_t - 0.028z_t, \tag{3.8}$$

where y_t is the time series of Kozosushi and z_t is of Renesas. Constant -0.028 is calculated by linear regression of y on z.

Here, we can see the time series described as (3.8) rounds around the straight line, 91.2 in Figure 3.13. This implies that the time series has stationarity with mean of 91.2.

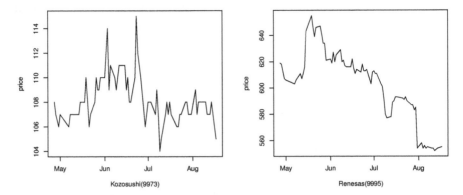

Figure 3.12: Time series of Kozosushi (left) and Renesas (right)

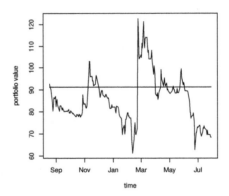

Figure 3.13: The time series combined with Kozosushi and Renesas.

This interesting feature also implies that it is difficult for us to find the combination of stocks having cointegration only by our intuition. Indeed, how do we find the relevance between sushi restaurant and semiconductor manufacture? The charts shown in Figure 3.12 do not show any intuitive relationship between these stocks. Nevertheless, the statistics shows the relationships and actually we can confirm it as in Figure 3.13. This is the interesting feature of statistics.

3.5 Application of the time series analysis to finance: Pairs trading

We have many applications of time series analysis for finance. Here, we discuss the method of pairs trading which is one of the applications of time series analysis for finance. The pairs trading is a method developed by the trading group managed by Nunzio Tartaglia at Morgan Stanley.

Usually, we consider whether the financial time series (or the combination of them) has strong trend or mean reverting.[19] If the mean reverting is observed, more precisely, if the difference or ratio of 2 stock price processes converges to a value, it is an opportunity for pairs trading.[20]

Convergence of asset price processes to a value, that is, mean reversion, implies stationarity which we intensively discussed in this chapter. For example, the AR model $y_t = c + a_1 y_{t-1} + \varepsilon_t$ has the mean reversion to the value, $\mu = c/(1 - a_1)$, where we assume $|a_1| < 1$ which assures stationarity of the time series. Indeed, by μ, AR model is rewritten as

$$y_t - \mu = a_1 (y_{t-1} - \mu) + \varepsilon_t.$$

As this equation shows, the stationary process implies the existence of mean-reversion. Pairs trading is a method utilizing the stationarity of cointegration. Consider 2 non-stationary processes y_t, z_t. If the combination of these processes has cointegration, then there exists a constant α such that the process x_t defined by

$$x_t = y_t - \alpha z_t$$

is stationary. At that time, the process x_t is mean reverting. In practice, the investor sets the position by purchasing (or short selling) a unit of y_t and short selling (or purchasing) α units of z_t, when x_t diverts from the mean. Then, by liquidating the position when x_t converges to the mean, the investor can make profit. This trading rule is the essence of pairs trading.

Such a simplicity of pairs trading looks nice and easy. However, for practical utilization of pairs trading, we have two problems. First is the mean-reversion; i.e., how do we derive where the value of the pair will converge? The simple answer is to apply the regression analysis for the time series of x_t. However, we have several alternatives: i.e., the application of Kalman filter for stochastic processes, like Ornstein-Uhlenbeck processes which also are mean-reverting (see

---

[19]The trading policy often depends on the investor's belief: Whether does the asset have strong trend or mean reverting? Of course, there are other criteria on the trading policy. For instance, we should consider whether the economy is in recession or not, whether the volatility is low or high, and so on. Especially, it is often said that the movement of volatility reflects the framework of economy. Thus, we have to pay attention on it.

[20]We have the extended version of the pairs trading, called statistical arbitrage. This method has been also animatedly developed, e.g., see [AL10].

[EVDHM05, LLW13]). The second problem is how to find the enter and exit points of the pairs trading. Even if the timing of exit is set as the value of the pair touches the mean, we are not sure the timing to enter the pairs trading. If we can find the point where the distance of the current value of the pair and the mean of the pair is the farthest, it may be a good timing to enter the pairs trading. However, it is not trivial. The application of optimal stopping may be a good candidate for this problem (see [ELT11, Yos17]).

BASIC THEORY
OF FINANCE

Chapter 4

Modern Portfolio Theory and CAPM

CONTENTS

Let us consider the situation where we have 1 million dollars and plan to purchase stocks by using such a large amount of money. Do we purchase only one stock? Probably not, because stocks are usually considered risky assets and the prices of stocks are not guaranteed to go up. We could lose all our investment if the stock goes bankrupt. Instead, we will purchase various stocks to avoid such a concentration of risk. Consider the stocks that we will purchase, for example, Google, Apple and Microsoft, with the respective number of shares $(3, 5, 1)$. The combination of stocks, where we set $(3, 5, 1)$, is called a *portfolio*. The problem is how to determine the stocks that we should purchase and in what ratio in keeping with our budget. Portfolio theory gives us some solutions to this problem.

In this chapter, we consider Modern Portfolio Theory which was developed by Harry M. Markowitz [Mar52]. To clarify the portfolio problem, modern portfolio theory assumes that the price movement of risky assets are random variables, their expected values as 'return' and the variances as 'risk'. Modern portfolio theory yields many fruitful results; the representative one Capital Asset Pricing Model (CAPM) developed by John Lintner [Lin65b, Lin65a], William F. Sharp [Sha64], and Jan Mossin [Mos66].[1] CAPM is now a basic concept widely used for trading in the stock market. Further, often used common trading strategies, like pairs trading, can be related back to CAPM.

CAPM assumes a relationship between the return of each stock and the return of the stock market such that

$$\mathbb{E}[R_i] = R_f + \beta (\mathbb{E}[R_M] - R_f),$$

where R_i, R_f, R_M are returns of each asset i, safe asset and the market portfolio, respectively. $\mathbb{E}$ is the expectation operator and β is a constant.

Some readers might not be familiar with the term 'market portfolio'. This is a hypothetical portfolio consisting of all the names (stocks) in the stock market. For example, on Tokyo stock exchange, many stocks are traded, such as Toyota, Nissan, Sony and so on. If the total value of these stocks are all summed up (i.e., the current price times the total number of shares outstanding), this adds up to the whole value of Tokyo stock exchange (also known as market capitalization). The portfolio the value of which is proportional to the market capitalization of the Tokyo stock exchange, is called the 'market portfolio'. The return of the market portfolio, R_M, is calculated by the return of the market capitalization of the stock market itself. The safe asset is the asset which makes a guaranteed profit in the future; e.g., governmental bonds or cash deposited in a bank account.[2] The return of the safe asset, R_f, may be considered the interest rate (yield) of governmental bonds or the interest rate one can earn on bank account desposits.

The formula of CAPM implies that returns of each stock, like Toyota, Google, etc., are derived linearly from the return of each respective market portfolio, e.g., the Tokyo stock exchange or NASDAQ. The return of each stock is typically different from each other. These differences are represented by different values of β. For example, if β is 0, the return of the stock is the same as the return of the safe asset. If β is 1, the return of the stock is the same as the return of the market portfolio. To purchase stocks with β greater than 1 means to try to make a larger profit with higher risk than the market portfolio. To make a smaller profit with less risk than the market portfolio, the investor should purchase stocks with β less than 1. The return of a stock with a large β will have a large sensitivity to small movements of the market portfolio. Thus, the main problem in CAPM is to determine the values of β. In summary, if we know the β of each stock, we can easily decide which stocks to pick given our trading view (bullish or bearish on the performance of the market).

---

[1]Fischer Black [Bla72] also developed CAPM without safe assets.

[2]Strictly, such assets also include risk because government or banks have the possibility of default, In this sense, the return is not guaranteed. However, for simplicity we assume that there exist safe assets with guaranteed return (and zero volatility).

Let us calculate an example. Suppose β of Google to be 1.5, the return of the safe asset to be 0.1% and the return of market portfolio to be 2%. Then the return of Google can be calculated by CAPM as follows,

```
> 0.1+1.5*(2-0.1)
[1] 2.95
```

This result shows that the return of Google is expected to be 2.95%. This simple structure of CAPM is one of the attractive features of this theory.

4.1   Mean-variance portfolio

Ideally we would like to have picked good stocks in our portfolio which will return a high profit with low risk. Here, 'risk' means how much the individual return of a particular stock deviates from its mean return. This is usually quantified by the standard error, which is called volatility in the context of finance. The problem is that the stock which might give us high returns often has high volatility, or risk. On the other hand, the stock with low volatility often makes only low returns. Thus, to make a high profit, we have to take high risk.

However, the construction of an appropriate portfolio might give us an opportunity to make a bigger profit with less risk, than trading a single stock. This is a basic idea of modern portfolio theory. The important problem is how to calculate the weights of the assets in the portfolio which generates a higher profit with less volatility than individual single stocks.

Here, we consider a portfolio of asset 1 and 2: Let the return of asset 1 be R_1, the return of asset 2 be R_2, the weight of asset 1 in the portfolio be t and that of asset 2 be $1 - t$. The expected values of each asset are given by μ_1, μ_2 and their volatilities are σ_1, σ_2. The return of portfolio is given by

$$tR_1 + (1-t)R_2.$$

The expected value of the portfolio μ_p is thus given by

$$\mu_p = t\mathbb{E}[R_1] + (1-t)\mathbb{E}[R_2] = t\mu_1 + (1-t)\mu_2. \tag{4.1}$$

The variance of the portfolio σ_p^2 is given by

$$\sigma_p^2 = t^2\sigma_1^2 + (1-t)^2\sigma_2^2 + 2t(1-t)\sigma_{1,2}, \tag{4.2}$$

where we used the covariance $\sigma_{1,2} := (\mathbb{E}[R_1R_2] - \mathbb{E}[R_1]\mathbb{E}[R_2])$. The larger the covariance, the larger $R_1 - \mathbb{E}[R_1]$ for given $R_2 - \mathbb{E}[R_2] > 0$.

Now, we will observe the relationship between μ_p and σ_p by using the following example. Let $\mu_1 = 0.1$, $\mu_2 = 0.05$, $\sigma_1 = 0.2$ and $\sigma_2 = 0.1$. In Figure 4.1, we depict μ_p on the vertical axis and σ_p on the horizontal axis for three cases of the covariance; i.e., $\sigma_{1,2}$ equal to -0.015, 0, and 0.015. More precisely, by constructing the portfolio with various ratio of these three stocks, the portfolio performs various means and volatilities. The "feasible area" depicts the combinations of means and volatilities.

```
> # sequence from -0.5 to 1.5 by increments of 0.05
> t <- seq(-0.5,1.5,by=0.05)
> mu_1 <- 0.1 # mean return of asset 1
> mu_2 <- 0.05 # mean return of asset 2
> sigma_1 <- 0.2 # volatility of asset 1
> sigma_2 <- 0.1 # volatility of asset 2
> cov1 <- -0.015 # covariance between asset 1 and asset 2
> cov2 <- 0
> cov3 <- 0.015
> # sequence of mean returns of the portfolio
> mu_p <- t*mu_1+(1-t)*mu_2
> # sequence of volatility of the portfolio
> sigma1_p <- sqrt(t^2*sigma_1^2+(1-t)^2*sigma_2^2+2*t*
+ (1-t)*cov1)
> sigma2_p <- sqrt(t^2*sigma_1^2+(1-t)^2*sigma_2^2+2*t*
+ (1-t)*cov2)
> sigma3_p <- sqrt(t^2*sigma_1^2+(1-t)^2*sigma_2^2+2*t*
+ (1-t)*cov3)
> plot(sigma1_p,mu_p,xlim=c(0.03,0.25),ylim=c(0.04,0.11),
+ xlab="sigma_p")
> points(sigma2_p,mu_p,pch=2)
> points(sigma3_p,mu_p,pch=3)
> # to add legend
> legend(0.05,0.11,legend=c("cov<0","cov=0","cov>0"),
+ pch=c(1,2,3))
```

In Figure 4.1, we can observe that the portfolio with covariance -0.15 can make the largest return for a given low volatility (more precisely, on the range of $0 < t < 1$). This is because the negative covariance implies that one asset works as a safety net (or 'hedge') for the plunge in price of another asset. This is called the portfolio effect, or diversification effect.

Further, we proceed to the case of 3 assets. Let the weights of the assets in the portfolio be t, s and $1 - t - s$. Then the expected return of the portfolio μ_p and the volatility of the portfolio σ_p can be written as follows,

$$\mu_p = t\mu_1 + s\mu_2 + (1 - t - s)\mu_3 \tag{4.3}$$

$$\sigma_p^2 = t^2\sigma_1^2 + s^2\sigma_2^2 + (1 - t - s)^2\sigma_3^2 + 2ts\sigma_{1,2} + 2t(1 - t - s)\sigma_{1,3} + 2s(1 - t - s)\sigma_{2,3} \tag{4.4}$$

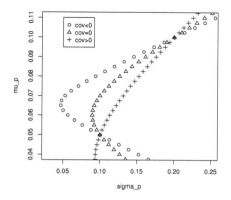

Figure 4.1: Feasible area of the portfolio

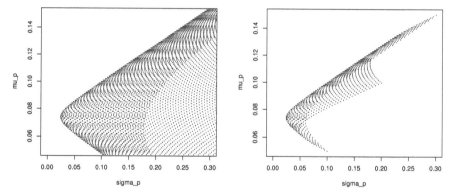

Figure 4.2: Feasible area of 3 assets portfolio (left) and feasible area with short selling constraint (right)

We depict the feasible area of the portfolio return and volatility in the left panel of Figure 4.2 by using the following example; $\mu_1 = 0.1$, $\mu_2 = 0.05$, $\mu_3 = 0.15$, $\sigma_1 = 0.2$, $\sigma_2 = 0.1$, $\sigma_3 = 0.3$, $\sigma_{1,2} = -0.015$, $\sigma_{13} = 0.01$ and $\sigma_{2,3} = -0.02$. By the construction of a portfolio with various ratio of these three stocks, the portfolio performance will have corresponding various mean returns and volatilities. The "feasible area" depicts the possible combinations of mean returns and volatilities.

```
> # sequence s,t with 101 points
> mu_p <- rep(0,101*101)
> var_p <- rep(0,101*101)
> mu_1 <- 0.1 # mean return of asset 1
> mu_2 <- 0.05 # mean return of asset 2
> mu_3 <- 0.15 # mean return of asset 3
> sigma_1 <- 0.2 # volatility of asset 1
```

```
> sigma_2 <- 0.1 # volatility of asset 2
> sigma_3 <- 0.3 # volatility of asset 3
> cov_12 <- -0.015 # covariance between asset 1 and 2
> cov_13 <- 0.01 # covariance between asset 1 and 3
> cov_23 <- -0.02 # covariance between asset 2 and 3
> i <- 1
> # to set -0.5 < s, t < 1.5
> for(t in -25:75){
+     t <- 0.02*t
+     for(s in -25:75){
+       s <- 0.02*s
+       # sequence of mean and variance of the portfolio
+       mu_p[i] <- t*mu_1 + s*mu_2 + (1-t-s)*mu_3
+       var_p[i] <- t^2*sigma_1^2+s^2*sigma_2^2+(1-t-s)
+       ^2*sigma_3^2+
+       2*t*s*cov_12+2*t*(1-t-s)*cov_13+2*s*(1-t-s)*cov_23
+       i <- i+1
+     }
+   }
> sigma_p <- sqrt(var_p) # the volatility of the portfolio
> plot(sigma_p,mu_p,xlim=c(0,0.3),ylim=c(0.05,0.15),pch=".")
>
```

In the left panel of Figure 4.2, the shaded area indicates the feasible portfolio. We consider this area.

The upper-left area on $\sigma_p - \mu_p$ plane is preferable due to the fact that the portfolio on the upper-left area can generate higher return with less volatility. This leads us to the idea of the *minimum variance frontier* which is the curve of (σ_p, μ_p) consisting of the smallest volatility for the same return. By this definition, it is clear that the border of the feasible area in the left panel of Figure 4.2 is the minimum variance frontier. Investors will try to select their portfolio such that it generates a larger return for the same volatility. Thus, an investor will choose a portfolio corresponding to the upper-half side of minimum variance frontier. Such an upper-half side of the minimum variance frontier is called the *efficient frontier*.

The above example implicitly assumed that investors can short sell assets.[3] If investors cannot short assets, the feasible area will be smaller and contained within the area without the short selling constraint (right panel of Figure 4.2).

---

[3] Short selling ('shorting', or 'short') means selling an asset which is not owned by the investor. In practice, to do this one has to first borrow the asset to sell. However, there may not be a counterparty willing to lend the investor the asset, or the investor may be restricted from such trading activity.

```
> mu_p <- rep(0,1326) #1326=1+2+...+51
> var_p <- rep(0,1326)
> mu_1 <- 0.1 # mean return of asset 1
> mu_2 <- 0.05 # mean return of asset 2
> mu_3 <- 0.15 # mean return of asset 3
> sigma_1 <- 0.2 # volatility of asset 1
> sigma_2 <- 0.1 # volatility of asset 2
> sigma_3 <- 0.3 # volatility of asset 3
> cov_12 <- -0.015 # covariance between asset 1 and 2
> cov_13 <- 0.01 # covariance between asset 1 and 3
> cov_23 <- -0.02 # covariance between asset 2 and 3
> i <- 1
> # loop for 0 < s, t < 1
> for(t in 0:50){
+     t <- 0.02*t
+     for(s in 0:(50-50*t)){
+       s <- 0.02*s
+       # sequence of mean and variance such that 1-t-s>0
+       mu_p[i] <- t*mu_1 + s*mu_2 + (1-t-s)*mu_3
+       var_p[i] <- t^2*sigma_1^2+s^2*sigma_2^2+(1-t-s)
+       ^2*sigma_3^2+
+       2*t*s*cov_12+2*t*(1-t-s)*cov_13+2*s*(1-t-s)*cov_23
+       i <- i+1
+     }
+ }
> sigma_p <- sqrt(var_p) # volatility of the portfolio
> plot(sigma_p,mu_p,xlim=c(0,0.3),ylim=c(0.05,0.15),pch=".")
```

Note that the minimum variance frontier depicts a hyperbola curve, according to (4.1) and (4.2), or (4.3) and (4.4) (we will prove it in the more general case in section 4.5).

We also note that the feasible area of the portfolio in the left panel of Figure 4.2 includes the curve depicted in 2 assets case. This implies that the addition of a third asset to the portfolio makes the possible portfolio selection wider. That is, investors can construct a better portfolio which generates larger returns for the same volatility than that of a 2 assets portfolio.

4.2 Market portfolio

Readers might wonder whether the addition of assets to the portfolio in general widens the feasible area or not. The answer is yes, the more assets included in the portfolio, the wider the feasible area of the portfolio. However, there is a limit of the number of assets traded in the market, because listed names of stocks are not infinite. For example, consider the tradeable assets available for us are only the stocks included in the Nikkei 225 stock index. Then, the portfolio which consists of all 225 stocks is the largest possible size of the portfolio that we are able to construct. The return and the volatility of this portfolio will limit the maximum area of the feasible portfolio.

Uniquely there exists within this area the most favourable portfolio which is called the market portfolio. Thus, our problem is to derive the market portfolio. To solve this, we consider the safe asset which generates a guaranteed return without any risk; i.e., the volatility of the safe asset is zero. Here, we introduce the safe asset with return R_f and a risky asset i with the (expected) return μ_i and the volatility σ_i. We consider the portfolio consisting of the safe and the risky asset i. Let the weight of this portfolio be $(t, 1 - t)$. Then, the return and the volatility of the portfolio is given by

$$\mu_p = tR_f + (1 - t)\mu_i$$
$$\sigma_p = (1 - t)\sigma_i,$$

where we used the fact that the volatility of the safe asset is zero. By solving the above equations simultaneously and elimintating t, it holds that

$$\mu_p = R_f + \frac{\mu_i - R_f}{\sigma_i}\sigma_p.$$

Thus, the return and the volatility of this portfolio is represented by the half-line through the points $(0, R_f)$ on $\sigma_p - \mu_p$ plane.

The same logic is applicable even if we replace the risky asset i in the portfolio consisting of several risky assets. Then, the feasible area is given by the connected line between the point $(0, R_f)$ and the points included in the area covered by the minimum variance frontier of the portfolio of risky assets.

This implies that the addition of the safe asset drastically changes the feasible area of the portfolio from that of a portfolio only consisting of risky assets. The portfolio of 3 assets widens the feasible area of the portfolio of 2 assets. The addition of the safe assets further widens the area such that it is covered by the tangent lines to the minimum variance frontier passing through the point $(0, R_f)$. Indeed, the area is given like Figure 4.3.

Here, we show R script to generate Figure 4.3 with $R_f = 0.07$ under the assumption that investors can borrow cash (a safe asset). This assumption allows that the investor to choose the portfolio of any point on the tangent line to the minimum variance frontier. However, if the investor cannot borrow cash, the tangent line is cut off at the contact points on the minimum variance frontier.

```
> R_f <- 0.07 # The return of safe asset
> # the positive tangency of the half-line
> a_max = max((mu_p-R_f)/sigma_p)
> # the negative tangency of the half-line
```

```
> a_min = min((mu_p-R_f)/sigma_p)
> x <- seq(0,3,by=0.01)
> lines(x,a_max*x+R_f)
> lines(x,a_min*x+R_f)
```

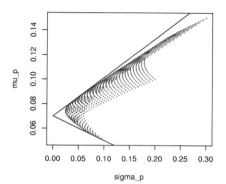

Figure 4.3: The feasible area of the portfolio containing a safe asset

The important point is that the safe asset changes the minimum variance frontier from a hyperbola to two half-lines. Further, the lines are tangent to the minimum variance frontier of the portfolio of risky assets. This implies that the optimal portfolio of risky assets is represented by the point of tangency to the efficient frontier, since the efficient portfolio of the safe asset and the portfolio of risky assets is given by this tangent line. When we use all tradeable risky assets in the market to construct a portfolio of risky assets, the portfolio given by the point of tangency should be the market portfolio.[4] This is the structure of the market portfolio. From the above discussion, the market portfolio is also called tangency portfolio.

In a nutshell, there exists a market portfolio which is regarded as a fund of all risky assets, and combining this portfolio with a safe asset induces the maximum efficient frontier. This property is called the 1-fund theorem.

Here, the half-line constructed by the safe asset and the market portfolio is called the capital market line (CML). Further, let the return and the volatility of the market portfolio be μ_M, σ_M. Then, the slope of the capital market line is given by $\frac{\mu_M - R_f}{\sigma_M}$, i.e., the ratio of the excess expected return (over that of the safe asset) to the volatility, which is called the market price of risk.

---

[4]Classical economics often assumes that all agents are rational such that their portfolios are efficient. Further, since the value of each stock is determined by transactions of rational agents, the market capitalization should reflect this efficiency. Thus, the market portfolio must be proportional to the market capitalization. This idea is applied for the construction of index funds corresponding to the performance of major stock market indexes such as S&P500, NIKKEI 225, etc.

4.3 Derivation of CAPM

The above discussion shows that the return and the volatility of the efficient portfolio is represented by the CML. In this section, we consider the relationship between the return and the volatility of each risky asset.

Let us consider the portfolio consisting of a risky asset i and the market portfolio with the ratio $(t, 1-t)$. Here, we write the return and the volatility of the market portfolio as μ_M and σ_M, respectively. The return and the volatility of the portfolio is given by

$$
\begin{aligned}
\mu_p &= t\mu_i + (1-t)\mu_M \\
\sigma_p^2 &= t^2\sigma_i^2 + (1-t)^2\sigma_M^2 + 2t(1-t)\sigma_{i,M}.
\end{aligned}
$$

Note that when $t = 0$, points given by μ_p and σ_p coincide with the market portfolio and cannot cross over the capital market line.[5] Thus, the curve of μ_p and σ_p tangents to the capital market line at $t = 0$ satisfy the following

$$
\frac{d\mu_p}{d\sigma_p}\bigg|_{t=0} = \frac{\mu_M - R_f}{\sigma_M}. \tag{4.5}
$$

On the other hand, it holds that

$$
\begin{aligned}
\frac{d\mu_p}{dt} &= \mu_i - \mu_M, \\
\frac{d\sigma_p}{dt} &= \frac{t\sigma_i^2 - (1-t)\sigma_M^2 + (1-2t)\sigma_{i,M}}{\sigma_p}.
\end{aligned}
$$

Therefore, we have

$$
\frac{d\mu_p}{d\sigma_p}\bigg|_{t=0} = \frac{(\mu_i - \mu_M)\sigma_M}{\sigma_{i,M} - \sigma_M^2}, \tag{4.6}
$$

where we used $\sigma_M = \sigma_p|_{t=0}$. Combining (4.5) and (4.6), it follows that

$$
\mu_i = R_f + \frac{\sigma_{i,M}}{\sigma_M^2}(\mu_M - R_f) = R_f + \beta_i(\mu_M - R_f).
$$

This is CAPM introduced in the beginning of this chapter.[6] The excess part of μ_i to R_f is called expected excess return of asset i. That is, the CAPM formula shows that the expected excess return $\mu_i - R_f$ is proportionate to the expected excess return $\mu_M - R_f$, and the proportionate coefficient is given by β.

---

[5]If it is possible to cross over the capital market line, this means that the portfolio on the CML is not efficient; i.e., there exists a more efficient portfolio.

[6]CAPM is often discussed in the context of the utility optimization problem of investors. In this regards, there are extended versions of CAPM; e.g., consumption based CAPM (CCPM) [Bre79] and intertemporal CAPM (ICAPM) [Mer73a].

4.4 The extension of CAPM: Multi-factor model

4.4.1 Arbitrage Pricing Theory

CAPM is considered as one of the standard theories in finance. However, the theory has not yet been empirically proven. On the contrary, this theory is often empirically rejected (see [CLM97, DT85, Fam91] and [JT95]). One of the reasons may be the simplistic form of this theory; i.e., CAPM is so-called one factor model which tries to explain the return of each stock only by the excess return of the market portfolio $u_M - R_f$. Multi factor models have been developed to overcome this drawback;[7] i.e., a multi factor model tries to explain the return of each stock by several factors not just by one factor. This is a natural extension of CAPM. Here, we present an overview of the multi factor model without R Programming.

We have to note that Arbitrage Pricing Theory (APT) as developed by Stephen Ross [Ros76] (see also [GL91] for an overview of the multi factor model), uses not only the return of market portfolio R_M, but also factors $(F_1, F_2, \cdots, F_n)$ to explain the returns of individual stocks. This has the following form,

$$\mathbb{E}[R_i] = \alpha_i + \beta_1 \mathbb{E}[F_1] + \beta_2 \mathbb{E}[F_2] + \cdots + \beta_n \mathbb{E}[F_n], \text{ for } i = 1, \cdots, m,$$

where α_i and $\beta_1, \cdots, \beta_n$ are constant (we will show how to determine these constants, later). Note that $n \leq m$ to avoid overfitting. Eliminating the expectation operator, we have the more general form,

$$R_i = \alpha_i + \beta_1 F_1 + \beta_2 F_2 + \cdots + \beta_n F_n + \varepsilon_i,$$

where ε_i is a random variable of mean zero and independent of $F_1, F_2, \cdots, F_n$ and ε_j $(j \neq i)$.

To model the return of each stock i, in addition to the excess return of the market portfolio, it might be good to adopt macro factors, like GDP, inflation rate P, or currency exchange rate USDJPY as factors $F_1, F_2, \cdots, F_n$.[8] Then, the model may be described as

$$R_i = \alpha_i + \beta_1 (R_M - R_f) + \beta_2 \text{GDP} + \beta_3 P + \beta_4 \text{USDJPY} + \varepsilon_i.$$

Here, we have to know that APT is not a theory to emphasize a goodness of fit between the model and marked data. APT requires us to find factors with strong explanatory power. At the same time, APT assumes that every stock in the market can be described by the same common factors. For example, if the return of a

---

[7] Although CAPM may not be rigorously proven empirically, it has theoretical attractiveness due to its simplicity. Asset pricing theories including the multi-factor models discussed in this section keep a similar form as CAPM. In this sense, CAPM has retained its significance.

[8] N. Chen, R. Roll and S. Ross [CRR86] suggests industrial production and inflation rate as the main macro factors.

stock can be described by GDP, inflation rate and currency exchange rate in addition to the excess return of market portfolio, APT requires that all other stock returns are also described by GDP, inflation rate, currency exchange ratio and excess return of market portfolio. Further, stock returns are determined so that they satisfy the no-arbitrage condition, which is the origin of the name of *arbitrage pricing theory*. No-arbitrage means that "there does not exist the opportunity to make a guaranteed profit in the future without cost at present." APT allows us to determine the coefficients that satisfy the no-arbitrage condition.

We show an example of how to determine the coefficients α_i and $\beta_1, \cdots, \beta_n$ which assure that the no-arbitrage condition holds. For simplicity, we set the number of factor be 1. Further, let the stock market have only 2 names of which returns are described by R_1 and R_2. APT implies that each return of these stocks are written as

$$R_1 = \alpha_1 + \beta_1 F_1 + \sigma_1 \varepsilon_1 \tag{4.7}$$
$$R_2 = \alpha_2 + \beta_2 F_1 + \sigma_2 \varepsilon_2, \tag{4.8}$$

where $\varepsilon_1, \varepsilon_2$ are random variables of mean zero, variance 1, independent of each other and of other factors. Consider a trading strategy with zero initial wealth. Borrowing cash at an interest rate R_f, let us use this cash to invest in asset 1 and asset 2 with weights in the portfolio of 70% and 30%, respectively. Then, the investor will expect a return $0.7R_1 + 0.3R_2 - R_f$ without any cost. More generally, the ratio of the investment to the asset 1 and 2 be w_1 and $w_2(= 1 - w_1)$, respectively. The return of this investment R_p is $R_p = w_1 R_1 + w_2 R_2 - R_f$. It is rewritten as

$$R_p = w_1 R_1 - w_1 R_f + w_2 R_2 - w_2 R_f$$
$$= (w_1, w_2) \begin{pmatrix} R_1 - R_f \\ R_2 - R_f \end{pmatrix}.$$

Recall this investment is done with zero initial wealth. Thus, if it is possible to construct the strategy (w_1, w_2) which certainly make profits; i.e., $R_p > 0$, then there exists arbitrage opportunities. Note that it is also possible to have an arbitrage opportunity if portfolio has a return of $R_p < 0$; selling asset 1 and 2 and lending the resulting cash at an interest rate R_f, the investor can make a profit without any cost. Therefore, the no-arbitrage condition leads to the requirement that $R_p = 0$.

The above equation and (4.7)-(4.8) implies that

$$R_p = (w_1, w_2) \begin{pmatrix} \alpha_1 + \beta_1 F_1 + \sigma_1 \varepsilon_1 - R_f \\ \alpha_2 + \beta_2 F_1 + \sigma_2 \varepsilon_2 - R_f \end{pmatrix}$$
$$= (w_1, w_2) \begin{pmatrix} \alpha_1 - R_f \\ \alpha_2 - R_f \end{pmatrix} + (w_1, w_2) \begin{pmatrix} \beta_1 \\ \beta_2 \end{pmatrix} F_1 + (w_1, w_2) \begin{pmatrix} \sigma_1 \varepsilon_1 \\ \sigma_2 \varepsilon_2 \end{pmatrix}.$$

The second factor F_1 is not sure in future, and the third factor is random. Thus, if the investor can make the first factor be strictly positive or negative and keep the second and third factors to be zero, then she can do arbitrage trading. The investor can make second factor be zero, by choosing a trading strategy with asset weights $w_2 = -\beta_1/\beta_2 w_1$.[9] The risk generated by this second factor is characterized by the factor F_1 which is common for all stocks. In this sense, it is called systematic risk. In the case of CAPM, the systematic risk is $R_M - R_f$.

Further, it is well known that the third term approximately approaches zero when the number of stocks in the portfolio is increased to infinity, because of the diversification effect.[10]

In brief, if we can construct the portfolio with a non-zero, first term is not zero, choose asset weights in the portfolio so that the second term is zero, and neglect the third term, then we can get an arbitrage opportunity. In other words, when we choose the strategy $w_2 = -\beta_1/\beta_2 w_1$ for the exposure of the systematic risk to be zero and the profit of this portfolio is zero, it holds no-arbitrage. Substituting $w_2 = -\beta_1/\beta_2 w_1$ into the above equation we have

$$R_p = (w_1, -\beta_1/\beta_2 w_1) \begin{pmatrix} \alpha_1 - R_f \\ \alpha_2 - R_f \end{pmatrix} = w_1 \left(\alpha_1 - R_f - \frac{\beta_1}{\beta_2}(\alpha_2 - R_f) \right).$$

Thus, if $w_1 \left(\alpha_1 - R_f - \frac{\beta_1}{\beta_2}(\alpha_2 - R_f) \right)$ is not zero, it is possible to make profit without risk. For this term to be zero, it is required that $\frac{\alpha_1 - R_f}{\beta_1} = \frac{\alpha_2 - R_f}{\beta_2}$. Defining a variable λ_1 as

$$\lambda_1 := F_1 + \frac{\alpha_1 - R_f}{\beta_1} = F_1 + \frac{\alpha_2 - R_f}{\beta_2},$$

(4.7)-(4.8) are rewritten as follows,

$$R_1 = R_f + \beta_1 \lambda_1 + \sigma_1 \varepsilon_1$$
$$R_2 = R_f + \beta_2 \lambda_1 + \sigma_2 \varepsilon_2,$$

where λ_1 is a factor making profit over R_f. Intuitively, it means the price of the risk corresponding to F_1. Thus, λ_1 is called the factor price. The profit ratio of each asset is determined by the sensitivity to the factor price. Further, choosing the excess return of the market portfolio to the safe asset as the factor price; i.e., setting $\lambda_1 = R_M - R_f$, we can see that the above equation is consistent with CAPM.

APT requires constraints on $\alpha_1, \alpha_2, \beta_1$ and β_2 such that they satisfy the equation derived above, keeping with the consistency of the no-arbitrage condition. It also holds in cases with more factors. Indeed, the general case is given as follows:

---

[9]Taking into account $w_1 + w_2 = 1$, it is clear that $w_1 = \beta_2/(\beta_2 - \beta_1)$ and $w_2 = \beta_1/(\beta_1 - \beta_2)$.

[10]The theoretical background of this is out of scope of this book. We just note that the name of this term is individual risk. That is why this risk is dependent on random variable ε_i proper to each asset i.

APT

For m assets, suppose $n \leq m$ factors exist. Let the return of each asset be

$$R_i = \alpha_i + \sum_{j=1}^{n} \beta_{i,j} F_j + \sigma_i \varepsilon_i.$$

We assume that the portfolio is well diversified such that ε_i can be neglected. Then there exist constants $\lambda_0, \lambda_1, \cdots, \lambda_n$ and it holds that

$$\mathbb{E}[R_i] = \lambda_0 + \sum_{j=1}^{n} \beta_{i,j} \lambda_j.$$

We summarize the above, using a case of 2 factors. Consider the investor has m assets with weight w_i in her portfolio such that

$$\sum_{i=1}^{m} w_i = 0, \quad \sum_{i=1}^{m} w_i \beta_{i,1} = 0, \quad \sum_{i=1}^{m} w_i \beta_{i,2} = 0.$$

The cost to construct this strategy is zero and the sensitivity to each factor is also zero. Therefore, the expected return should be zero to satisfy the no-arbitrage condition; i.e.,

$$\sum_{i=1}^{m} w_i R_i = 0.$$

Considering m dimensional vectors

$$\mathbf{1} = (1, 1, \cdots, 1), \quad \boldsymbol{\beta}_1 = (\beta_{1,1}, \beta_{2,1}, \cdots, \beta_{m,1}), \quad \boldsymbol{\beta}_2 = (\beta_{1,2}, \beta_{2,2}, \cdots, \beta_{m,2}),$$
$$\mathbf{w} = (w_1, w_2, \cdots, w_m), \quad \mathbf{R} = (R_1, R_2, \cdots, R_m),$$

with $\mathbf{w}$ orthogonal to $\mathbf{1}, \boldsymbol{\beta}_1, \boldsymbol{\beta}_2$ and $\mathbf{R}$. This means that $\mathbf{R}$ is linearly dependent on $\mathbf{1}, \boldsymbol{\beta}_1, \boldsymbol{\beta}_2$. Thus, there exist constants $\lambda_0, \lambda_1, \lambda_2$ satisfying $\mathbf{R} = \lambda_0 \mathbf{1} + \lambda_1 \boldsymbol{\beta}_1 + \lambda_2 \boldsymbol{\beta}_2$. If a safe asset is present in the portfolio, then it holds that $\lambda_0 = R_f$.

It is important how we choose to specify factors, because APT itself does not show us how to do so. To choose factors, we often either (1) use observable variables like macro economic factors, or (2) utilize a statistical method, like principal component analysis, on price movements. The first method (1) is interpretable because the factors have an economic basis, but the choice is subjective in how we weigh the importance. The second method (2) allows us to specify factors without any subjectivity, even if it might be difficult to give an economic interpretation of the model.

4.4.2 Fama-French's 3 factor model

Eugene Fama and Kenneth French [FF93] suggested a model with the drastic abstraction of APT. As the name of 3 factor model suggests, the model proposed by Fama and French includes only 3 factors to explain the stock returns.[11] These 3 factors are chosen as the return of the market portfolio, 'small minus big' (SMB) and 'high minus low' (HML). SMB is so-called small-cap effect and defined by the return of a stock with the big market capitalization subtracted from the return of a stock with small market capitalization. HML is the return of the discounted stock subtracted from the return of the stock with a high growth rate, where the discounted stock price is relatively cheap in comparison to the true value of this stock. It is in general difficult to evaluate which stocks are growth stocks and which stocks are discounted stocks. However, it is often used the Earnings Per Share (EPS) or the ratio of stock price-to-book value (Price Book-value Ratio, short form is PBR) as a criterion of growth and discounted stocks.[12]

The 3 factor model describes the return of a stock as follows,

$$\mathbb{E}[R_i] = R_f + \beta_1(\mathbb{E}[R_M] - R_f) + \beta_2 SMB + \beta_3 HML.$$

The 3 factor model is a specification of APT, and is thus based on the no-arbitrage principle. However, strictly speaking there is no rigorous theoretical ground as to why SMB and HML in particular are chosen as factors. In this sense, the selection of factors may be an art rather than a theory. We have to note that in finance we often use methods which are closer to art rather than theory, as long as the result has some pragmatic applicability to the real market.

4.5 The form of the efficient frontier

In this section, we show that the form of the efficient frontier is given by a hyperbola curve. First, we formalize the minimum variance frontier of the Markowits mean variance portfolio. Let w be a vector of the ratio of each asset in the portfolio, μ be a vector of the expected returns of each assets, and V be the variance-covariance matrix. The minimum variance frontier is given by the minimization problem of

$$\sigma_p^2 = w'Vw, \tag{4.9}$$

with the following constraints

$$w'\mu = \mu_p, \quad w'1 = 1.$$

---

[11] Similar to the extension of the 3 factor model, there are more models with a higher number of factors, such as 4 factor models (see [Car97]), and 5 factor models (see [FF14]).

[12] The following link has data for EPS and PBR of stocks in the US market
http://mba.tuck.dartmouth.edu/pages/faculty/ken.french/data_library.html

This problem can be solved by using Lagrange multipliers. We define the Lagrange function as follows,[13]

$$L(w, \lambda, \gamma) = \frac{1}{2} w'Vw - \lambda (w'\mu - \mu_p) - \gamma (w'1 - 1).$$

The first order condition of the above is

$$\frac{\partial L}{\partial w} = Vw - \lambda \mu - \gamma 1 = 0.$$

Rearranging terms, it follows that

$$w = \lambda V^{-1}\mu + \gamma V^{-1}1.$$

Here, defining $A = 1'V^{-1}\mu = \mu'V^{-1}1$, $B = \mu'V^{-1}\mu$ and $C = 1'V^{-1}1$, we can rewrite the constraints as follows,

$$\mu_p = \lambda B + \gamma A, \quad 1 = \lambda A + \gamma C.$$

Further, defining $D = BC - A^2$, it follows that

$$
\begin{aligned}
\lambda &= \frac{C\mu_p - A}{D}, \quad \gamma = \frac{B - A\mu_p}{D}, \\
w &= \left(\frac{C}{D}V^{-1}\mu - \frac{A}{D}V^{-1}1 \right) \mu_p + \left(\frac{B}{D}V^{-1}1 - \frac{A}{D}V^{-1}\mu \right).
\end{aligned}
$$

Substituting the above into (4.9), we can find that σ_p^2 is given by

$$
\begin{aligned}
\sigma_p^2 &= \left(\frac{C^2}{D^2}B - 2\frac{AC}{D^2}A + \frac{A^2}{D^2}C \right) \mu_p^2 + 2 \left(\frac{BC}{D^2}A - \frac{AC}{D^2}B - \frac{AB}{D^2}C + \frac{A^2}{D^2}A \right) \mu_p \\
&\quad + \left(\frac{B^2}{D^2}C - 2\frac{AB}{D^2}A + \frac{A^2}{D^2}B \right) \\
&= \frac{C}{D} \left(\mu_p - \frac{A}{C} \right)^2 + \frac{1}{C}.
\end{aligned}
$$

Rearranging this, we attain the following relation

$$\frac{\sigma_p^2}{1/C} - \frac{\left(\mu_p - \frac{A}{C} \right)^2}{D/C^2} = 1.$$

---

[13]Using 1/2 in the first term of the right hand side gives a clearer form of the solution.

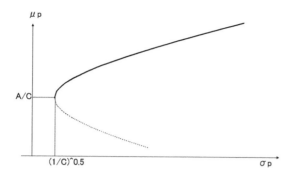

Figure 4.4: The efficient frontier

This shows that the minimum variance frontier is given by a hyperbola curve. Since the efficient frontier consists of the minimum variance portfolio, it is depicted as the upper half of this hyperbola curve. This is shown as the bold line in Figure 4.4.

Note that we allow the weights w_i to have negative values. However, in practice, a short selling constraint often restricts the weights to positive values.[14] In this case, additional constraints are added on the optimization problem. This is the optimization problem in which the objective function is given by a quadratic equation and the constraint is given by linear equality and linear inequality. This type of optimization problem is called the quadratic programming problem. There are numerical algorithms for solving this type of problem, and R is equipped with functions to solve quadratic programming problems (see Appendix A).

---

[14]Even if short selling is allowed, the fee for borrowing stocks (borrow cost) is often charged. The rate of the borrow cost may be even higher than the risk free rate. This breaks the symmetry between long and short asset positions in the portfolio and changes the feasible area. However, for simplicity here we do not consider borrow costs and assume that there is no difference in cost between a long and short position in assets.

Chapter 5

Interest Rate Swap and Discount Factor

CONTENTS

5.1   Interest rate swap

Interest rate swap is the representative instrument in interest rate derivatives.[1] A simple interest rate swap is an exchange of two cash flows, one stream of interest based on a fixed rate and the other stream of interest based on a periodically-resetting floating rate tied to a benchmark. Interest rate swaps are used to manage (hedge) exposure that investors are exposed to fluctuations in interest rates or borrowing costs.[2] This is used to derive the discount factor, which represents the present value of future cash flows and is used to price various derivatives. Thus, we need to understand the properties of interest rate swaps and the method to derive the discount factor.

     Let us consider borrowing cash at short term interest rate and purchasing a long term governmental bond or lending cash for long term. Before the end of long term contracts of governmental bond or the long term fund, the short term

---

[1]This derivative first appeared 1981 at first [KS98]. See, [DH96, Hul12, LX08] and [Lit92], for more details on the structure of the interest rate swap market.

[2]Exposure to interest rates can come from expected future cash flows or obligations.

fund ends. We renew the short term contract (this is called *rolling*), holding the contract of the governmental bond or the long term fund. We continue rolling the short term contract until we reach the expiration (maturity) of the longer term contract. An interest rate swap generates the same cash flow as the transaction where we roll the short term contract against a longer term one.

Consider the case where we borrow 1 billion dollars at 6 month interest rate and at the same time purchase 10 years governmental bond or lend a fund for 10 years. At each 6 month maturity, we roll the short term funds borrowed at short-term interest rate and receive a fixed coupon of the bond, or the long term fund deposit. That is, by 6 months, we pay the short term interest rate which is different from each term and receive the fixed interest rate. Thus, the short term interest rate is called floating rate. The transaction of interest rate swap is based on such an exchange of floating rates and fixed rates. For instance, a rate is called 10 years swap rate when it is the fixed rate appropriate to exchange 6 month floating rate[3] for 10 years. This fixed rate is also called *par rate* and interpreted as the average expected interest rate for 10 years. The difference between interest rate swap and purchasing governmental bond or lending funds is the deal of the principal amount; i.e., the transaction of governmental bond requires the actual payment of 1 billion dollars. On the other hand, the transaction of interest rate swap does not, but just requires to exchange the floating rate and fixed rate. Then, instead of the principal amount, the notional principal amount of 1 billion dollars is set for the interest rate swap as a hypothetical principal amount. We also call receiving fixed rate 'to receive the swap' and paying fixed rate 'to pay the swap'.

Since an interest rate swap contract does not require an exchange of the principal amount (notional), it is possible to apply a high degree of *leverage*. Using leverage, investors can make speculative transactions in interest rates, without having to deal with governmental bonds (which would require the investor to spend the cash to buy the bond). The other effect of interest rate swap is to hedge the risk on the change of interest rates (floating rates). Taking into account for that the economy is strongly related to interest rates, investors might be able to hedge risks related to the economy.

Similarly to the yields of governmental bond of different maturities, swap rates also differ depending on maturity. It is usual in the yield curve that the longer the term, the higher the swap rate. That is, the yield curve of interest rate swaps usually shows the forward yield. This implies that the fixed rate is higher than floating rate and is interpreted as the cost to hedge the risk of change of floating rates.

---

[3] In this book, we use the 6 month floating rate, which is the standard benchmark floating rate used for yen-denominated interest rate swaps. Other benchmark rates, such as 3 month floating rate, are used for other interest rate swaps denominated in other currencies. LIBOR (The London Inter-bank Offered Rate) is typically used as the benchmark for the resets of the floating rate.

We also note that the floating rate was considered to be risk free before the Lehman crisis. However, the Lehman crisis revealed that even LIBOR includes risks, in particular the credit risk of banks.

The pricing of interest rate swaps is discussed in the following section. Note that, pricing a new interest rate swap means determining the appropriate fixed rate in the swap agreement. We often use the market prices of swap rates and the pricing formula of interest rate swap to derive discount factors and forward rates. Once we know the discount factors, we can calculate the value of any interest rate swap as well as price various types of derivatives.

5.2 Pricing of interest rate swaps and the derivation of discount factors

Interest rate swap rates, or "swap rates", are set so as to equate 'the present value of receiving (paying) fixed rates' and 'the present value of paying (receiving) floating rates' for the duration of the contract.[4] Thus, at the beginning of the swap contract, the value of the interest rate swap which is given by the difference between the present expected values of the receiving and paying cash flows is zero. However, as time passes, the difference may widen.

The exchange of interest rates is done at times $t_1, t_2, \cdots, t_i, \cdots, t_N$ (for a period $\tau_i = t_i - t_{i-1}$). Let the fixed rate (swap rate) be S, the floating rate exchanged at time t_i be F_i, the discount factor from time t_i to present be D_i,[5] and the principal amount (notional) be 1 (Figure 5.1). The present value of the cash flow on fixed rate side is described by the sum of cash flows $\tau_i S$ at time t_i discounted by D_i; i.e.,

$$\text{Fix} = \sum_{i=1}^{N} \tau_i S D_i. \tag{5.1}$$

Likewise, the floating side is also evaluated by the sum of the cash flow $\tau_i F_i$ at time t_i discounted by D_i; i.e.,

$$\text{Float} = \sum_{i=1}^{N} \tau_i F_i D_i.$$

Note that the F_is are determined at future times. As usual, a floating rate F_i is calculated by its forward rate and is related to the discount factor as follows,

$$D_i = D_{i-1}/(1 + \tau_i F_i) \quad \Leftrightarrow \quad F_i = \frac{1}{\tau_i}\left(\frac{D_{i-1}}{D_i} - 1\right).$$

---

[4] If one of them is worth more than the other, then investors will buy the more valuable one at a cheaper price until the two reach an equilibrium in value. Thus the fixed and floating streams in the interest rate swap market will ideally have equal value.
[5] By convention, the floating rate paid at t_i is determined at the start of the the period, t_{i-1}.

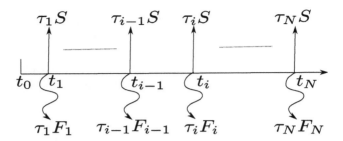

Figure 5.1: Cash flow of interest rate swap. Time proceeds to the right. Fixed rate cash flows received are the straight arrows pointing up, while the squiggly arrows pointing down represent the variable floating rate cash flows paid.

This means that the discount factor from t_i to present is equivalent to the value discounted by $(1 + \tau_i F_i)^{-1}$ from t_i to t_{i-1} and discounted by D_{i-1} from t_{i-1} to present. Here, D_0 is a discount factor from present to present, which is of course not discounted, and thus $D_0 = 1$. In brief, the present value of floating side is given by

$$\text{Float} = \sum_{i=1}^{N} (D_{i-1} - D_i) = 1 - D_N. \tag{5.2}$$

Equations (5.1) and (5.2) have to be equivalent with each other so that the swap rate S equates the value of floating side to the fixed side. Thus, S satisfies

$$S = (1 - D_N) \Big/ \sum_{i=1}^{N} \tau_i D_i. \tag{5.3}$$

The market prices of swap rates and (5.3) are used to derive discount factors and forward rates for contracts of various durations. Using the discount factors, we can calculate the present values of interest rate swaps which terms were set in the past and the prices of various derivatives.

We derive discount factors by using market swap rates as follows. Consider the 6 month floating rate as a reference rate; and let the exchange of receiving and paying interest rates be done at each 6 month interval (semi-annually). We consider an example of the swap rates at each period (T) in Table 5.1.

First, we calculate the swap rate (par rate) at each 6 months (0.5 year) by interpolating the above data. Interest rate swap rates that trade in the market vary smoothly between contracts close to maturity and thus a smooth function for interpolation, such as a spline, is appropriate. In R, we can perform a spline interpolation by first making an object `smooth.spline()` and then calculating the interpolated values with the function `predict()`.

Table 5.1: An example of the market prices of swap rates

T (Year)	0.5	1	1.5	2	3	4	5	6	7
Swap %	0.345	0.349	0.353	0.359	0.378	0.416	0.479	0.567	0.674
T (Year)	8	9	10	12	15	20	25	30	
Swap %	0.795	0.916	1.031	1.238	1.479	1.716	1.811	1.853	

```
> # maturity in years
> T <- c(0.5,1,1.5,2,3,4,5,6,7,8,9,10,12,15,20,25,30)
> Swap <- c(0.345,0.349,0.353,0.359,0.378,0.416,0.479,0.567,0.674,
+ 0.795,0.916,1.031,1.238,1.479,1.716,1.811,1.853)# the unit is %
> sp <- smooth.spline(T,Swap)
> T1 <- seq(0.5,30,length=60) # periods by 0.5 year for 30 years
> Yield <- predict(sp,T1) # values of the interpolated swap rates
```

We plot the market swap rates and the spline interpolation in Figure 5.2.

```
> plot(T,Swap) # plot the market swap rates
> lines(Yield) # plot the spline interpolated swap rates
```

Swap rates for specified years can be calculated. For example, the swap rate for 17 years is calculated as follows,

```
> Y <- predict(sp,x=17)
> cat("T =", Y$x, ", Rate = ", Y$y, "\n")
T = 17, Rate =  1.595982
```

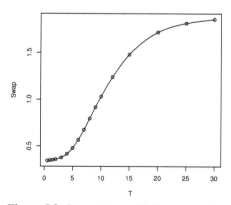

Figure 5.2: Swap rates and their interpolation

We introduce the method to calculate discount factors using the bootstrap method. If discount factors up to t_{N-1}, that is, D_{N-1} are known, then D_N can be calculated according to (5.3), such that

$$D_N = \left(1 - S \sum_{i=1}^{N-1} \tau_i D_i\right) \Big/ (1 + \tau_N S), \qquad (5.4)$$

where S is the swap rate for year t_N. Thus we have an iterative relation from D_1 at t_1 to D_N at t_N.

```
> DF <- rep(0,60) # sequence for discount factors
> Par <- Yield$y/100 # conversion from 1% to 0.01
> # discount factor D_1 by 0.5 year par rate
> DF[1] <- 1/(1+0.5*Par[1])
```

According to (5.4), discount factors up to 30 years are calculated as follows,

```
> for(i in 2:60){
+ DF[i]<-(1-Par[i]*sum(0.5*DF[1:i-1]))/(1+0.5*Par[i])
+ }
```

and we plot the discount factors in Figure 5.3.

```
> plot(T1,DF)
```

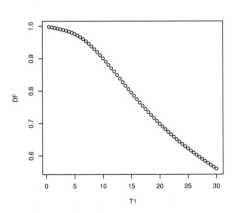

Figure 5.3: Discount factors versus time to maturity

Once discount factors D_i are given, spot (as of today) and forward rates (implied rates at future times) defined as below are also derived.

$$D_i \;=\; 1/(1+\text{Spot}_i)^{t_i} \quad \Leftrightarrow \quad \text{Spot}_i = \left(\frac{1}{D_i}\right)^{1/t_i} - 1,$$

$$D_i \;=\; D_{i-1}/(1+\tau_i F_i) \quad \Leftrightarrow \quad F_i = \frac{1}{\tau_i}\left(\frac{D_{i-1}}{D_i} - 1\right).$$

Using R, we can calculate them as follows,

```
> Spot <- (1/DF)^(1/T1)-1
> DF1 <- c(1,DF[1:59])
> FWD <- (DF1/DF-1)/0.5
```

We plot them in Figure 5.4.

```
> plot(T1,100*Par,xlab="T",ylab="Rate(%)",ylim=c(0,3),
+ type="l")
> lines(T1,100*Spot,lty=2)
> lines(T1,100*FWD,lty=3)
> legend(1,3,legend=c("Par","Spot","Forward"),lty=c(1,2,3))
```

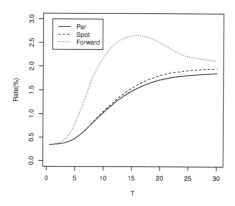

Figure 5.4: Par rate (solid line), spot rate (dashed line), forward rate (dotted line)

5.3   Valuation of interest rate swaps and their risk

Once the discount factors are known, we can evaluate the present value of interest rate swaps and calculate their risk. As discussed above, when the terms of an interest rate swap is set, the swap rate is such that the present value of the interest rate swap is zero. However, the value of the interest rate swap will in general move over time as the swap rate market moves.

Consider a receiver swap (receives a fixed rate and pays a floating rate) with a notional of 10,000, time to maturity 4.5 years, and fixed rate is 0.45%. The market value of the swap rate is given in Table 5.1. We calculate the interpolated swap rate of 4.5 year maturity as follows

```
> predict(sp,x=4.5)$y
[1] 0.4442288
```

The swap rate is approximately 0.44%, which implies that this receiver swap has a positive value since the fixed rate of the contract 0.45% is greater than the current swap rate in the market.

According to (5.1) and (5.2), R_{PV}, the present value of receiving fixed swap rates, and P_{PV}, the present value of paying floating interest rates, are calculated as follows,

$$
\begin{aligned}
R_{PV} &= 10000 \sum_{i=1}^{9} \tau_i SD_i \\
P_{PV} &= 10000 \left(1 - D_9\right).
\end{aligned}
$$

The present value (PV) of the receiver swap is given by the difference; i.e.,

$$PV = R_{PV} - P_{PV}.$$

Using R, we calculate the above. The discount factors from 0.5 year to 4.5 year are

```
> DF[1:9]
[1] 0.9982780 0.9965191 0.9947235 0.9928516 ......
```

Thus, R_{PV} and P_{PV} are calculated as follows,

```
> # the present value of receiving amount
> R_PV <- 10000*0.5*0.0045*sum(DF[1:9])
> R_PV
[1] 200.5199
> # the present value of the cash flow paying floating rates
> P_PV <- 10000*(1-DF[9])
> P_PV
[1] 197.9483
> PV <- R_PV - P_PV # the present value of the interest
+ # rate swap
> PV
[1] 2.571666
```

For a payer swap (paying the fixed rate), the sign is opposite (negative in this case). Next, we consider the calculation of the interest rate risk of an interest rate swap. The risk shows how large the present value of interest rate swap changes when the swap rates are deviated from the present rates. We calculate $PV_\pm$, which are present values calculated by the same method introduced above for the swap rates changed from the current rates to $\pm$1bp ($= \pm$0.01%). The risk sensitivity delta (Δ) and gamma (Γ) are defined as follows,

$$\Delta = \frac{PV_+ - PV_-}{2 \times 1\text{bp}},$$

$$\Gamma = \frac{PV_+ - 2PV + PV_-}{(1\text{bp})^2}.$$

These equations show that the delta is the first order differential of the swap rate and the gamma is the second order differential of it. If we want to know the value of the interest rate swap for dx, the infinitesimal change of the swap rate, it is given approximately by Taylor expansion,

$$PV_{dx} = PV + \Delta(dx) + \frac{1}{2}\Gamma(dx)^2.$$

Although we can calculate the exact value of PV_{dx} by applying the change of dx for the yield curve, it is often tedious, especially when we have a portfolio consisting of various positions of interest rate swaps. In this case, we calculate the delta and gamma of the portfolio, instead of each position, and manage the risk at the portfolio level. Further, this formula makes it possible to calculate the amount of risk by the change of each swap rate, not the change of the yield curve. This analysis is done for checking whether the amount of risk is biased on the specific year on the yield curve.

The following script is an example of the calculation of the risk amount.

```
> # the yield curve shifted by +1bp (the unit is %)
> Swap_p <- Swap+0.01
> # the yield curve by shifted by -1bp (the unit is %)
> Swap_m <- Swap-0.01
>
> # Spline interpolation of each curve
> sp_p <- smooth.spline(T,Swap_p)
> sp_m <- smooth.spline(T,Swap_m)
> Par_p <- predict(sp_p,T1)$y/100
> Par_m <- predict(sp_m,T1)$y/100
>
> # discount factors for each curve
> DF_p <- rep(0,60)
> DF_m <- rep(0,60)
> DF_p[1] <- 1/(1+0.5*Par_p[1])
> DF_m[1] <- 1/(1+0.5*Par_m[1])
```

```
> for(i in 2:60){
+ DF_p[i] <- (1-0.5*Par_p[i]*sum(DF_p[1:i-1])))/
+ (1+0.5*Par_p[i])
+ }
> for(i in 2:60){
+ DF_m[i] <- (1-0.5*Par_m[i]*sum(DF_m[1:i-1])))/
+ (1+0.5*Par_m[i])
+ }
>
> # present values for +1bp and -1bp changes in swap rates
> PV_p <- 10000*(0.5*0.0045*sum(DF_p[1:9])-(1-DF_p[9]))
> PV_m <- 10000*(0.5*0.0045*sum(DF_m[1:9])-(1-DF_m[9]))
> PV_p
[1] -1.883863
> PV_m
[1] 7.029414
```

The delta and gamma are calculated as follows,

```
> Del <- (PV_p-PV_m)/(2*0.0001) #1bp=0.01%=0.0001
> Del
[1] -44566.39
> Gam <- (PV_p-2*PV+PV_m)/0.0001^2
> Gam
[1] 221844.9
```

An increase of 10bp in the swap rates makes the present value of interest rate swap approximately change as follows,

```
> PV+Del*0.001+0.5*Gam*0.001^2
[1] -41.8838
```

This result shows that the change of 10bp makes the PV decrease 41.884bp.

In this chapter, we discussed issues on the interest rate swap, including the structure of the interest rate swap, discount factor, the deduction of spot, par and forward rates. In addition, we considered the calculation of the risk sensitivity of interest rate swaps.

Although this book does not step into the calculation of more complicated interest derivatives, the interest rate swap is the most basic product in interest rate derivatives. Further, since the discount factor is used for pricing various derivatives, the ideas discussed here is very important. Readers who are interested in these fields, may refer to books including more comprehensive discussion on interest rate models (e.g., [BF06], [JW00] and [MR05]).

Chapter 6

Discrete Time Model: Tree Model

CONTENTS

Along with asset pricing, derivative pricing is one of the most important subjects in finance theory. Derivatives are financial instruments, or contracts, whose values, or pay-offs, are derived from the value of other basic assets called underlying assets. Derivative pricing usually starts with modelling the dynamics of the underlying safe and risky assets. One of the most intuitive methods to understand derivative pricing is the binomial model which was developed by John C. Cox, Stephen Ross, Mark Rubinstein [CRR79] and Richard J. Rendleman and Brit J. Bartter [RB79]. We thus focus on the binomial model in this section as an introduction to the pricing of derivatives.

6.1 Single period binomial model

The single period model describes a price movement to be captured in only one period from initial time 0 to terminal time 1. The binomial model assumes that price movement has only two possible outcomes. Here, we let them be 'up' and 'down', for simplicity, denoted by events ω_u and ω_d, which occur with probability $P(\omega_u)$ and $P(\omega_d)$, respectively. If event ω_u happens, then the risky asset price S changes to $(1+u)S$. If event ω_d happens, then price S changes to $(1+d)S$, where $d < u$. The magnitude of the 'up' and 'down' movements, u and d, thus correspond to the percent return of the risky asset during the period. We also assume the existence of a safe asset, which moves deterministically. The return from the safe asset is constant for either event ω_u and ω_d. More precisely, the value of the safe asset is given by 1 at initial time 0, and the value will be $1+r$ at time 1.

We give further crucial assumptions for derivative pricing.

Model assumptions

■ Frictionless markets: e.g., no transaction costs, no tax, no short selling constraints, and infinite liquidity.

■ The market in the assets satisfies the no-arbitrage condition.

We have already discussed the no-arbitrage condition in Chapter 4. In the single period binomial model, the no-arbitrage condition requires $d < r < u$. The reason is as follows: Let the initial wealth of an investor be zero at time 0; i.e., she does not hold any safe and risky assets. Borrowing S units of the safe asset, the investor purchases 1 unit of the risky asset with price S. The net value of the investor's portfolio is $S - S = 0$ at time 0. However, the value at time 1 has two possibilities. If event ω_u happens, the risky asset price S increases, and the new portfolio value is given by $-(1+r)S + (1+u)S = (u-r)S$. If ω_d happens, the risky asset price S decreases, and the portfolio value becomes $-(1+r)S + (1+d)S = (d-r)S$. If $u-r > 0$ and $d-r > 0$, the investor can make a profit with zero cost and zero risk. This would imply that there is an arbitrage opportunity. Investors would thus borrow money and buy S to make a profit. They would be able to continue to do this until the price of S becomes too high or the cost of borrowing too high to be able to guarantee a profit. Thus, for no arbitrage opportunity to exist, it is necessarily that $u-r > 0$ and $d-r < 0$, i.e., $d < r < u$.

6.1.1 Derivative pricing

Now, we turn to the discussion of derivative pricing. The simplest derivative is known as Arrow-Debreu securities [Arr64, Deb59].[1] This is a security generating a pay-off of 1 for an event and 0 otherwise. For instance, this generates the pay-off 1 when the event ω_u happens, else the pay-off is 0. The security which generates the pay-off 1 when the event ω_d happens and the pay-off 0 otherwise, is also Arrow-Debreu security. Let the former type of Arrow-Debreu security be ϕ_u and the latter be ϕ_d.[2] Arrow-Debreu securities are called derivatives because the present value of Arrow-Debreu security is completely determined (i.e., 'derived') by underlying safe and risky assets. As we described them, Arrow-Debreu securities are the simplest derivative securities and most fundamental derivative securities. The reason is all other derivatives can be priced by Arrow-Debreu securities, to be discussed later. In this sense, it is important to understand the derivation of prices of Arrow-Debreu securities.

Let us do pricing with Arrow-Debreu securities. The basis of pricing in finance theory is applying the no-arbitrage condition. For this, we use the comparison between the pay-off of the underlying assets and the pay-off of the derivative and determine the value of the derivative satisfying no-arbitrage.

First, we consider the portfolio of the safe asset and Arrow-Debreu securities.

■ Portfolio 1: $1/(1+r)$ unit of safe asset at time 0

■ Portfolio 2: 1 unit each of Arrow-Debreu securities ϕ_u, ϕ_d, respectively

The value of these portfolios at time 1 will both be 1 for events ω_u and ω_d.

The movement of the value of portfolio 1 is depicted in Figure 6.1. The movement of the value of portfolio 2 is also depicted in Figure 6.2.

At time 1, both portfolios are the same. To exclude arbitrage opportunities, the values of both portfolios at 0 have also to be same as each other; i.e., it holds

$$\phi_u + \phi_d = 1/(1+r). \tag{6.1}$$

Next, we consider the following portfolios, comparing the risky asset with Arrow-Debreu securities.

■ Portfolio 3: 1 unit of risky asset S at time 0

■ Portfolio 4: $(1+u)S$ unit of Arrow-Debreu security ϕ_u and $(1+d)S$ unit of Arrow-Debreu security ϕ_d

---

[1]More precisely, Arrow-Debreu securities are not necessarily derivatives, but primitive and hypothetical securities which are not traded on any real market. However, they work as the intermediate securities between underlying assets and any other derivatives. Thus, it is reasonable to interpret Arrow-Debreu securities as derivatives in this context.

[2]In this section, we deal with the binomial model which assumes only two types of future events. Thus, it is sufficient to set two types of Arrow-Debreu securities, ϕ_u, ϕ_d. If we extend binomial model to more complicated one, then we need to consider more types of Arrow-Debreu securities.

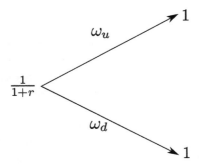

Figure 6.1: The movement of the value of portfolio 1

Values of these portfolios are given at time 1 as follows:

■ The value of portfolio 3 is given by $(1+u)S$ for event ω_u and $(1+d)S$ for event ω_d.

■ The value of portfolio 4 is given by $(1+u)S$ for event ω_u and $(1+d)S$ for event ω_d.

The movement of portfolio 3 is depicted in Figure 6.3. The movement of portfolio 4 is depicted in Figure 6.4.

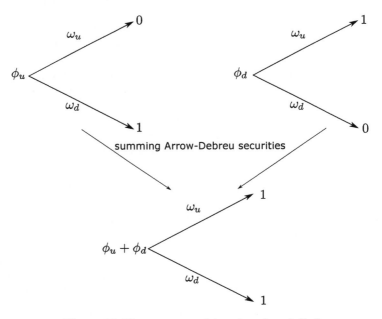

Figure 6.2: The movement of the value of portfolio 2

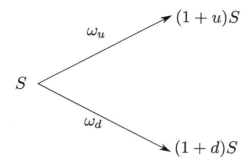

Figure 6.3: The movement of the value of portfolio 3

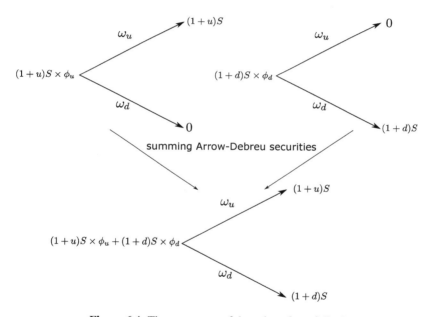

Figure 6.4: The movement of the value of portfolio 4

Similar to the preceding case, values of portfolio 3 and portfolio 4 are the same as each other. Thus, the no-arbitrage condition requires that

$$(1+u)S\phi_u + (1+d)S\phi_d = S. \tag{6.2}$$

Solving (6.1) and (6.2), it holds

$$\phi_u = \frac{1}{1+r}\frac{r-d}{u-d} \tag{6.3}$$

$$\phi_d = \frac{1}{1+r}\frac{u-r}{u-d}. \tag{6.4}$$

They are the prices of Arrow-Debreu securities.

We show a numerical example to derive Arrow-Debreu securities. Here, let $u = 0.2, d = -0.1, r = 0.1$ and calculate the Arrow-Debreu securities. First, we define a function to derive the price of Arrow-Debreu security.

```
> arrow_debreu <- function(r,u,d)
+ {
+   phi_u <- (r-d)/((1+r)*(u-d))
+   phi_d <- (u-r)/((1+r)*(u-d))
+   return(c(phi_u,phi_d))
+ }
```

Run this script as follows:

```
> arrow_debreu(0.1,0.2,-0.1)
[1] 0.6060606 0.3030303
```

Next thing we want to do is to replicate the Arrow-Debreu securities using safe and risky assets. The replication means to construct a portfolio of safe and risky assets which generates the same cash flow as Arrow-Debreu securities. Once the price of Arrow-Debreu securities is given, the replication is easy. For instance, the Arrow-Debreu securities ϕ_u can be replicated by the portfolio of $\frac{1}{(u-d)S}$ unit of risky asset and $-\frac{1+d}{(1+r)(u-d)}$ unit of safe asset (note that the sign of them is opposite to each other). Indeed, the value of this portfolio at time 0 coincides with (6.3) and (6.4). Further, when the event ω_u happens, the portfolio value is

$$\frac{1}{(u-d)S}(1+u)S - \frac{1+d}{(1+r)(u-d)}(1+r) = 1.$$

When the event ω_d happens, the value is

$$\frac{1}{(u-d)S}(1+d)S - \frac{1+d}{(1+r)(u-d)}(1+r) = 0.$$

This shows that the portfolio $\left(\frac{1}{(u-d)S}, -\frac{1+d}{(1+r)(u-d)}\right)$ replicates the Arrow-Debreu securities ϕ_u. Similarly, the Arrow-Debreu securities ϕ_d is also replicable by the portfolio of $-\frac{1}{(u-d)S}$ unit of risky asset and $\frac{1+u}{(1+r)(u-d)}$ unit of safe asset.

Let us try the following numerical example as an exercise.

```
> repli <- function(r,u,d,S)
+ {
+   # the replication of Arrow-Debreu securities phi_u
+   phi_u_S <- 1/((u-d)*S) # the unit of risky asset
+   phi_u_B <- -(1+d)/((1+r)*(u-d)) # the unit of safe asset
+
+   # the replication of Arrow-Debreu securities phi_d
+   phi_d_S <- -1/((u-d)*S) # the unit of risky asset
+   phi_d_B <- (1+u)/((1+r)*(u-d)) # the unit of safe asset
+
+   return(rbind(
+   "The replicating portfolio of phi_u"=c(phi_u_S, phi_u_B),
+   "The replicating portfolio of phi_d"=c(phi_d_S, phi_d_B)))
+ }
```

Let $r = 0.1, u = 0.2, d = -0.1, S = 100$ and run this script, then we get the following.

```
> repli(0.1,0.2,-0.1,100)
                                        [,1]        [,2]
The replicating portfolio of phi_u   0.03333333 -2.727273
The replicating portfolio of phi_d  -0.03333333  3.636364
```

Arrow-Debreu securities make us possible to price any derivative. That is why derivatives with any pay-off can be replicated by Arrow-Debreu securities. We see it, here.

Let C_0 be the price of a derivative at time 0 and the pay-off of this derivative be given by (C_u, C_d) at time 1; i.e., when the event ω_u happens, the pay-off C_u is generated and when the event ω_d happens, the pay-off C_d is generated. This derivative can be replicated by the portfolio of C_u unit of Arrow-Debreu securities ϕ_u and C_d unit of Arrow Debreu securities ϕ_d. Since ϕ_u and ϕ_d are prices of these Arrow-Debreu securities at time 0, the value of this portfolio is represented by

$$\phi_u C_u + \phi_d C_d. \tag{6.5}$$

This portfolio replicates the derivative C_0. Indeed, when the event ω_u happens, the derivative C_0 generates the pay-off C_u and the portfolio of Arrow-Debreu securities of (6.5) generates the pay-off $1 \times C_u + 0 \times C_d$. When the event ω_d happens, the derivative C_0 generates the pay-off C_d and the portfolio of Arrow-Debreu securities of (6.5) generates the pay-off $0 \times C_u + 1 \times C_d$. This shows that the portfolio of (6.5) replicates the derivative C_0. Since the pay-off of this derivative, (C_u, C_d), is arbitrarily given, any derivative can be replicated by Arrow-Debreu securities. Here, we consider simple probability space consisting of only

2 events (ω_u, ω_d). However, this can be extended to more general spaces. On the extended space, we can extend the pay-off of Arrow-Debreu securities. Thus, a similar discussion is possible.

In brief, we see any derivative can be replicated by Arrow-Debreu securities. Further, the Arrow-Debreu securities can be replicated by underlying assets. That is, any derivatives can be replicated by underlying assets.

6.1.2 Pricing by risk neutral measure

The preceding section shows that any derivative can be replicated by Arrow-Debreu securities. However, if the price of a derivative C_0 is different from the value of the portfolio by Arrow-Debreu securities $\phi_u C_u + \phi_d C_d$ at time 0 then it generates arbitrage opportunities. Therefore, it requires that $C_0 = \phi_u C_u + \phi_d C_d$. That is, a derivative price is determined by replication of the derivative. However, this procedure is sometimes tedious. To avoid it, we often use a pricing method using risk neutral measure [HK79, HP81].

According to (6.3) and (6.4), it holds

$$
\begin{aligned}
C_0 &= \phi_u C_u + \phi_d C_d \\
&= \frac{1}{1+r}\frac{r-d}{u-d}C_u + \frac{1}{1+r}\frac{u-r}{u-d}C_d.
\end{aligned}
\tag{6.6}
$$

We define

$$
Q(w_u) = \frac{r-d}{u-d}
\tag{6.7}
$$

$$
Q(w_d) = \frac{u-r}{u-d},
\tag{6.8}
$$

and substitute them into (6.6), then it follows

$$
C_0 = \frac{C_u}{1+r}Q(w_u) + \frac{C_d}{1+r}Q(w_d).
\tag{6.9}
$$

We can interpret Q as a probability measure satisfying the definition of probability; i.e.,

$$
Q(w_u) + Q(w_d) = 1,
\tag{6.10}
$$

$$
0 < Q(w_u), Q(w_d) < 1
\tag{6.11}
$$

and being equivalent to the original probability measure P.[3] This implies that any derivative can be evaluated by the expected value under the probability measure Q; i.e., (6.9) implies

$$C_0 = \mathbb{E}^Q \left[\frac{C_1}{1+r} \right],$$

where C_1 is the pay-off of the derivative at time 1 such that

$$C_1 = \begin{cases} C_u & \text{if } \omega_u \text{ happened} \\ C_d & \text{if } \omega_d \text{ happened} \end{cases}.$$

In other words, it can be described as

$$\frac{C_0}{B_0} = \mathbb{E}^Q \left[\frac{C_1}{B_1} \right], \tag{6.12}$$

where, to make the time clear, we write B_0, B_1 and $B_0 = 1$ and $B_1 = 1 + r$ as the price dynamics of safe asset. The probability measure Q is called risk neutral measure and (6.12) implies the discounted process of the derivative value C/B is martingale which is discussed in the following.

The relationship between risky asset S and risk neutral measure Q

The probability measure Q discussed above is, in a sense, artificial measure. Here, we clarify the economic interpretation of the measure Q. (6.2) can be rewritten by Q as follows,

$$\frac{S_1(\omega_u)}{1+r} Q(\omega_u) + \frac{S_1(\omega_d)}{1+r} Q(\omega_d) = S_0. \tag{6.13}$$

To make the time clear, we describe S_0, S_1. Further, this can be rewritten as

$$\frac{S_0}{B_0} = \mathbb{E}^Q \left[\frac{S_1}{B_1} \right]. \tag{6.14}$$

---

[3]The equivalence of probability measures means that the null set of both of probability measures is equal. That is, the event of which probability is zero under the probability measure P also deduces the probability zero under the probability measure Q and vice versa. In the binomial model, the event with probability 0 under the probability measure P is "both the event ω_u and ω_d does not happen". Now, the conceivable events are $\{\omega_u\}, \{\omega_d\}, \emptyset, \Omega$ and these events are disjoint with each other. Even under the probability measure Q, the probability will be 0 for only $Q(\emptyset)$. Thus, the probability measures P and Q are equivalent.

For a more comprehensive discussion of probability theory, [Bil86, CK05, JP04] and [Wil91] will be good guidances.

This equation shows that the expected value of the discounted price of risky asset at time 1, S_1/B_1, is equivalent to the discounted price of the risky asset at time 0, S_0/B_0. Such a random variable, S/B, is called martingale and the probability measure satisfying the relationship of (6.14) is called martingale measure. More precisely, since Q and P is equivalent, Q is called an equivalent martingale measure.[a]

Note that the probability measure Q is also called risk neutral measure in the context of finance. Under the probability measure Q, the expected return of the risky asset seems to be equal to the return of the safe asset. This is the origin of the name of *risk neutral measure*. However, the returns of risky asset and safe asset are not necessarily equal in real financial market (if equal, everyone does not want to invest their capital to safe assets). This implies that the probability measure Q is artificial and different from the real probability measure P.

Interestingly, even under more extended models than binomial model, any derivative price is given by the expected value of the discounted pay-off at maturity under risk neutral measure. The requirement on us is only no-arbitrage condition. Therefore, it is important to specify the dynamics of underlying assets under the risk neutral measure Q for derivative pricing.

Further, the pricing method using risk neutral measure makes us possible to price derivatives without specifying Arrow-Debreu securities. The method only requires us to derive the probability measure such that the discounted price process of underlying asset is martingale under this measure. Then, we can derive derivative price by calculating the expected value of the pay-off at maturity under this risk neutral measure.

For instance, when we write the upward probability under risk neutral measure as q, it holds

$$\frac{(1+u)S}{1+r}q + \frac{(1+d)S}{1+r}(1-q) = S.$$

This induces that $q = \frac{r-d}{u-d}$. Next, we can easily derive the derivative price by calculating the expected value of the pay-off at maturity under the probability $q, 1-q$. This is much easier than taking account for no-arbitrage condition, replication conditions or Arrow-Debreu securities.

---

[a]The idea of martingale was created by [Doo42].

Next, we show the numerical example to derive the derivative price using risk neutral measure. Let $r = 0.02, u = 0.1, d = -0.09$ and the pay-off of the derivative at maturity be $(C_u, C_d) = (50, 0)$. Then, we calculate the risk neutral measure q and derivative price at time 0.

```
> mart_call_1 <- function(r,u,d,Cu,Cd)
+ {
+   # the risk neutral measure
+   q <- (r-d)/(u-d)
+   # the expected value under risk neutral measure
+   C0 <- (q*Cu + (1-q)*Cd)/(1+r)
+   return(c("risk neutral measure q_u"=q,
+   "derivative price"=C0))
+ }
```

Run this script.

```
> mart_call_1(0.02,0.1,-0.09,50,0)
risk neutral measure q_u          derivative price
                0.5789474                 28.3797730
```

6.2 Multi period binomial model

We extend the single period model which consists only of present time 0 and maturity 1, to the multi period model which includes multiple time steps between the present time and maturity. Further, we consider pricing call option which is one of the most representative derivatives in finance.

6.2.1 *Generalization to the multi period model*

Consider a derivative with a time to maturity $T = N\Delta t$. We divide the time interval from present time 0 to maturity T by Δt into N units. We assume that the price of a risky asset $\{S_{i\Delta t}\}_{i \in N}$ moves from $S_{i\Delta t}$ to $(1+u)S_{i\Delta t}$ with probability p_u and moves from $S_{i\Delta t}$ to $(1+d)S_{i\Delta t}$ with probability p_d on the time interval between $i\Delta t$ and $(i+1)\Delta t$. Thus, the price of the risky asset at maturity T is governed by the binomial distribution; i.e., if the price of the risky asset at time 0, given by S_0, moves upward at j times by the maturity T, then the price S_T at time T is given by $S_T = (1+u)^j(1+d)^{N-j}S_0$. The probability for this move is given by[4]

$$P[S_T = (1+u)^j(1+d)^{N-j}S_0] = \binom{N}{j} p_u^j p_d^{N-j}. \tag{6.15}$$

We also assume that a safe asset moves from $B_{i\Delta t}$ to $(1+r\Delta t)B_{i\Delta t}$ with probability 1 on the time interval between $i\Delta t$ and $(i+1)\Delta t$. During the N time steps from time 0 to maturity T, the price of the safe asset evolves from B_0 to $B_T = (1+rT)B_0$.

---

[4]In this section, we denote a combination $_NC_j$ as $\binom{N}{j}$ to avoid the confusion with the option pay-off C.

The above discussion for the time interval between $i\Delta t$ and $(i+1)\Delta t$ on the multi period model is equivalent to that for the single time step between 0 and 1 in the single period model. Thus, similarly to single period model, the risk neutral measure in one unit of the time interval in multi period model is given by

$$q_u = \frac{r\Delta t - d}{u - d}$$

$$q_d = \frac{u - r\Delta t}{u - d}.$$

Further, the risk neutral measure of the movement from time 0 to T is just replaced by p_u, p_d in (6.15) into q_u, q_d. Thus, it holds that

$$Q[S_T = (1+u)^j (1+d)^{N-j} S_0] = \binom{N}{j} q_u^j q_d^{N-j}.$$

Consider a derivative C_0. Let the pay-off of this derivative be determined by the number of events ω_u (or event ω_d) that happen by the maturity T. If event ω_u happens j times, the pay-off of this derivative is denoted by $C(j)$. Note that the price of the risky asset is given by $S_T = (1+u)^j (1+d)^{N-j} S_0$ in this case. Figure 6.5 shows an example of the dynamics of the multi period binomial model, where $N = 3$.

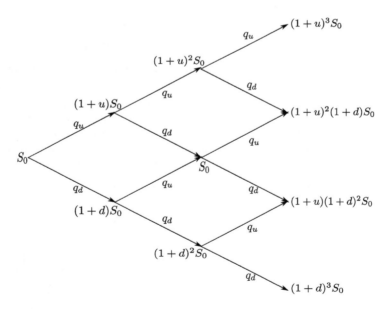

Figure 6.5: Price movement in multi period binomial model

The derivative price can be derived if the pay-off at the maturity and the risk neutral measure are known, and is given as follows,

$$C_0 = B_0 \mathbb{E}^Q \left[\frac{C_T}{B_T} \right] \tag{6.16}$$

$$= \sum_{j=0}^{N} \frac{C_T(j)}{1+rT} \binom{N}{j} q_u^j q_d^{N-j}, \tag{6.17}$$

where the subscript 0 and T of C is the time for its pay-off.

Let's now try a numerical example with R. We define the below function, with the pay-off of the derivative $C_T(j) = 10 \times j$. We calculate the risk neutral measure and the derivative price at time 0.

```
> deriv_price <- function(r,u,d,N,dt)
+ {
+   # the risk neutral measure in the single time interval
+   q <- (r*dt-d)/(u-d)
+   C0 <- 0 # initialization of the derivative price as 0
+   for (j in 0:N) # to set a loop from 0 to N
+   {
+       C0 <- C0 + 10*j*choose(N,j)*q^j*(1-q)^(N-j)/(1+r*dt)^N
+   }
+   return(c("risk neutral measure q_u"=q,
+   "derivatives price"=C0))
+ }
```

We run the above function with $r = 0.02, u = 0.1, d = -0.09$, and $N = 5, \Delta t = 0.2$, and we get the following result

```
> deriv_price(0.02,0.1,-0.09,5,0.2)
risk neutral measure q_u        derivatives price
           0.4947368                 24.2479871
```

If you don't use for-loop, but use the vectorized version, the following code is also possible:

```
> deriv_price_vec <- function(r,u,d,N,dt)
+ {
+   # the risk neutral measure in the single time interval
+   q <- (r*dt-d)/(u-d)
+   C0 <- 0 # initialization of the derivative price as 0
+   tmp_seq <- 0:N
+   C0 <- sum(10*tmp_seq*choose(N,0:N)*q^tmp_seq
+   *(1-q)^(N-tmp_seq))
```

```
+   CO <- CO/(1+r*dt)^N
+   return(c("risk neutral measure q_u"=q,
+   "derivatives price"=CO))
+ }
```

We can get the above result by using the no-arbitrage condition. Indeed, similarly to (6.6), the no-arbitrage condition in the single period model requires

$$C_0 = \frac{1}{1+r}\frac{r-d}{u-d}C_u + \frac{1}{1+r}\frac{u-r}{u-d}C_d.$$

In the multi period model, we have $i+1$ possible outcomes of the derivative price at time $i\Delta t$. We give numbers $j = 0, \cdots, i$ by sorting them from lower to higher to the value of the derivative at time $i\Delta t$ and denote it as $C_{i,j}$. Then the above no-arbitrage condition can be rewritten as

$$
\begin{aligned}
C_{i,j} &= \frac{1}{1+r\Delta t}\frac{r\Delta t - d}{u-d}C_{i+1,j+1} + \frac{1}{1+r\Delta t}\frac{u-r\Delta t}{u-d}C_{i+1,j} \\
&= q_u\frac{C_{i+1,j+1}}{1+r\Delta t} + q_d\frac{C_{i+1,j}}{1+r\Delta t}.
\end{aligned}
$$

Since $C_0 = C_{0,0}$ in this notation, we have the following

$$C_{0,0} = q_u\frac{C_{1,1}}{1+r\Delta t} + q_d\frac{C_{1,0}}{1+r\Delta t},$$

and recursively attain the following result

$$C_{0,0} = \sum_{j=0}^{N}\frac{C_T(j)}{1+rT}\binom{N}{j}q_u^j q_d^{N-j}.$$

6.2.2 Pricing call options

A European call option is one of the most common derivatives contracts.[5] A call option is a contract in which the holder has the right to buy an underlying asset at a predetermined, or strike price. If the asset value is higher than the strike price, the option is said to be "in the money". If the asset value is lower than the strike price, then the option is said to be "out of the money". If the holder exercises the right to buy, then the contract is deemed to have been exercised. Typically, the holder will only exercise an option if the asset value is higher than the strike price, i.e., if the option is in the money. Indeed, most commonly traded option contracts are automatically exercised if they are in the money at maturity.

---

[5]Options can be categorized by the time which they are allowed to be exercised. Those which can be exercised only at maturity are referred to as 'European' style options. 'American' style options allow the holder to exercise at any time until maturity. We assume European exercise style options, here.

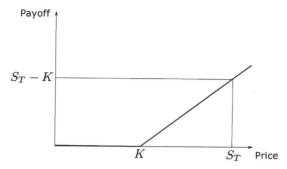

Figure 6.6: The pay-off of call option

The payoff at maturity T of a call option with strike price K can be written as follows[6]

$$\max(S_T - K, 0). \tag{6.18}$$

Figure 6.6 depicts the pay-off of a call option at maturity. In Figure 6.6, we can see that the pay-off of call option is zero when the underlying asset price S_T is less than strike price K at maturity T. However, the pay-off is positive when S_T exceeds K at maturity T.

If an investor can purchase a call option for free, there will be an arbitrage opportunity such that the investor can own the positive excess return without any risk. Indeed, such an one-sided favourable contract is impossible to come by because we will not find in practice a counter party to sell a call option, or any option contract, for free. Thus, if an investor wants to purchase a call option, they must pay a fee for it. Such a fee is referred to as the option premium and is the price of the option at the initiation of the contract at time 0. To calculate how much the premium is, we use the pricing method of derivatives discussed in the preceding sections. We can price the call option using (6.17) as follows,

$$C_0 = \sum_{j=0}^{N} \frac{\max((1+u)^j(1+d)^{N-j}S_0 - K, 0)}{1+rT} \begin{pmatrix} N \\ j \end{pmatrix} q_u^j q_d^{N-j}. \tag{6.19}$$

We can calculate this option price using the following function in R. As before, we calculate the risk neutral measure q in the function and calculate the price of the call option at time 0.

---

[6]The call option contract can be either physical settled or cash settled. Physical settlement means that the holder of the option receives the physical asset in exchange for a cash payment of the strike price (an exchange of K units of cash per unit of asset). If the option is cash settled, only then a cash payment is exchanged which corresponds to the difference in the price of the asset and the strike price.

```
> mart_call <- function(r,u,d,S0,K,T,dt)
+ {
+   q <- (r*dt-d)/(u-d) # the risk neutral measure
+   N <- T/dt
+   N <- trunc(N)
+   # trunc() is a function to take the integer part of
+   # the argument
+   C0 <- 0 # initialization of the call option price
+   for (j in 0:N) # loop from 0 to N
+   {
+     # all pay-off at maturity
+     CT <- max((1+u)^j*(1+d)^(N-j)*S0-K,0)
+     # substitution of the above into the expected values
+     # under risk neutral measure
+     C0 <- C0 + CT*choose(N,j)*q^j*(1-q)^(N-j)/(1+r*dt)^N
+   }
+   return(c("risk neutral measure q_u"=q,
+   "call option price"=C0))
+ }
```

In the above function, we have N price movements to maturity, giving `N<-T/dt`. However, `T/dt` is not necessarily an integer. To avoid having a non-integer number of time steps, we use the built-in R function `trunc()` and take the integer part of `T/dt`.

Run the above function with inputs $r = 0.02, u = 0.1, d = -0.09, S_0 = 100, T = 1$, $\Delta t = 0.02$ and the strike price $K = 80$, we get the following result.

```
> mart_call(0.02,0.1,-0.09,100,80,1,0.02)
risk neutral measure q_u   call option price
            0.4757895                35.7330892
```

For readers not using for-statement, we present the following R code.

```
> mart_call_vec <- function(r,u,d,S0,K,T,dt)
+ {
+   q <- (r*dt-d)/(u-d) # the risk neutral measure
+   N <- T/dt
+   N <- trunc(N)
+   # trunc() is a function to truncate integer part of
+   # the argument
+   C0 <- 0 # initialization of the call option price
+   tmp_seq <- 0:N
+   # all pay-off at maturity
```

```
+   CT <- ((1+u)^tmp_seq*(1+d)^(N-tmp_seq)*S0-K)*
+   choose(N,tmp_seq)*q^tmp_seq*(1-q)^(N-tmp_seq)
+   pos_CT <- CT[CT>0]
+   C0 <- sum(pos_CT)/(1+r*dt)^N
+   return(c("risk neutral measure q_u"=q,
+   "call option price"=C0))
+ }
```

Using the above, we have the same result as `mart_call_2`. Indeed, it follows that

```
> mart_call_vec(0.02,0.1,-0.09,100,80,1,0.02)
risk neutral measure q_u          call option price
           0.4757895                    35.7330892
```

Next, let us try a numerical example of recursive calculation in the region where the pay-off takes positive values, i.e., where the option is in-the-money. Of course, it should output the same result as above. To implement this algorithm, we rewrite the formula for the price of a call option as follows,

$$
C_0 = \sum_{j=a}^{N} \frac{((1+u)^j(1+d)^{N-j}S_0 - K)}{1+rT} \binom{N}{j} q_u^j q_d^{N-j}
$$

$$
= \frac{S_0}{1+rT} \sum_{j=a}^{N} (1+u)^j(1+d)^{N-j} \binom{N}{j} q_u^j q_d^{N-j} - \frac{K}{1+rT} \sum_{j=a}^{N} \binom{N}{j} q_u^j q_d^{N-j},
$$

where $a = \min\{0 \le j \le N | (1+u)^j(1+d)^{N-j}S_0 > K\}$. That is, we define a as the minimum value of j at which the price of risky asset exceeds the strike price K.

```
> mart_call_2 <- function(r,u,d,S0,K,T,dt)
+ {
+   N <- trunc(T/dt)
+   pay_off <- 0
+   q <- (r*dt -d)/(u-d)
+   # The minimum value of j which the price of risky asset
+   # exceeds the strike price
+   a <- 0
+   while((1+u)^a*(1+d)^(N-a)*S0 <= K)
+   {
+     a <- a+1
+   }
```

```
+  for(j in a:N) # loop from a to N
+  {
+    # addition of the pay-off of call option
+    pay_off <- pay_off+
+      S0*(1+u)^j*(1+d)^(N-j)*choose(N,j)*q^j*(1-q)^(N-j)-
+      K*choose(N,j)*q^j*(1-q)^(N-j)
+  }
+  # for avoiding the for-loop, use the following code
+  # tmp_seq <- a:N
+  # pay_off <- sum(((1+u)^tmp_seq*(1+d)^(N-tmp_seq)*S0-K)*
+  # choose(N,tmp_seq)*q^tmp_seq*(1-q)^(N-tmp_seq))
+
+  # the discount by the pay-off of safe asset
+  pay_off <- pay_off/(1+r*dt)^N
+  return(c("risk neutral measure q_u"=q,
+    "call option price"=pay_off))
+ }
```

Running this function with the same inputs as above, we get the following result.

```
> mart_call_2(0.02,0.1,-0.09,100,80,1,0.02)
risk neutral measure q_u  call option price
            0.4757895            35.7330892
```

6.3 Trinomial model

We have considered the binomial model in the preceding sections; i.e., the price movement of the risky asset price has two possible outcomes in the time interval. Here, we add the additional type of price movement, which is, 'no change'. This is called trinomial model.

Similarly to binomial model, we denote the upward change of risky asset price S to $(1+u)S$ and the downward change to $(1+d)S$. Further, we denote the risk neutral probability of upward change as q_u, of downward change as q_d, and of no change as q_n. Note that (q_u, q_n, q_d) satisfies the condition $0 \le q_u, q_n, q_d \le 1$ and

$$q_u + q_n + q_d = 1. \tag{6.20}$$

Note that, for the risk neutral measure q_u, q_d, q_n and the risk free rate r, it holds that

$$S_{i\Delta t} = (q_u(1+u)S_{i\Delta t} + q_n S_{i\Delta t} + q_d(1+d)S_{i\Delta t})/(1+r\Delta t). \tag{6.21}$$

Hereafter, we denote the risky asset price $S_{i\Delta t}$ at time $i\Delta t$ as S_i, for simplicity. Figure 6.7 shows the price movement from $i\Delta t$ to $(i+1)\Delta t$ in the trinomial model.

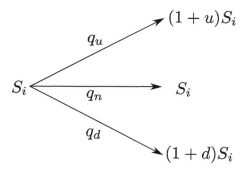

Figure 6.7: Price movement in trinomial model

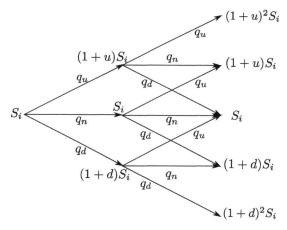

Figure 6.8: Two step price movement in trinomial model

Further, we add a condition that the two step price movement of 'up and down', 'down and up' and 'no-change and no-change' coincide with each other in the trinomial model. The Figure 6.8 shows the possible paths for two sequential time steps. This recombination condition requires that

$$1 + u = \frac{1}{1+d}. \tag{6.22}$$

Now, we have 5 unknown variables to be determined, q_u, q_n, q_d, u, d. However, we are only given 3 equations of (6.20)–(6.22). Thus, we cannot derive these 5 unknown model parameters completely.[7] To overcome this problem, it is often used as a method to exogenously define volatility σ and add a condition such that the standard error of the return under risk neutral measure coincides

---

[7]In the binomial model, we give u, d exogenously. Thus, we can easily derive the solution.

with the volatility. Hull [Hul12] introduces a method to add the further condition, $1 + u = e^{\sigma\sqrt{3\Delta t}}$, to derive the following solution

$$q_u = -\sqrt{\frac{\Delta t}{12\sigma^2}}\left(r - \frac{\sigma^2}{2}\right) + \frac{1}{6} \tag{6.23}$$

$$q_n = \frac{2}{3} \tag{6.24}$$

$$q_d = \sqrt{\frac{\Delta t}{12\sigma^2}}\left(r - \frac{\sigma^2}{2}\right) + \frac{1}{6}. \tag{6.25}$$

There is another method to complete trinomial model (trinomial tree); i.e., Frittelli [Fri00] introduces the minimal entropy martingale measure which enable us to complete the trinomial model. Although both methods are more complicated than the binomial model, they give us interesting results. For readers who are interested in this, it is good to follow these literatures.[8]

Once the risk neutral measure is determined, the same procedure as before can be taken for calculating the option price. Similarly to (6.19), the price of a call option is given by

$$C_0 = \sum_{i+j+k=N} \frac{\max((1+u)^i(1+d)^k S_0 - K, 0)}{1+rT}\begin{pmatrix} N \\ i \end{pmatrix}\begin{pmatrix} N-i \\ j \end{pmatrix}q_u^i q_n^j q_d^k. \tag{6.26}$$

The formula (6.26) implies that i upward movements and k downward movements of the stock price consists of the combination of i chosen from N grids and j chosen from $N - i$ grids; i.e., $\begin{pmatrix} N \\ i \end{pmatrix}\begin{pmatrix} N-i \\ j \end{pmatrix}$.

The part of $\begin{pmatrix} N \\ i \end{pmatrix}\begin{pmatrix} N-i \\ j \end{pmatrix}$ can be simplified as:

$$\begin{pmatrix} N \\ i \end{pmatrix}\begin{pmatrix} N-i \\ j \end{pmatrix} = \frac{N!}{i!(N-i)!}\frac{(N-i)!}{j!(N-j)!} = \frac{N!}{i!j!(N-j)!}.$$

However, R is equipped with the function choose(). Hence, it may not necessarily to be simplified as above. It is dependent on the preference of readers.

---

[8]In the following chapter, we will discuss implied volatility. Related to this issue, [DKC96] and [DK98] show us a good navigation for utilizing the trinomial tree.

This algorithm is easily implemented as follows:

```
> call_trino <- function(r,S0,K,T,dt,sigma)
+ {
+   N <- trunc(T/dt)
+   tmp <- 0
+   # upward and downward width
+   u <- exp(sigma*sqrt(3*dt))-1
+   d <- 1/(1+u) - 1
+   # risk neutral measure
+   q_u <- -sqrt(dt/12)*(r-0.5*sigma*sigma)/sigma+1/6
+   q_n <- 2/3
+   q_d = 1-q_u-q_n
+
+   for(i in 0:N) # loop from 0 to N
+   {
+     for(j in 0:N-i){
+       # add the pay-off of call option
+       tmp<-tmp+max(S0*(1+u)^i*(1+d)^(N-i-j)-K,0)*choose(N,i)*
+       choose(N-i,j)*q_u^i*q_n^j*q_d^(N-i-j)
+     }
+     # for avoiding double loop, use the following code
+     #   tmp_seq <- 0:N-i
+     #   tmp_tmp <- (S0*(1+u)^i*(1+d)^(N-i-tmp_seq)-K)*choose(N,i)*
+     #   choose(N-i,tmp_seq)*q_u^i*q_n^tmp_seq*q_d^(N-i-tmp_seq)
+     #   tmp <- tmp + sum(tmp_tmp[tmp_tmp>0])
+   }
+   # discount by the pay-off of safe asset
+   tmp <- tmp/(1+r*dt)^N
+   return(c("risk neutral measure q_u"=q_u,"call option price"=tmp))
+ }
```

Here, we used the risk neutral measure given by (6.23)–(6.25). Running the above function with parameters $r = 0.02$, $S_0 = 100$, $K = 80$, $T = 1$, $\Delta t = 0.02$ and $\sigma = 0.4$, we get the following result.

```
> call_trino(0.02,100,80,1,0.02,0.4)
risk neutral measure q_u          call option price
              0.1727904                  38.0138895
```

Except for the parameter σ, the above parameters are same as the numerical example used in the binomial model. Although the call option price 38.01 is similar to the result of the binomial model, the risk neutral measure $q_u = 0.17$ is less than this in the binomial model due to the large $q_n = 2/3$.

Chapter 7

Continuous Time Model and the Black-Scholes Formula

CONTENTS

In this chapter, we extend the discrete time model to the continuous time model and derive the Black-Scholes formula developed by Fischer Black, Myron Scholes [BS73] and Robert C. Merton [Mer73b, Mer77], which is one of the most important formulae in finance theory. We have shown that the price of a financial derivative can be calculated by introducing a risk neutral measure Q in the binomial model, defined for discrete, finite time intervals. We extend this discrete model to the continuous model by increasing the discrete time interval N to infinity.

7.1 Continuous rate of return

First, we consider the rate of return of safe and risky assets in the binomial model and then extend them to continuous version. The binomial model describes the price of safe asset moves from $B_{i\Delta t}$ to $(1 + r\Delta t)B_{i\Delta t}$ in the time interval from $i\Delta t$ to $(i+1)\Delta t$. Let $t = i\Delta t$. Then, we can rewrite $B_{t+\Delta t} = (1 + r\Delta t)B_t$. Thus, the rate of return of a safe asset is given by

$$\frac{B_{t+\Delta t} - B_t}{B_t} = \frac{(1 + r\Delta t)B_t - B_t}{B_t} = r\Delta t.$$

Let us consider the following manipulation of time interval, i.e., $\Delta t \to 0$. This implies that the time interval is made vanishingly small. Then, the above becomes,

$$\frac{dB_t}{B_t} = rdt. \tag{7.1}$$

This is easily solved as follows,

$$B_t = B_0 e^{rt}, \tag{7.2}$$

where we assume $B_0 \equiv 1$, for simplicity. Next, we consider the rate of return of a risky asset. The price movement of the risky asset is given by

$$S_{(i+1)\Delta t} = \begin{cases} (1+u)S_{i\Delta t} & \text{if event } \omega_u \text{ occurs} \\ (1+d)S_{i\Delta t} & \text{if event } \omega_d \text{ occurs.} \end{cases}$$

This implies that the rate of return of the risky asset is described by

$$\frac{S_{t+\Delta t} - S_t}{S_t} = \frac{\Delta S_t}{S_t} = \begin{cases} u & \text{if event } \omega_u \text{ occurs} \\ d & \text{if event } \omega_d \text{ occurs.} \end{cases}$$

The expected value of this is given under a risk neutral measure such that

$$\mathbb{E}^Q\left[\frac{\Delta S_t}{S_t}\right] = q_u u + q_d d,$$

where q_u and q_d are the risk neutral measures discussed in the previous chapter; i.e.,

$$q_u = \frac{r\Delta t - d}{u - d}$$

$$q_d = \frac{u - r\Delta t}{u - d}.$$

Note that q_u and q_d work as the probabilities of ω_u and ω_d occurring. The variance is given by

$$\begin{aligned} \text{Var}^Q\left[\frac{\Delta S_t}{S_t}\right] &= q_u u^2 + q_d d^2 - (q_u u + q_d d)^2 \\ &= q_u q_d (u - d)^2. \end{aligned}$$

Note that the rate of return of the risky asset under a risk neutral measure is equal to the rate of return of the safe asset.[1] Thus, it holds that

$$q_u u + q_d d = r\Delta t.$$

Further, let $\sigma^2 \Delta t$ be the variance of the rate of return of the risky asset in the time interval, Δt, under a risk neutral measure; i.e.,

$$q_u q_d (u - d)^2 = \sigma^2 \Delta t.$$

The equation given above can be solved for u and d as

$$u = r\Delta t + \sigma \sqrt{\frac{q_d \Delta t}{q_u}}$$
$$d = r\Delta t - \sigma \sqrt{\frac{q_u \Delta t}{q_d}},$$

where we have used $u > r\Delta t > d$.

Now, we have rates of upward and downward for given r and σ. That is, in the binomial model, for given r, σ, we can determine u and d.

Based on this, we derive the continuous version of the rate of return. Note that

$$\frac{\Delta S_t}{S_t} = \begin{cases} \left(r\Delta t + \sigma \sqrt{\frac{q_d \Delta t}{q_u}} \right) & \text{if event } \omega_u \text{ occurs} \\ \left(r\Delta t - \sigma \sqrt{\frac{q_u \Delta t}{q_d}} \right) & \text{if event } \omega_d \text{ occurs.} \end{cases}$$

Using the following indicator functions,

$$\mathbf{1}_u := \begin{cases} 1 & \text{if event } \omega_u \text{ occurs} \\ 0 & \text{otherwise,} \end{cases}$$

and

$$\mathbf{1}_d := \begin{cases} 1 & \text{if event } \omega_d \text{ occurs} \\ 0 & \text{otherwise,} \end{cases}$$

the above equation on S is rewritten as follows,

$$\begin{aligned} \frac{\Delta S_t}{S_t} &= r\Delta t + \left(\sqrt{\frac{q_d}{q_u}} \mathbf{1}_u - \sqrt{\frac{q_u}{q_d}} \mathbf{1}_d \right) \sigma \sqrt{\Delta t} \\ &= r\Delta t + \left(\frac{q_d \mathbf{1}_u - q_u \mathbf{1}_d}{\sqrt{q_u q_d}} \right) \sigma \sqrt{\Delta t}. \end{aligned}$$

In the above equation, we have a random variable $\left(\frac{q_d \mathbf{1}_u - q_u \mathbf{1}_d}{\sqrt{q_u q_d}} \right)$. Let us calculate the mean and variance of this. Taking into consideration $\mathbb{E}^Q[\mathbf{1}_u] = q_u 1 + (1 - q_u) \times 0 = q_u$ and $\mathbb{E}^Q[\mathbf{1}_u^2] = q_u 1^2 + (1 - q_u) \times 0^2 = q_u$, we can calculate the mean

---

[1] See the discussion on the relationship between risky asset S and risk neutral measure Q on pp.147.

and variance, i.e., the 1st and 2nd moments of the distribution of the random variable.[2]

$$\mathbb{E}^Q\left[\frac{q_d\mathbf{1}_u - q_u\mathbf{1}_d}{\sqrt{q_u q_d}}\right] = \left(\frac{q_d\mathbb{E}^Q\left[\mathbf{1}_u\right] - q_u\mathbb{E}^Q\left[\mathbf{1}_d\right]}{\sqrt{q_u q_d}}\right) = \left(\frac{q_d q_u - q_u q_d}{\sqrt{q_u q_d}}\right) = 0,$$

and

$$Var^Q\left[\left(\frac{q_d\mathbf{1}_u - q_u\mathbf{1}_d}{\sqrt{q_u q_d}}\right)\right] = \mathbb{E}^Q\left[\left(\frac{q_d\mathbf{1}_u - q_u\mathbf{1}_d}{\sqrt{q_u q_d}}\right)^2\right]$$

$$= \mathbb{E}^Q\left[\frac{q_d^2\mathbf{1}_u^2 - 2q_d q_u\mathbf{1}_u\mathbf{1}_d + q_u^2\mathbf{1}_d^2}{q_u q_d}\right]$$

$$= \mathbb{E}^Q\left[\frac{q_d^2\mathbf{1}_u^2 + q_u^2\mathbf{1}_d^2}{q_u q_d}\right]$$

$$= \frac{q_d^2 q_u + q_u^2 q_d}{q_u q_d} = 1.$$

For $t_i = i\Delta t$ where $i = 1\cdots,N$ (note that $t_N = N\Delta t = T$), we define $\Delta w_{t_i} := \frac{q_d\mathbf{1}_u - q_u\mathbf{1}_d}{\sqrt{q_u q_d}}\sqrt{\Delta t}$. Then we can rewrite $\Delta S_t/S_t$ by using Δw_{t_i}, as follows,

$$\frac{\Delta S_{t_i}}{S_{t_i}} = r\Delta t + \sigma\Delta w_{t_i}.$$

By definition, Δw_{t_i} satisfies following properties,

$$\mathbb{E}^Q[\Delta w_{t_i}] = 0,$$
$$Var^Q(\Delta w_{t_i}) = \Delta t.$$

Further, it holds that for $w_{t_{n_1}} := \sum_{i=1}^{n_1}\Delta w_{t_i}$ and $w_{t_{n_2}} := \sum_{i=1}^{n_2}\Delta w_{t_i}$,

$$Cov(w_{t_{n_1}}, w_{t_{n_2}}) = \sum_{i=1}^{n_1}\mathbb{E}^Q[(\Delta w_{t_i})^2] = n_1\Delta t.$$

where we set $n_1 < n_2$ and used the independence of Δw_i and Δw_j for $i \neq j$.

---

[2] We can also calculate higher moments. For the 3rd and 4th moments of this random variable, we have

$$\mathbb{E}^Q\left[\left(\frac{q_d\mathbf{1}_u - q_u\mathbf{1}_d}{\sqrt{q_u q_d}}\right)^3\right] = \mathbb{E}^Q\left[\frac{q_d^3\mathbf{1}_u^3 - q_u^3\mathbf{1}_d^3}{q_u q_d\sqrt{q_u q_d}}\right] = \frac{q_d^3 q_u - q_u^3 q_d}{q_u q_d\sqrt{q_u q_d}} = \frac{q_d^2 - q_u^2}{\sqrt{q_u q_d}},$$

and

$$\mathbb{E}^Q\left[\left(\frac{q_d\mathbf{1}_u - q_u\mathbf{1}_d}{\sqrt{q_u q_d}}\right)^4\right] = \mathbb{E}^Q\left[\frac{q_d^4\mathbf{1}_u^4 + q_u^4\mathbf{1}_d^4}{(q_u q_d)^2}\right] = \frac{q_d^4 q_u + q_u^4 q_d}{(q_u q_d)^2} = \frac{q_d^3 + q_u^3}{q_u q_d}.$$

Considering a convergence of $N \to \infty$, that is, $\Delta t \to 0$, it is well known that a random variable, $dW_t := \lim_{\Delta t \to 0} \Delta w_{t_i}$ approaches a Brownian motion (in some contexts, this is called a Wiener process[3]). A stochastic process $\mathcal{B}(t)$ is called standard Brownian motion if the process satisfies

$$\mathbb{E}[\mathcal{B}(t)] = 0, \quad Var[\mathcal{B}(t)] = t,$$
$$Cov(\mathcal{B}(t), \mathcal{B}(s)) = \min\{t, s\}.$$

From the dynamics of Δw_t above, we can conjecture that Δw_t approaches a Brownian motion.[4]

From above, for $N \to \infty$, using a dynamics of Brownian motion (or, Wiener process) W_t under the risk neutral measure Q, the dynamics of the underlying asset can be expressed as follows,

$$\frac{dS_t}{S_t} = rdt + \sigma dW_t. \tag{7.3}$$

The parameter σ, which coincides with the standard deviation (i.e., the square root of the variance) of the return of risky asset, is called the volatility. Since this parameter means the magnitude of fluctuation of the risky asset, it implies the magnitude of risk of the risky asset. Volatility plays the important role of deriving prices of derivatives.[5]

7.2 Itô's lemma

The continuous version of the dynamics of safe and risky assets is given by the differential equations (7.1) and (7.3), respectively. In these equations, we have dt, the infinitesimal difference of time, and dW_t, the infinitesimal difference of a stochastic process. Understanding the order of magnitude of these two differentials is important to deal with a stochastic differential equation. We can conjecture that there is a relationship between dt and dW, noting the fact that $Var(dW_t) = dt$. This relationship is summarized by Itô's lemma [Itô44, Itô51] which is one of the most important theories in stochastic calculus.

---

[3]Wiener formulated a rigorous construction of Brownian motion in [Wie23]. The origin of Brownian motion goes back to the observation of the apparent random motion of microscopic particles by the botanist Robert Brown in 1828. The idea of Brown was mathematically formulated by Einstein [Ein05]. The application of Brownian motion to finance was first developed by [Bac00].

[4]More precisely, we need an additional assumption, $q_u = q_d = 1/2$ to derive it. The reason is easily conjectured by the calculation of 3rd and 4th moments of Δw_t.

[5]Some readers might be interested in the return of the risky asset, not the standard deviation of it. If we consider the physical measure P, not the risk neutral measure Q, then the dynamics of dS/S is written by replacing r in (7.3) by μ, which is the return of the risky asset. However, it is difficult to empirically estimate μ from real market data. Thus, as discussed later, the fact that the price of financial derivatives can be calculated without using μ is one of the merits of the Black-Scholes formula.

Itô's lemma

Let $F(t, X_t)$ be a continuous function, differentiable in time t, and twice differentiable in a stochastic process X_t, where X_t is given by

$$dX_t = a_t dt + \sigma_t dW_t.$$

Then, we have

$$
\begin{aligned}
dF_t &= \frac{\partial F}{\partial t} dt + \frac{\partial F}{\partial X_t} dX_t + \frac{1}{2} \frac{\partial^2 F}{\partial X_t^2} dX_t^2 \\
&= \frac{\partial F}{\partial t} dt + \frac{\partial F}{\partial X_t} dX_t + \frac{1}{2} \frac{\partial^2 F}{\partial X_t^2} \sigma_t^2 dt \\
&= \left[\frac{\partial F}{\partial t} + \frac{\partial F}{\partial X_t} a_t + \frac{1}{2} \frac{\partial^2 F}{\partial X_t^2} \sigma_t^2 \right] dt + \frac{\partial F}{\partial X_t} \sigma_t dW_t,
\end{aligned}
$$

where the above equality holds in the sense of the convergence in mean square.

In the stochastic world, we cannot neglect the second order of infinitesimal difference of the stochastic variable. This is the noteworthy point of Itô's lemma; that is, the second order of dW_t cannot be neglected in the third term of first and second lines of the above equation. That is because the second order of dW has the same order as the first order of dt.[6]

We show one of the most famous examples in finance; i.e., we calculate $d \ln S_t$ by using (7.3). By Taylor expansion, it holds that

$$
\begin{aligned}
d \ln S_t &= \frac{dS_t}{S_t} - \frac{1}{2} \frac{dS_t^2}{S_t^2} + \cdots \\
&= \left(r - \frac{\sigma^2}{2} \right) dt + \sigma dW_t.
\end{aligned}
$$

Let the initial value of S_t be S_0. Then, at $t = T$, we have

$$S_T = S_0 \exp\left[\left(r - \frac{\sigma^2}{2} \right) T + \sigma W_T \right],$$

$$\mathbb{E}^Q\left[\ln \frac{S_T}{S_0} \right] = \left(r - \frac{\sigma^2}{2} \right) T, \quad Var^Q\left[\ln \frac{S_T}{S_0} \right] = \sigma^2 T.$$

---

[6]Note that the variance of the stochastic variable is first order in the time differential, i.e., $Var(dW_t) = \mathbb{E}[dW_t^2] = dt$.

They imply that $\ln(S_T/S_0) \sim \mathcal{N}((r - \frac{1}{2}\sigma^2)T, \sigma^2 T)$ under risk neutral measure. Since W_T is normally distributed with mean zero and variance T, it also holds that

$$
\begin{aligned}
\mathbb{E}^Q[S_T] &= S_0 \exp\left[\left(r - \frac{\sigma^2}{2}\right)T\right] \int_{-\infty}^{\infty} e^{\sigma x} \frac{1}{\sqrt{2\pi T}} e^{-x^2/2T} dx \\
&= S_0 \exp\left[\left(r - \frac{\sigma^2}{2}\right)T\right] e^{\sigma^2 T/2} \int_{-\infty}^{\infty} \frac{1}{\sqrt{2\pi T}} e^{-(x-\sigma T)^2/2T} dx \\
&= S_0 e^{rT}.
\end{aligned}
$$

Note that the expected value of the risky asset depends on the deterministic risk-free rate, and does not depend on the variance of its returns. As its name of "risk neutral measure", the volatility σ does not appear in the above expected value. Note that the risk is often measured by the magnitude of the volatility σ. This is an interesting feature using Itô's lemma.

7.3   The Black-Scholes formula

We now turn to the derivation of one of the most widely used formulae in pricing derivatives. Since $\ln(S_T/S_0) \sim \mathcal{N}((r - \frac{1}{2}\sigma^2)T, \sigma^2 T)$, the density function is given by

$$
f(x) = \frac{1}{\sqrt{2\pi\sigma^2 T}} \exp\left[-\frac{1}{2}\left(\frac{x - \left(r - \frac{\sigma^2}{2}\right)T}{\sigma\sqrt{T}}\right)^2\right].
$$

From this, the price of European call option[7] is written as follows,

$$
\begin{aligned}
C_0 &= \mathbb{E}^Q\left[B_T^{-1}\max(S_T - K, 0)\right] \\
&= e^{-rT}\mathbb{E}^Q\left[\max\left(S_0 e^{\ln S_T/S_0} - K, 0\right)\right] \\
&= e^{-rT}\int_{-\infty}^{\infty}\max(S_0 e^x - K, 0)f(x)dx \\
&= e^{-rT}\int_{\ln(K/S_0)}^{\infty}\left[S_0 e^x f(x) - Kf(x)\right]dx, \quad\quad (7.4)
\end{aligned}
$$

where B_T is the value of the safe asset at $t = T$ (See (7.2)). We define the following

$$
X := \frac{x - \left(r - \frac{\sigma^2}{2}\right)T}{\sigma\sqrt{T}}, \quad Y := X - \sigma\sqrt{T},
$$

$$
d_1 := \frac{\ln\frac{S_0}{K} + \left(r + \frac{\sigma^2}{2}\right)T}{\sigma\sqrt{T}}, \quad d_2 := d_1 - \sigma\sqrt{T}.
$$

---

[7]Recall that the payoff of a call option at expiry is $\max(S_T - K, 0)$.

Then, (7.4) is rewritten as follows,

$$
\begin{aligned}
C_0 &= \int_{-d_2}^{\infty} \left[\frac{S_0}{\sqrt{2\pi}} \exp\left(-\frac{1}{2}\left(X - \sigma\sqrt{T} \right)^2 \right) - e^{-rT} \frac{K}{\sqrt{2\pi}} \exp\left(-\frac{X^2}{2} \right) \right] dX \\
&= \int_{-d_1}^{\infty} \frac{S_0}{\sqrt{2\pi}} e^{-Y^2/2} dY - e^{-rT} \int_{-d_2}^{\infty} \frac{K}{\sqrt{2\pi}} e^{-X^2/2} dX \\
&= S_0 \Phi(d_1) - e^{-rT} K \Phi(d_2), \tag{7.5}
\end{aligned}
$$

where $\Phi(x)$ is the standard normal cumulative distribution function;[8] i.e.,

$$
\Phi(x) = \int_{-\infty}^{x} \frac{1}{\sqrt{2\pi}} e^{-x^2/2} dx.
$$

Equation (7.5) is the Black-Scholes formula for the price of European call option.

We define a function to calculate the price of a European call option using the Black-Scholes formula.

```
> black_scholes_1 <- function(S,K,r,sigma,T)
+ {
+   d1 <- (log(S/K) + (r+sigma^2/2)*T)/(sigma*sqrt(T))
+   d2 <- d1 - sigma*sqrt(T)
+
+   CO <- S*pnorm(d1) - exp(-r*T)*K*pnorm(d2)
+   return(c("Call option price"=CO))
+ }
```

Let's calculate the price of a call option for which $S_0 = 100, K = 100, r = 0.01, \sigma = 0.2, T = 1$.

```
> black_scholes_1(100,100,0.01,0.2,1)
Call option price
         8.433319
```

Similarly, we can also derive the price of a European put option. A put option is a contract that grants the right to sell an asset at an agreed upon strike price, K at expiry. The resulting value (pay-off) of a put option at maturity is $\max(K - S_T, 0)$, shown in Figure 7.1. If the underlying price is above the strike price K at maturity, then the put will not be exercised and the pay-off of the put option is zero. However, if the underlying asset price is below the strike price at maturity, the put option will be exercised and the pay-off of the put option will be non-zero. Thus put options are used to hedge against drops in the asset price. We can

---

[8]Let a random variable $X \sim \mathcal{N}(0, 1)$. Then the probability $P(X \le x)$ is given by the standard normal cumulative distribution function $\Phi(\cdot)$; i.e.,

$$
P(X \le x) = \Phi(x).
$$

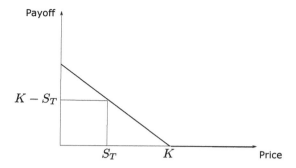

Figure 7.1: The pay-off of put option as a function of asset price at expiry S_T for a fixed strike K, $\max(K - S_T, 0)$.

derive the analytical solution to Black-Scholes formula for a put option is similar to that for a call option. The price of put option P_0 is given by

$$P_0 = e^{-rT} K\Phi(-d_2) - S_0\Phi(-d_1).$$

We can derive a well-known relationship between call options and put options by examining the difference in their pay-off.

$$\max(S_T - K, 0) - \max(K - S_T, 0) = S_T - K$$
$$\leftrightarrow e^{-rT}(\max(S_T - K, 0) - \max(K - S_T, 0)) = e^{-rT}(S_T - K)$$
$$\leftrightarrow C_0 - P_0 = S_0 - e^{-rT}K,$$

where we take the expected value under a risk neutral measure on the third line. This implies that

$$P_0 = C_0 - S_0 + e^{-rT}K.$$

The above equation is *Put-Call Parity*, which allows us to simultaneously derive the prices of call and put options. The put-call parity implies significant features; e.g., puts and calls with the same expiry and strike have the same implied volatility[9] (assuming a symmetry of transaction, exercise costs). Puts and calls are also interchangeable in a delta-neutral portfolio. Here, the delta-neutral portfolio is the no sensitive portfolio for changes of the price of the underlying asset. More precisely, the value of the delta-neutral portfolio does not change, even if the price of the underlying asset changes.

Let $S_0 = 100, K = 100, r = 0.01, \sigma = 0.2, T = 1$ and calculate the prices of call and put options.

---

[9]On the implied volatility, we describe it in the following section.

```
> black_scholes_2 <- function(S,K,r,sigma,T)
+ {
+   d1 <- (log(S/K) + (r+sigma^2/2)*T)/(sigma*sqrt(T))
+   d2 <- d1 - sigma*sqrt(T)
+
+   C0 <- S*pnorm(d1) - exp(-r*T)*K*pnorm(d2)
+   P0 <- C0 - S + exp(-r*T)*K
+
+   return(c("call option price"=C0, "put option price"=P0))
+ }
```

Running the above script, we get the following result.

```
> black_scholes_2(100,100,0.01,0.2,1)
call option price put option price
         8.433319          7.438302
```

7.4   Implied volatility

Once parameters of current price of underlying asset, strike price, interest rate, maturity and volatility are given, we can calculate the price of an option using the relevant Black-Scholes formula. However, in financial service industries, it is important to calculate volatilities backward from Black-Scholes formula and market prices of the option. These volatilities are considered as the future volatilities based on the agreement of investors. This is called implied volatility.

For a given model, we often need to estimate model parameters such that the model with these parameters fits well with the market values. This procedure is called calibration. For the calibration, we usually use optimization. R is equipped with a function for optimization, optimize(). Here, we introduce this function to derive implied volatility in the following numerical example (we also introduce other methods for optimization in R, later. See Appendix A).

Let the price of underlying asset $S_0 = 100$, the strike price $K = 100$, the risk free rate $r = 0.01$, the time to maturity $T = 1$ and the market price of the call option be 8.43, as we calculated in the previous section. We calculate the implied volatility of this option. We write the option price by Black-Scholes formula, C_0, as

$$C_0 = C_0(S_0, K, r, \sigma, T).$$

In this example, we need to calculate σ satisfying $8.43 = C_0(100, 100, 0.01, \sigma, 1)$. We define a function $f(\sigma) = |8.43 - C_0(100, 100, 0.01, \sigma, 1)|$, which is the difference between the market price and the numerically calculated option price using the Black-Scholes formula. We then calculate σ by minimizing $f(\sigma)$ in R using the optimizing function.

```
> # The function calculating the error, i.e.
> # difference, between the given market price
> # and the price of Black-Scholes formula
> err <- function(S,K,r,sigma,T,MktPrice)
+ {
+   tmp <- abs(MktPrice - black_scholes_1(S,K,r,sigma,T))
+   return(tmp)
+ }
>
> # minimization of err() by using optimize()
> optimize(err,interval=c(0,5),maximum=FALSE,MktPrice=8.43,
+ S=100,K=100,r=0.01,T=1)
```

Note that the argument `interval` in `optimize()` restricts the range of `sigma`, in this case, between 0 and 5. For minimization, we have to set `maximum=FALSE`. By specifying only values of `MktPrice`, `S`, `K`, `r` and `T`, we implicitly instruct the optimizing function that we want to calculate the optimization on the remaining variable, i.e., `sigma`. The following result is shown by running the above script.

```
$minimum
[1] 0.1999261

$objective
[1] 0.0004032324
```

The optimized variable is output as `minimum`, and the value of the objective function (i.e., `err()`) evaluated with the optimized variable is `objective`. The above result shows that the implied volatility found is 0.1999261 (approximately 20%); i.e., the above result shows that the value of objective function is given by 0.0004032324. We can check the result and confirm that $f(0.1999261) = 0.0004032324$, which is very close to zero.

The above numerical example uses one strike price K for estimating the implied volatility. However, real markets have options with various strike prices and various times to maturity. Let the strike price be K, the maturity be T and the market price of call option be $\tilde{C}(K,T)$. Consider the market prices as follows,

$$\tilde{C}(80,1) = 22.75, \quad \tilde{C}(90,1) = 15.1, \quad \tilde{C}(100,1) = 8.43,$$
$$\tilde{C}(110,1) = 4.72, \quad \tilde{C}(120,1) = 3.28$$

Strike price	70	80	90	100	110	120	130
IV(%)	27.18	24.38	22.8	20	20.28	23.0	24.2

For example, we can see in real market the following forms of implied volatilities (IV) for a time to maturity with various strike prices.[10] Implied volatilities for different strike prices are not necessarily on a horizontal line, but take the form of the right decreasing or smile curve (decreasing and increasing). This phenomenon is called volatility skew or volatility smile. This feature contradicts the assumption of Black-Scholes formula which assumes that volatilities is a constant parameter across different strike prices. To give interpretations, several extended models are suggested. The most representative ones are local volatility model [Dup94, DK94] and stochastic volatility models [Hes93, HKLW02].[11]

---

[10]The ratio of strike price and underlying asset price, i.e., moneyness, is often used instead of strike price alone in standard market conventions.

[11]See [Gat06] for more comprehensive discussion.

NUMERICAL METHODS IN FINANCE

Chapter 8

Monte Carlo Simulation

CONTENTS

We discuss methods of pricing derivatives using Monte Carlo simulation in this chapter. The idea of Monte Carlo simulation is based on the law of large numbers and the fact that pricing derivatives is reduced to the calculation of expected values. As we discussed in preceding chapters, the price of a derivative is given by the expected value of the pay-off under a risk neutral measure. Thus, we have to know how the underlying assets move under the risk neutral measure. Once we have the dynamics of underlying assets, we can price the derivative. According to the law of large numbers, Monte Carlo simulation leads us to the approximate price of the derivative by generating random variables consistent with the risk neutral measure.[1]

---

[1]Monte Carlo simulation with application for option pricing is given by many papers; e.g., [Boy77, BBG97, DG95, Fri07, Gla04] and [PT95].

8.1 The basic concept of Monte Carlo simulation

Consider a random variable Y and its expected value $\mathbb{E}[Y]$. According to the law of large numbers, for a sequence of random variables Y_n which are independent but taken from the same distribution in Y, the variable

$$\frac{1}{N}\sum_{n=1}^{N}Y_n$$

converges to $\mathbb{E}[Y]$ with probability 1 as $N \to \infty$.[2] Let the price of underlying asset be S and the pay-off function of the derivative be f. Then, the price of the derivative is given by the discounted expected value of the payoff of the contract as follows,

$$e^{-rT}\mathbb{E}^{Q}[f(S_T)],$$

where r is the risk free interest rate and T is the maturity of the derivative. The Monte Carlo simulation uses this fact; i.e., generating a sequence of random variables $\{S_T^n, n = 1, \cdots, N\}$ which are distributed by the risk neutral measure Q, the Monte Carlo simulation gives us the following approximation,

$$\mathbb{E}^{Q}[f(S_T)] \approx \frac{1}{N}\sum_{n=1}^{N}f(S_T^n).$$

The name of 'simulation' is derived from the process generating the sequence of random numbers. The above value is considered the approximated price of the derivative. We can thus reduce the problem of pricing a derivative to that of simulating the price of the underlying asset.

The price at maturity S_T is written under the risk neutral measure Q as

$$S_T = S_0 e^{\left(r-\frac{1}{2}\sigma^2\right)T+\sigma W_T},$$

where W_T is a Brownian motion under the risk neutral measure Q. In numerical simulation, it is convenient to standardize random variables to the variance 1. So, defining $\varepsilon = W_T/\sqrt{T} \sim \mathcal{N}(0,1)$, we rewrite the above equation as follows,

$$S_T = S_0 e^{\left(r-\frac{1}{2}\sigma^2\right)T+\sigma\sqrt{T}\varepsilon}. \tag{8.1}$$

Therefore, the price of the derivative is given by

$$e^{-rT}\mathbb{E}\left[f\left(S_0 e^{\left(r-\frac{1}{2}\sigma^2\right)T+\sigma\sqrt{T}\varepsilon}\right)\right]. \tag{8.2}$$

To avoid confusion, we simply describe the expectation operator under the risk neutral measure Q as $\mathbb{E}$, hereafter, not $\mathbb{E}^{Q}$.

---

[2]The law of large numbers implies the existence of the convergence.

Generating independent and identically distributed random numbers, $\varepsilon_1, \varepsilon_2, \cdots, \varepsilon_N$ of $\mathcal{N}(0,1)$,[3] we calculate

$$\frac{1}{N} \sum_{n=1}^{N} f\left(S_0 e^{\left(r - \frac{1}{2}\sigma^2\right)T + \sigma\sqrt{T}\varepsilon_n}\right).$$

According to the law of large numbers, for $N \to \infty$, the above value approaches $\mathbb{E}\left[f\left(S_0 e^{\left(r - \frac{1}{2}\sigma^2\right)T + \sigma\sqrt{T}\varepsilon}\right)\right]$. Since we cannot treat infinite number of random numbers, we need to generate a sufficiently large number N of random numbers and calculate the approximate value of the expected value.

Let's now try an example of Monte Carlo simulation in R to price a simple derivative contract. Using the pay-off of call option $f(x) = \max(x - K, 0)$, we generate a function to value the derivative price described above. We use the function rnorm(N,0,1) to generate random numbers from a normal distribution.

```
> # function to price a call option using Monte
> # Carlo simulation
> call.monte1<- function(S,K,r,sigma,T,N)
+ {
+   C0 <- 0
+   # N iterations for Monte Carlo simulation
+   for(n in 1:N)
+   {
+     C0 <- C0 + max(S*exp((r-0.5*sigma^2)*T+sigma*sqrt(T)*
+     rnorm(1,0,1))-K,0)
+   }
+   C0 <- exp(-r*T)*C0/N
+   return(c("Price calculated by Monte Carlo simulation"=C0))
+ }
```

As an example, letting $S_0 = 100, K = 100, r = 0.01, \sigma = 0.2, T = 1$,[4] we calculate the price of call option by using the function defined above. Although it is a subtle problem how to define the number of iterations of Monte Carlo simulation, we let the number of iterations be 10,000. Then, run the script and we get the result below,

---

[3]Monte Carlo simulation does not assume the type of distribution. So, we may generate random numbers of uniform distribution or some other distribution. However, we consider the Brownian motion, here. So, we use random numbers of the normal distribution.

[4]This corresponds to a call option of strike 100, 1-year maturity, assuming a risk free interest rate of 1% per annum, implied volatility of the underlying asset of 20% and initial asset price of 100.

```
> call.monte1(100,100,0.01,0.2,1,10000)
Price calculated by Monte Carlo simulation
                8.353214
> call.monte1(100,100,0.01,0.2,1,10000)
Price calculated by Monte Carlo simulation
                8.23827
> call.monte1(100,100,0.01,0.2,1,10000)
Price calculated by Monte Carlo simulation
                8.692412
> call.monte1(100,100,0.01,0.2,1,10000)
Price calculated by Monte Carlo simulation
                8.401362
```

Here, we have repeated the same calculation four times. Notice that the results are slightly different from each other. The function `call.monte1()` generates different random numbers, and thus the results are also dependent on the random numbers generated at each time. We can calculate the analytical solution of the call option price, which is 8.433319. The results above by `call.monte1()` vary around the analytical solution. We can also confirm that the solution by Monte Carlo simulation converges to the analytical solution by increasing the number of iterations N. However, increasing the number of simulations also increases the calculation time. In summary, the accuracy of the calculation is trade-off to the time of calculation. The above script uses a for-loop for the iterated calculation, which is easy to read but can be slow for a large number of iterations. We can instead use a vectorized version which generates all the random numbers we need for N simulations in a single line as follows.

```
> call.monte1.vec <- function(S,K,r,sigma,T,N)
+ {
+   # N normal random numbers of mean 0 and standard error 1
+   x <- rnorm(N,0,1)
+   y <- S*exp((r-0.5*sigma^2)*T+sigma*sqrt(T)*x)-K
+   # calculation of the price of call option taking sum of
+   # positive parts of y
+   C0 <- sum(y[y>0])*exp(-r*T)/N
+   return(c("Price calculated by Monte Carlo simulation"=C0))
+ }
```

Run this script with same parameters of the above example.

```
> call.monte1.vec(100,100,0.01,0.2,1,10000)
Price calculated by Monte Carlo simulation
                8.54221
```

There are other techniques to get more accurate approximation by using better sequences of random numbers. It is often recommended to use a sequence of random numbers called Mersenne Twister [MN98] which is considered a better sequence of random numbers. We show an example using Mersenne Twister.

```
> call.monte1.2 <- function(S,K,r,sigma,T,N)
+ {
+   # Use Mersenne-Twister to generate random numbers
+   RNGkind("Mersenne-Twister")
+   # initialization of the seed of random numbers
+   ini <- 1
+   set.seed(ini)
+
+   x <- rnorm(N,0,1)
+   y <- S*exp((r-0.5*sigma^2)*T+sigma*sqrt(T)*x)-K
+   C0 <- sum(y[y>0])*exp(-r*T)/N
+   return(c("Price calculated by Monte Carlo simulation"=C0))
+ }
```

Run the `call.monte1.2()`.

```
> call.monte1.2(100,100,0.01,0.2,1,10000)
Price calculated by Monte Carlo simulation
                  8.468332
```

In this case, even if we run the above script several times, the result will be same, because we fix the seed of the random numbers in the script `ini <- 1`. If we change the value of `ini`, the result of the calculation is also changed.

Figure 8.1 shows the convergences of the option prices calculated by the normal Monte Carlo simulation and the Monte Carlo simulation using Mersenne Twister. The convergence of the Monte Carlo simulation using Mersenne Twister to the analytical call option price 8.433319 is higher than that of the normal Monte Carlo simulation. This may be a good reason to use Mersenne Twister.

8.2 Variance reduction method

The basic idea of Monte Calro simulation was described in the previous section. Next, we discuss methods to improve the accuracy of Monte Carlo simulation.

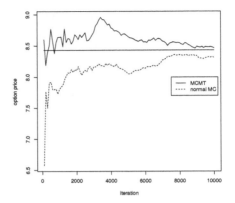

Figure 8.1: Convergence of option prices by the Monte Carlo simulation using Mersenne Twister (MCMT) and the normal Monte Carlo simulation (normal MC)

8.2.1 Antithetic variates method

We have to use random numbers in Monte Carlo simulation. The random number is assumed $\varepsilon \sim \mathcal{N}(0, 1)$. Thus, it theoretically holds

$$\mathbb{E}[\varepsilon] = 0, \tag{8.3}$$

$$Var[\varepsilon] = 1. \tag{8.4}$$

However, in practice, the approximated value of the moments of a numerically generated sequence of random numbers $\{\varepsilon_n\}$ does not necessarily satisfy the above equations. Indeed, although the following values

$$\frac{1}{N}\sum_{n=1}^{N}\varepsilon_n,$$

$$\frac{1}{N}\sum_{n=1}^{N}\varepsilon_n^2 - \left(\frac{1}{N}\sum_{n=1}^{N}\varepsilon_n\right)^2$$

should approach 0 and 1, respectively, when $N \to \infty$, it is not necessarily the case or the convergence might be slow (i.e., we would need a very large N). In practice, due to computational time constraints we cannot generate an infinite number of random numbers and so we might not see good convergence. Thus, we consider the method generating random numbers satisfying (8.3) (8.4). We can then ensure by construction that the moments of random numbers with a finite number of N coincides with the theoretical moment. This should give us a more accurate result with less iterations of Monte Carlo simulation. More precisely, we first calculate the following sequence of random numbers $\{\varepsilon_n\}$. At the same time, we calculate another sequence of random numbers with opposite sign $\{-\varepsilon_n\}$.

Consider a sequence $\tilde{\varepsilon}_n$ which is the union of these two sequences $\{\varepsilon_n\}$ and $\{-\varepsilon_n\}$. It is clear that this sequence $\tilde{\varepsilon}_n$ satisfies

$$\frac{1}{2N}\sum_{n=1}^{2N}\tilde{\varepsilon}_n = 0.$$

Thus, the sequence $\tilde{\varepsilon}_n$ satisfies (8.3) by construction. The price of an option with this set of random numbers is thus given as follows,

$$\frac{1}{2N}\sum_{n=1}^{2N}f\left(S_0 e^{\left(r-\frac{1}{2}\sigma^2\right)T+\sigma\sqrt{T}\tilde{\varepsilon}_n}\right).$$

This is called antithetic variates method. Let us calculate the price of call option by this method. Setting $S_0 = 100, K = 100, r = 0.01, \sigma = 0.2, T = 1$, we calculate the price of call option with iterated number $N = 10,000$.

```
> call.monte2 <- function(S,K,r,sigma,T,N)
+ {
+   epsi <- rnorm(N,0,1)
+   for(n in 1:N)
+   {
+     CO <- CO +
+       (max(S*exp((r-0.5*sigma^2)*T+sigma*sqrt(T)*epsi[n])-K,0) +
+             max(S*exp((r-0.5*sigma^2)*T-sigma*sqrt(T)*epsi[n])-K,0))
+     # The sign of sigma*sqrt(T)*eps in first term is opposite to
+     # the sign of sigma*sqrt(T)*epsi in second term.
+   }
+   CO <- exp(-r*T)*CO/(2*N)
+   return(c("Price calculated by Monte Carlo simulation"=CO))
+ }
```

We run this script and get the following result.

```
> call.monte2.1(100,100,0.01,0.2,1,10000)
Price calculated by Monte Carlo simulation
                  8.543737
```

If you don't use for-loop, but use the vectorized version, the following script is a candidate.

```
> call.monte2.vec <- function(S,K,r,sigma,T,N)
+ {
+   CO <- 0
+   epsi <- rnorm(N,0,1)
+   pos <- S*exp((r-0.5*sigma^2)*T+sigma*sqrt(T)*epsi)-K
+   neg <- S*exp((r-0.5*sigma^2)*T-sigma*sqrt(T)*epsi)-K
```

```
+   CO <- sum(pos[pos>0])+sum(neg[neg>0])
+   CO <- 0.5*CO*exp(-r*T)/N
+
+   return(c("Price calculated by Monte Carlo simulation"=CO))
+ }
```

Unfortunately, the antithetic variates method does not necessarily show the remarkable improvement. Indeed, Figure 8.2 depicts the speed of the convergence of the Monte Carlo simulation using the antithetic variates method to the analytical option price which is similar to the normal Monte Carlo simulation. Thus, we proceed to the more sophisticated variance reduction method, called the moment matching method.

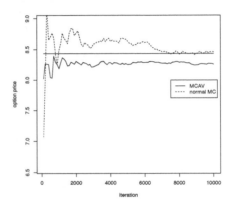

Figure 8.2: Convergence of option prices by the Monte Carlo simulation using the antithetic variates method (MCAV) and the normal Monte Carlo simulation (normal MC)

8.2.2 Moment matching method

The antithetic variates method is used to make a sequence of random numbers consistent with 1st moment. We can advance this discussion; i.e., we consider the method which makes a sequence consistent with 1st and 2nd moments.

The sample mean and variance of a set of random numbers is as follows,

$$\bar{\varepsilon} = \frac{1}{N}\sum_{n=1}^{N}\varepsilon_n$$

$$\bar{\sigma}^2 = \frac{1}{N}\sum_{n=1}^{N}\varepsilon_n^2 - \left(\frac{1}{N}\sum_{n=1}^{N}\varepsilon_n\right)^2.$$

We define a sequence of random numbers $\{\hat{\varepsilon}_n\}$ as

$$\hat{\varepsilon}_n = \frac{\varepsilon_n - \bar{\varepsilon}}{\bar{\sigma}}.$$

This sequence of random numbers satisfy the following properties by construction,

$$\frac{1}{N} \sum_{n=1}^{N} \hat{\varepsilon}_n = 0,$$

$$\frac{1}{N} \sum_{n=1}^{N} \hat{\varepsilon}_n^2 - \left(\frac{1}{N} \sum_{n=1}^{N} \hat{\varepsilon}_n \right)^2 = 1.$$

This shows that the sequence $\hat{\varepsilon}$ has its 1st and 2nd moments consistent with ε. We calculate the price of call option using this sequence of random numbers. Let $S_0 = 100, K = 100, r = 0.01, \sigma = 0.2, T = 1$ and the number of iterations N be 10,000.

```
> call.monte3 <- function(S,K,r,sigma,T,N)
+ {
+   x <- rnorm(N,0,1) # random numbers
+   # transformation of x to a random numbers with mean 0
+   # and standard error 1
+   y <- (x - mean(x))/sd(x)
+   # the pay-off of call option
+   z <- S*exp((r-0.5*sigma^2)*T+sigma*sqrt(T)*y)-K
+   # the price of option by Monte Carlo simulation
+   C0 <- sum(z[z>0])*exp(-r*T)/N
+   return(c("Price calculated by Monte Carlo simulation"=C0))
+ }
```

Running this script, we have the following result.

```
> call.monte3(100,100,0.01,0.2,1,10000)
Price calculated by Monte Carlo simulation
                    8.415985
```

Figure 8.3 depicts the improvement of the speed of the convergence by introducing the moment matching method. Indeed, about 3000 iteration of the moment matching method shows the good convergence in Figure 8.3. This result shows that moment matching method decreases the error between the results by Monte Carlo simulation and the analytical solution.

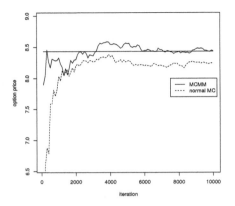

Figure 8.3: Convergence of option prices by the Monte Carlo simulation using the moment matching method (MCMM) and the normal Monte Carlo simulation (normal MC)

8.3 Exotic options

In the preceding section, we used Monte Carlo simulation to calculate the price of a call option. However, it is not computationally efficient, because there is an analytical solution to the price of a call option. The merit of using Monte Carlo simulation is to price options for which no analytical solution exists. In general, exotic options have payoffs which are path dependent or depend upon multiple, potentially correlated, assets.[5] To clarify the difference from exotic options, the call and put option discussed in preceding sections are, especially, called plain option, vanilla option or plain vanilla option. Hereafter, we consider the method to price exotic options by Monte Carlo simulation.

First, we consider a digital option. A digital option is an option of which pay-off is 1 (or the multiple of 1) if the option is exercised in the money and is 0, otherwise. The pay-off can be written as

$$\text{Payoff} = 1_{S_T > K},$$

---

[5]Note that some exotic options have analytical solutions. One of the good examples is the European barrier option which is categorized by the knock-out and knock-in types. The pay-off of the barrier option is defined whether the underlying asset touches a certain boundary or not by the maturity; e.g., up-and-in option which is one of the barrier options of the knock-in type which pay-off function is given by

$$\text{Pay-off} = (S_T - K)^+ 1_{\sup\{S_t; 0 < t < T\} \geq H},$$

where S_t is the underlying asset, K is the strike, T is the maturity and H is the barrier. Various types are included in the barrier option, like up-and-out, down-and-in, and down-and-out option.

Digital option is also an exotic option with the analytical solution which is discussed immediately later in this section with numerical example.

where S_T is the underlying asset price at maturity and K is the strike of the option.[6] We define a function to calculate the digital option by R.

```
> digital.monte1 <- function(S,K,r,sigma,T,N)
+ {
+   x <- rnorm(N,0,1)  # random numbers
+   # transformation of x to y consistent with 1st and 2nd
+   # moments
+   y <- (x - mean(x))/sd(x)
+
+   P <- 0 # initialization of the price P of digital
+   # option to be 0
+   for(n in 1:N)
+   {
+     # the pay-off of the digital option if it is exercised
+     if(S*exp((r-0.5*sigma^2)*T+sigma*sqrt(T)*y[n])>K)
+     {
+       P <- P + 1
+     }
+   }
+   P <- exp(-r*T)*P/N
+   return(c("price of digital option"=P))
+ }
```

We calculate the price of the digital option letting the price of the underlying asset $S_0 = 100$, the strike price $K = 100$, the risk free rate $r = 0.01$, the volatility $\sigma = 0.2$, the maturity $T = 1$ and the number of iterations of Monte Carlo simulation $N = 10{,}000$.

```
> digital.monte1(100,100,0.01,0.2,1,10000)
price of digital option
              0.4716597
```

If you do not want to use for-statement and if-statement, it is possible to modify the above script as follows,

```
> digital.monte.vec <- function(S,K,r,sigma,T,N)
+ {
+   x <- rnorm(N,0,1)
+   y <- (x - mean(x))/sd(x)
+   z <- S*exp((r-0.5*sigma^2)*T+sigma*sqrt(T)*y)-K
```

---

[6]The pay-off of a digital option looks similar to the Arrow-Debreu securities discussed in Section 6.1.1. However, they differ in the sense that the pay-off of a digital option corresponds to a specific event (at maturity), while the Arrow-Debreu securities correspond to all possible events.

```
+  # Only when z is positive, we add the pay-off which is
+  # normalized by dividing z by z
+  P <- sum(z[0<z]/z[0<z])*exp(-r*T)/N
+  return(c("price of digital option"=P))
+ }
```

We calculate the price of digital option by using this function.

```
> digital.monte.vec(100,100,0.01,0.2,1,10000)
price of digital option
              0.471661
```

In the case of digital option, we can also have the analytical solution by using the probability density function defined in section 7.3 as follows,

$$e^{-rT} \int_{\ln(K/S_0)}^{\infty} f(x)dx = e^{-rT}\Phi(d_2).$$

By the implementation of the above, the analytical solution with the parameters given above is 0.4752845. The R code for this is as follows:

```
> digital.analytic <- function(S,K,r,sigma,T)
+ {
+  d<- (log(S/K)+(r+0.5*sigma^2)*T)/(sigma*sqrt(T))-
+  sigma*sqrt(T)
+  P <- exp(-r*T)*pnorm(d)
+  return(c("price of digital option"=P))
+ }
>
> digital.analytic(100,100,0.01,0.2,1)
price of digital option
              0.4752845
```

Next, we consider look-back options. The look-back option is an option of which pay-off depends on the path that the underlying assets take from the inception of the option until maturity [And98]. Although there are several types of the pay-off of look-back option, we consider here a look-back call option where the underlying price used to calculate the payout is the maximum price during the life of the option as follows

$$\text{Payoff} = \max\left(\max\{S_t\}_{t \in [0,T]} - K, 0\right).$$

We define a function to price the look-back option.

```
> lookback.option <- function(S,K,r,sigma,T,N,M)
+ {
+  P <- 0
```

```
+   # M is the number of observation points;
+   # i.e., we divide the period to maturity by M of grids.
+   dt <- T/M
+
+   # N iterations of Monte Carlo simulation
+   for(n in 1:N)
+   {
+     # The price of underlying asset at time t which
+     # is initialized by the price of underlying
+     # asset S at time 0
+     St <- S
+     # Smax is the maximum value of St by maturity
+     # which is initialized by S
+     Smax <- S
+     # random numbers of observation points
+     x <- rnorm(M,0,1)
+
+     for(m in 1:M)
+     {
+       # simulation of St at each observation points
+       St <- St*exp((r-0.5*sigma^2)*dt+sigma*sqrt(dt)*x[m])
+       if(St>Smax)
+       # If the price St at time t is larger than the
+       # maximum value of St before t,
+       {
+         Smax <- St # update of the maximum value
+       }
+     }
+     P <- P + max(Smax-K,0)
+   }
+   P <- exp(-r*T)*P/N
+   return(c("price of look-back option"=P))
+ }
```

We run this script.

```
> lookback.option(100,100,0.01,0.2,1,10000,100)
price of look-back option
                16.05403
```

Here, we show only digital and look-back options as exotic options. In the following sections, we discuss other exotic options, like basket, rainbow and average options. However, there are many options other than those discussed here; e.g., American, Bermudan, compound, binary options. Further, we have various interesting derivatives like variance swaps, VIX index, CDS (credit default swap), CDO (collateralized debt obligation), and so forth. Readers who are interested in this field may be good to see, for example, [BO10, CS97] and [Hul12].

8.4 Multi asset options

Exotic option includes contracts which have multiple underlying assets.[7] The representative ones are basket option and rainbow option. The basket call option has the pay-off which simultaneously refers to the portfolio consisting of several assets such as

$$\text{Payoff} = \max\left(\frac{1}{M}\sum_{m=1}^{M}S_T^m - K, 0\right).$$

For simplicity, we set the ratio of assets in the portfolio equally given by $1/M$. Of course, this assumption can be relaxed.

The rainbow call option has the pay-off which refers to the maximum or minimum value of several assets such as

$$\text{Payoff} = \max\left(\max\{S_T^m\}_{m=1,\cdots,M} - K, 0\right).$$

We price these types of options using Monte Carlo simulation. The difficulty of this is due to the pay-off of these options simultaneously referring to several underlying assets. We need to evolve the underlying assets simultaneously, not independently, because they might have correlated with each other. Consider an example such that the prices of underlying assets $\{S_t^1, \cdots, S_t^M\}$ are described under the risk neutral measure as follows,

$$\begin{pmatrix} dS_t^1/S_t^1 \\ \vdots \\ dS_t^M/S_t^M \end{pmatrix} = \begin{pmatrix} r \\ \vdots \\ r \end{pmatrix} dt + \begin{pmatrix} \sigma_{11} & \cdots & \sigma_{1M} \\ \vdots & \ddots & \vdots \\ \sigma_{M1} & \cdots & \sigma_{MM} \end{pmatrix} \begin{pmatrix} dW_t^1 \\ \vdots \\ dW_t^M \end{pmatrix}.$$

Assume that Brownian motions are independent of each other; i.e., $\mathbb{E}[W_t^i W_t^j] = \mathbb{E}[W_t^i]\mathbb{E}[W_t^j]$, if $i \neq j$. We can solve the above stochastic equation by Itô's lemma; i.e., for $m = 1, \cdots, M$,

$$S_t^m = S_0^m e^{\left(r - \frac{1}{2}\|\sigma_m\|^2\right)t + \sigma_m \mathbf{W}_t},$$

where $\sigma_m = (\sigma_{m1}, \cdots, \sigma_{mM})$, $\|\sigma_m\|$ is the Euclidean norm and $\mathbf{W}_t = \left(W_t^1, \cdots, W_t^M\right)'$.

---

[7][Bar95, Boy90] and [BEG89] are classical papers for this issue.

Here, we generate a sequence of independent normal random numbers; $\varepsilon^{mn} \sim \mathcal{N}(0,1)$, $m = 1, \cdots, M$, $n = 1, \cdots, N$. We have this by the matrix form and define

$$\varepsilon^n := (\varepsilon^{1n}, \cdots, \varepsilon^{Mn})'.$$

For the ε^n, we generate a sequence of random variables S_T^m as follows,

$$S_T^{mn} = S_0^m e^{\left(r - \frac{1}{2}\|\sigma_m\|^2\right)t + \sqrt{T}\sigma_m \varepsilon^n}, \quad n = 1, \cdots, N.$$

We apply this sequence consisting of N random numbers for Monte Carlo simulation; i.e., we calculate

$$\mathbb{E}\left[f(S_T^1, \cdots, S_T^M)\right] = \frac{1}{N}\sum_{n=1}^{N} f(S_T^{1n}, \cdots, S_T^{Mn}).$$

We can calculate this pay-off function in both cases of basket option and rainbow option. The method of calculation is similar to each other. The above is the basic idea of the application of Monte Carlo simulation for multi asset options.

Consider an example of the basket option with 2 underlying assets. Let $S_0 = (100, 50)$, $K = 75$, $r = 0.01$, $\Sigma = \begin{pmatrix} 0.2 & 0.4 \\ 0.1 & 0.5 \end{pmatrix}$, $T = 1$ and the number of iterations of Monte Carlo simulation 10,000.

```
> basket.option <- function(S,K,r,Sigma,T,N)
+ {
+   # S consists of referenced underlying assets
+   M <- length(S) # M is the number of underlying assets
+
+   # Euclidean norm of each row of the matrix Sigma
+   v <- rep(0,M)
+   for(m in 1:M)
+   {
+     v[m] <- sqrt(Sigma[m,]%*%Sigma[m,])
+   }
+   # The above for-statement can be written as simpler form;
+   # v <- sqrt(diag(Sigma%*%t(Sigma)))
+   payoff <- 0
+   for(n in 1:N)
+   {
+     tmp <- 0
+     # M-dimensional standard normal random numbers
+     x<-rnorm(M,0,1)
+     for(m in 1:M)
+     {
```

```
+     # calculation of sum(S^m(t))
+     tmp <- tmp+S[m]*exp((r-0.5*v[m]^2)*T+
+     Sigma[m,]%*%x*sqrt(T))
+     }
+     # the above calculation without for-statement
+     # tmp <- S%*%exp((r-0.5*v^2)*T+Sigma%*%x*sqrt(T))
+     payoff <- payoff + max(tmp/M-K,0)
+   }
+   # the basket option price
+   ans <- payoff/N*exp(-r*T)
+   return(ans)
+ }
```

We run this script.

```
> Sigma <- matrix(c(0.2,0.1,0.4,0.5),2,2)
> basket.option(c(100,50),75,0.01,Sigma,1,10000)
[1] 14.01399
```

Similarly, we describe a function to calculate the price of rainbow call option and calculate the price by letting $S_0 = (100, 100)$, $K = 100$, $r = 0.01$, $\begin{pmatrix} \sigma_{11} & \sigma_{12} \\ \sigma_{21} & \sigma_{22} \end{pmatrix} = \begin{pmatrix} 0.2 & 0.4 \\ 0.1 & 0.5 \end{pmatrix}$, $T = 1$ and the number of iterations of Monte Carlo simulation be 10,000.

```
> rainbow.option <- function(S,K,r,Sigma,T,N)
+ {
+   # the number of underlying assets
+   M <- length(S)
+
+   # Euclidean norm of each row of the matrix Sigma
+   v <- rep(0,M)
+   for(m in 1:M)
+   {
+     v[m] <- sqrt(Sigma[m,]%*%Sigma[m,])
+   }
+
+   payoff <- 0
+   for(n in 1:N)
+   {
+     tmp1 <- 0
+     # M-dimensional standard random number
+     x<-rnorm(M,0,1)
+     for(m in 1:M)
+     {
```

```
+    # calculation of S^m(t)
+    tmp2 <- S[m]*exp((r-0.5*v[m]^2)*T+
+    Sigma[m,]%*%x*sqrt(T))
+    if(tmp1<tmp2)
+    {
+      tmp1 <- tmp2 # update of the maximum value
+    }
+    }
+    # calculation of tmp1 without for-statement;
+    # tmp1 <- max(S*exp((r-0.5*v^2)*T+Sigma%*%x*sqrt(T)))
+    payoff <- payoff + max(tmp1-K,0)
+    }
+    # the rainbow option price
+    ans <- exp(-r*T)*payoff/N
+    return(ans)
+ }
```

Run this script.

```
> Sigma <- matrix(c(0.2,0.1,0.4,0.5),2,2)
> rainbow.option(c(100,100),100,0.01,Sigma,1,10000)
[1] 22.58603
```

8.5 Control variates method

In the final section of this chapter, we briefly discuss control variates method. The control variates method is also one of variance reduction methods, like antithetic variates method and moment matching method. This gives us the value of exotic options with high accuracy [HW88]. The idea is nice and simple.

As we described, the value of option is calculated by the expected value $\mathbb{E}[f(S_T)]$ for the pay-off function $f(S_T)$. Here, we consider Monte Carlo simulation. Then, the approximated expected value is given by

$$\frac{1}{N}\sum_{n=1}^{N}f(S_T^n). \tag{8.5}$$

To calculate the above, control variates method requires to introduce a pay-off function $g(S_T)$ of which the option price can be analytically calculated and to define the expected value as follows,

$$\frac{1}{N}\sum_{n=1}^{N}(f(S_T^n)-g(S_T^n))+\mathbb{E}[g(S_T)]. \tag{8.6}$$

Note that this formulation is essentially the same as the value of (8.5). Thus, (8.6) also leads to the option price of pay-off $f(\cdot)$.

The accuracy of a method may be defined by how the variance derived by Monte Carlo simulation is small. In this sense, we should compare the variance of the option price based on control variates method (8.6) with the variance of the option price based on normal Monte Carlo simulation (8.5).

The variance by control variates method is given as follows.

$$Var\left(\frac{1}{N}\sum_{n=1}^{N}(f(S_T^n)-g(S_T^n))+\mathbb{E}[g(S_T)]\right)$$

$$=Var\left(\frac{1}{N}\sum_{n=1}^{N}f(S_T^n)-\frac{1}{N}\sum_{n=1}^{N}g(S_T^n)+\mathbb{E}[g(S_T)]\right)$$

$$=Var\left(\frac{1}{N}\sum_{n=1}^{N}f(S_T^n)-\frac{1}{N}\sum_{n=1}^{N}g(S_T^n)\right)$$

$$=Var\left(\frac{1}{N}\sum_{n=1}^{N}f(S_T^n)\right)+Var\left(\frac{1}{N}\sum_{n=1}^{N}g(S_T^n)\right)-2Cov\left(\frac{1}{N}\sum_{n=1}^{N}f(S_T^n)\frac{1}{N}\sum_{n=1}^{N}g(S_T^n)\right).$$

To calculate the more accurate value of the option by control variate method, the above value of the variance must be smaller than the value of variance of (8.5); i.e.,

$$Var\left(\frac{1}{N}\sum_{n=1}^{N}f(S_T^n)\right) > Var\left(\frac{1}{N}\sum_{n=1}^{N}f(S_T^n)\right)+Var\left(\frac{1}{N}\sum_{n=1}^{N}g(S_T^n)\right)$$

$$- 2Cov\left(\frac{1}{N}\sum_{n=1}^{N}f(S_T^n)\frac{1}{N}\sum_{n=1}^{N}g(S_T^n)\right).$$

If the above inequality holds, it is meaningful to introduce $g(S_T)$ into the Monte Carlo method to calculate $\mathbb{E}[f(S_T)]$, because the variance (the magnitude of error) of the option price gets smaller.

We rearrange the above inequality,

$$2Cov\left(\frac{1}{N}\sum_{n=1}^{N}f(S_T^n)\frac{1}{N}\sum_{n=1}^{N}g(S_T^n)\right) > Var\left(\frac{1}{N}\sum_{n=1}^{N}g(S_T^n)\right).$$

This is further rewritten as

$$\frac{Cov\left(\frac{1}{N}\sum_{n=1}^{N}f(S_T^n)\frac{1}{N}\sum_{n=1}^{N}g(S_T^n)\right)}{Var\left(\frac{1}{N}\sum_{n=1}^{N}g(S_T^n)\right)} > \frac{1}{2}.$$

To simplify further, we introduce the correlation coefficient between $\frac{1}{N}\sum_{n=1}^{N} f(S_T^n)$ and $\frac{1}{N}\sum_{n=1}^{N} g(S_T^n)$; i.e.,

$$\rho_{fg} = \frac{Cov\left(\frac{1}{N}\sum_{n=1}^{N} f(S_T^n) \frac{1}{N}\sum_{n=1}^{N} g(S_T^n)\right)}{\sqrt{Var\left(\frac{1}{N}\sum_{n=1}^{N} f(S_T^n)\right)}\sqrt{Var\left(\frac{1}{N}\sum_{n=1}^{N} g(S_T^n)\right)}}.$$

Then the above inequality is finally reduced to

$$\rho_{fg}\frac{\sqrt{Var\left(\frac{1}{N}\sum_{n=1}^{N} f(S_T^n)\right)}}{\sqrt{Var\left(\frac{1}{N}\sum_{n=1}^{N} g(S_T^n)\right)}} > \frac{1}{2}.$$

This implies that the more similar the dynamics of f and g are, the smaller the variance (error) of the option price is such that the above condition sufficiently holds. That is, we should choose the pay-off function $g(x)$ sufficiently satisfying the above inequality.

The control variates method is often applied for average option which pay-off depends on the averaged value of the underlying asset in the fixed time period. The reason of this is that the value of the arithmetic average option cannot be calculated analytically, although the value of the geometric average option can be analytically calculated. Of course, the arithmetic average value and the geometric one are similar to each other. Using this relationship, we often adopt the control variates method. More precisely, we let the pay-off function $f()$ be the pay-off of arithmetic average option and the pay-off function $g()$ be the pay-off of geometric average option.

Due to the attractive feature of the average option,[8] there are many references; e.g., [CC90, KV90, CV91, TW91, BBC94, GY93, RS95, And98, Vec1, Vec2] and [VX04]. Although we have the PDE approach and analytical approximation for pricing the average option, the Monte Carlo approach may be the most simple method, but it may be the most time consuming to attain the accurate value. Thus, the control variates method is useful in this context.

Let us define the pay-off of the average option. We fix the sampling time $t_1 < t_2 \cdots < t_M = T$ and observe the underlying asset price $S_{t_1}, S_{t_2}, \cdots, S_{t_M}$. For simplicity, we assume time interval $\Delta t = t_m - t_{m-1}$ is same for all $m = 1, \cdots, M$.

---

[8]Indeed, the average options are less expensive than the plain options. These types of options are often used in the foreign exchange rate and commodity futures markets. Further, the average option is also called Asian option. The name "Asian" is derived from the fact that such types of options are firstly written on stock trading on Asian exchanges.

The average value calculated at $t = T$ is given by

$$S_T^{ave} := \frac{1}{M} \sum_{m=1}^{M} S_{t_m}$$

For this average value, the pay-off of the average call option is given by

$$f(S_T^{ave}) = \max(S_T^{ave} - K, 0),$$

and the pay-off of the average put option is given by

$$f(S_T^{ave}) = \max(K - S_T^{ave}, 0).$$

The pay-off of the average option looks like the basket option. However, the "average" is calculated in the fixed time period. Thus, it is path-dependent options like look-back option.

The essence of pricing the average option via Monte Carlo method is to generate $(S_T^{ave,n})_{n=1,\cdots,N}$ and calculate the mean value of the pay-off, where $S_T^{ave,n}$ is defined by the sample $S_{t_1}^n, S_{t_2}^n, \cdots, S_{t_M}^n$ for $n = 1, \cdots, N$; i.e., $S_T^{ave,n} = \frac{1}{M} \sum_{m=1}^{M} S_{t_m}^n$.

Let us calculate the average call option price via normal Monte Carlo method which is used for the comparison with the Monte Carlo method via the control variates method.

First, we define the function for calculating average call option price via normal Monte Carlo method as follows:

```
> average.option <- function(S,K,r,sigma,T,N,M)
+ {
+ P <- 0
+ # M is the number of the observation points;
+ # i.e., we divide the period to maturity by M number of grid.
+ dt <- T/M
+
+ # N is the number of iterations of Monte Carlo simulation
+ for(n in 1:N)
+ {
+ # the price of underlying asset at time t which is initialized
+ # by the price of underlying asset S at time 0
+ St <- S
+ # Save is the average value of St by maturity
+ # which is initialized by 0.0
+ Save <- 0.0
+ # generate random numbers with the number
```

```
+ # of observation points
+ x <- rnorm(M,0,1)
+
+ for(m in 1:M)
+ {
+ # simulate St at each observation points
+ # which consist of M points
+ St <- St*exp((r-0.5*sigma^2)*dt+sigma*sqrt(dt)*x[m])
+ Save <- Save + St # update the average value
+ }
+ P <- P + max(Save/M-K,0)
+ }
+ P <- exp(-r*T)*P/N
+ return(c("price of average call option"=P))
+ }
```

Let $S_0 = 100$, $K = 100$, $r = 0.01$, $\sigma = 0.2$, $T = 1$ and $M = 100$. Then, the average option price is given with 10,000 number of iterations is given as follows:

```
> average.option(100,100,0.01,0.2,1,10000,100)
price of average call option
                 4.817254
```

The plain call option for parameters $S_0 = 100$, $K = 100$, $r = 0.01$, $\sigma = 0.2$, $T = 1$ is 8.43. Indeed, the average option price is less expensive than plain option.

For the control variates method, we need the analytical solution of the geometric average option price, which is given by [Vor92] (see [KV90] for continuous geometric average value). Note that the geometric average is defined by

$$
S_T^{g.ave} = \left(\prod_{m=1}^{M} S_{t_m} \right)^{1/M} .
$$

Further, we need to give the drift μ_G and volatility σ_G for the geometric average value $S_T^{g.ave}$ such that

$$
\mu_G = \ln S_0 + \left(r - \frac{1}{2}\sigma^2 \right) \frac{T + \Delta t}{2},
$$

$$
\sigma_G = \sigma \sqrt{ \Delta t \frac{(2M+1)(M+1)}{6M} } .
$$

Then, the analytical value of the geometric call option price is given by

$$\mathbb{E}[g(S_T^{g.ave})] = e^{-rT}\left(e^{\mu_G + \frac{1}{2}\sigma_G^2}\Phi(d_1) - K\Phi(d_2)\right),$$

where $g(S_T^{g.ave}) := \max(S_T^{g.ave} - K, 0)$ and

$$d_1 = \frac{\mu_G - \ln K + \sigma_G^2}{\sigma_G},$$

$$d_2 = d_1 - \sigma_G.$$

According to this, we first define the function for calculating the geometric average option.

```
> analytical.geometric.average.option <- function(S,K,r,sigma,T,M)
+ {
+   # M is the number the observation points;
+   # i.e., we divide the period to maturity by M number of grid.
+   dt <- T/M
+
+   # drift of geometric average value
+   mu_G <- log(S) + (r-0.5*sigma^2)*0.5*(T+dt)
+   # volatility of geometric average value
+   sigma_G <- sigma*sqrt(dt*(2*M+1)*(M+1)/(6*M))
+
+   d1 <- (mu_G - log(K) + sigma_G*sigma_G)/sigma_G
+   d2 <- d1 - sigma_G
+
+   P <- exp(-r*T)*(exp(mu_G + 0.5*sigma_G^2)*pnorm(d1)-
+   K*pnorm(d2))
+   return(P)
+ }
```

Now, we can calculate the average option price via control variates method.

```
> average.option.control <- function(S,K,r,sigma,T,N,M)
+ {
+   # calculate analytical price of geometric average option
+   P_ana <- analytical.geometric.average.option(S,K,r,sigma,T,M)
+
+   P <- 0
+   # M is the number of the observation points;
+   # i.e., we divide the period to maturity by M number of grid.
+   dt <- T/M
+
+   # N is the number of iterations of Monte Carlo simulation
+   for(n in 1:N)
```

```
+  {
+    # the price of underlying asset at time t which is initialized
+    # by the price of underlying asset S at time 0
+    St <- S
+    # Save and Save_geo are the arithmetic average value and
+    # the geometric average value of St by maturity
+    # which are initialized by 0.0 and 1.0
+    Save <- 0.0
+    Save_geo <- 1.0
+    # generate random numbers with the number
+    # of observation points
+    x <- rnorm(M,0,1)
+
+    for(m in 1:M)
+    {
+      # simulate St at each observation points
+      # which consist of M points
+      St <- St*exp((r-0.5*sigma^2)*dt+sigma*sqrt(dt)*x[m])
+      # update the arithmetic average value
+      Save <- Save + St
+      # update the geometrical average value
+      Save_geo <- Save_geo*St
+    }
+    P <- P + max(Save/M-K,0)-max(Save_geo^(1/M)-K,0)
+  }
+  P <- exp(-r*T)*P/N + P_ana
+  return(c("price of average call option"=P))
+ }
```

Using parameter $S_0 = 100$, $K = 100$, $r = 0.01$, $\sigma = 0.2$, $T = 1$ and $M = 100$ which is same as the above numerical example via normal Monte Carlo method, we calculate the average option price:

```
> average.option.control(100,100,0.01,0.2,1,10000,100)
price of average call option
                4.887256
```

Since the option price calculated by the normal Monte Carlo method is 4.817254, the option price by the Monte Carlo method via control variates method is similar to each other. To confirm the efficiency of the control variates method, we show the speed of the convergence of both methods. Figure 8.4 depicts the convergence of the option price for the number of iterations. The option price via control variates method looks stable with less number of iterations.

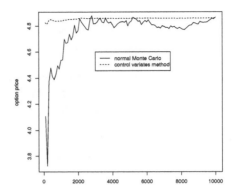

Figure 8.4: Convergence of option prices

In addition to methods discussed here, there are many methods of variance reduction methods (see, for example, [Leh97]); e.g., regression analysis method, approximating Martingales for variance reduction method, conditional Monte Carlo method, stratification. If readers are interested in them, refer to the books focussing on Monte Carlo simulation; e.g., [Fis96, HH64, KW86].

Chapter 9

Derivative Pricing with Partial Differential Equations

CONTENTS

We have seen a few different methods for calculating the prices of derivatives, assuming various dynamical behaviour of the underlying assets. However, it is also possible to describe the dynamics of derivative prices by partial differential equations and as such partial differential equations are very useful for pricing derivatives. We can turn the problem of calculating derivative prices into that of solving partial differential equations. One of the most common methods used is the finite difference method, which we briefly illustrate in this chapter.[1]

---

[1] For more detailed issues on finite difference method, see e.g., [BS78, Cou82, HW93, PTVF92, RM67, Smi85, TR00, TR00] and [Wil97].

Partial differential equation for the Black-Scholes formula

Let the price of a derivative $V(t,S)$ be a function of time t and the price of an underlying risky asset S. The price of the risky asset S is described by the following form under the risk neutral measure Q:

$$dS = rSdt + \sigma SdW_t.$$

Then, by Itô's lemma it holds that

$$
\begin{aligned}
dV &= \frac{\partial V}{\partial t}dt + \frac{\partial V}{\partial S}dS + \frac{1}{2}\frac{\partial^2 V}{\partial S^2}dS^2 \\
&= \frac{\partial V}{\partial t}dt + \frac{\partial V}{\partial S}(rSdt + \sigma SdW_t) + \frac{1}{2}\frac{\partial^2 V}{\partial S^2}\sigma^2 S^2 dt \\
&= \left(\frac{\partial V}{\partial t} + rS\frac{\partial V}{\partial S} + \frac{1}{2}\sigma^2 S^2 \frac{\partial^2 V}{\partial S^2}\right)dt + \sigma S\frac{\partial V}{\partial S}dW_t.
\end{aligned}
$$

Further, taking into account the expected value under the risk neutral measure

$$\mathbb{E}^Q[dV] = rVdt,$$

we arrive at the following partial differential equation

$$\frac{\partial V}{\partial t} + rS\frac{\partial V}{\partial S} + \frac{1}{2}\sigma^2 S^2 \frac{\partial^2 V}{\partial S^2} - rV = 0,$$

which is the Black-Scholes partial differential equation.

As the name implies, the essence of the finite difference method is to approximate derivatives by finite differences. Instead of directly approximating the above Black-Scholes partial differential equation, we try to simplify the equation by using a variable transformation.

1. Introducing a variable x satisfying $S = e^x, dS = Sdx$, we use the following relationships:

$$\frac{\partial V}{\partial S} = \frac{1}{S}\frac{\partial V}{\partial x}, \quad \frac{\partial^2 V}{\partial S^2} = -\frac{1}{S^2}\frac{\partial V}{\partial x} + \frac{1}{S^2}\frac{\partial^2 V}{\partial x^2}.$$

2. We introduce a function $f(x,t)$ satisfying $V = fe^{-r(T-t)}$, where T is the maturity of the option. Then, it holds that

$$\frac{\partial V}{\partial t} = \frac{\partial f}{\partial t}e^{-r(T-t)} + rfe^{-r(T-t)}.$$

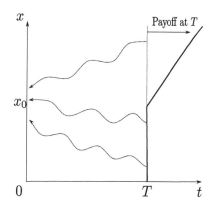

Figure 9.1: The concept of pricing a derivative by partial differential equation, with the boundary condition of the payoff at expiry.

The above variable transformation reduces the Black-Scholes partial differential equation to

$$\frac{\partial f}{\partial t} + \left(r - \frac{\sigma^2}{2}\right)\frac{\partial f}{\partial x} + \frac{\sigma^2}{2}\frac{\partial^2 f}{\partial x^2} = 0. \tag{9.1}$$

Since the pay-off function $f(x,T)$ at the maturity $t = T$ is known, the partial differential equation (9.1) can be solved with the initial condition on $f(x,T)$ by backward from $t = T$ to $t = 0$ on the time interval $(t : T \to 0)$. Then we attain $f(x,0)$, which is the price of the derivative at the present time (see Figure 9.1).

To solve numerically (9.1) with a finite difference method, we need to define the region for the calculation over x,t and divide the region of x,t into an appropriate grid. First, we define an arbitrary grid interval $\Delta x, \Delta t$ and describe x,t by them as follows:

$$\begin{cases} x_i = i\Delta x \\ t_j = j\Delta t \end{cases} ,i = 0, 1, \cdots, N, j = 0, 1, \cdots, M.$$

The value of f at $x = x_i, t = t_j$ is described by $f(x_i, t_j) = f_{i,j}$. According to (9.1), we recursively calculate the status $f_{i,j}$ at t_j by using information of $f_{i,j+1}$ at t_{j+1}. This procedure is iterated until $j = 0$ $(t : T \to 0)$. Then, we attain the price of the derivative at time 0.

In the following sections, we introduce the two most common methods of solving partial differential equations by finite differences, the explicit finite difference method (explicit method) and the implicit finite difference method (implicit method).

9.1   The explicit method

Using the definition of a derivative $\partial f/\partial x = [f(x+\Delta x,t) - f(x,t)]/\Delta x$, $(\Delta x \to 0)$, the explicit method approximates the differential by the finite differences as follows [ABR97, HW90]:

$$\left\{ \begin{array}{l} \dfrac{\partial f}{\partial t} = \dfrac{f_{i,j+1} - f_{i,j}}{\Delta t} \\[3mm] \dfrac{\partial f}{\partial x} = \dfrac{f_{i+1,j+1} - f_{i-1,j+1}}{2\Delta x} \\[3mm] \dfrac{\partial^2 f}{\partial x^2} = \dfrac{f_{i+1,j+1} - 2f_{i,j+1} + f_{i-1,j+1}}{\Delta x^2} \end{array} \right. .$$

Substituting these difference approximations into the partial differential equation (9.1), it holds that

$$\frac{f_{i,j+1} - f_{i,j}}{\Delta t} + \left(r - \frac{\sigma^2}{2} \right) \frac{f_{i+1,j+1} - f_{i-1,j+1}}{2\Delta x} + \frac{\sigma^2}{2} \frac{f_{i+1,j+1} - 2f_{i,j+1} + f_{i-1,j+1}}{\Delta x^2} = 0.$$

We define $\Delta t/\Delta x^2 = \delta$ and solve the above on $f_{i,j}$. Then we have

$$\begin{aligned} f_{i,j} = & \frac{\delta}{2} \left[\sigma^2 - \Delta x \left(r - \frac{\sigma^2}{2} \right) \right] f_{i-1,j+1} + (1 - \delta\sigma^2) f_{i,j+1} \\ & + \frac{\delta}{2} \left[\sigma^2 + \Delta x \left(r - \frac{\sigma^2}{2} \right) \right] f_{i+1,j+1} \\ = & a f_{i-1,j+1} + b f_{i,j+1} + c f_{i+1,j+1}, \end{aligned}$$

where we define a, b, c as the coefficients of the terms on the right hand side. From this equation, we can calculate backwards in time from the known variables $f_{i,j+1}$ at time $j+1$ to unknown $f_{i,j}$ at time j. Continuing this procedure to time 0 leads us to the present value of the derivative (see Figure 9.2[2]).

Next, we show the numerical example to price the call option by explicit method. Before this, we have to note that there are methods to sophisticate the construction of computational grids and the region of variables on finite difference methods including both of explicit and implicit methods. Furthermore, we have to take into consideration of the boundary condition when we use the finite difference method. Indeed, although it is natural to define the finite region of time interval $[0,T]$ for time t, it is controversial how to define the region of the price of underlying asset S of variable x, because theoretically it can take infinite values. However, it is impossible for numerical calculation to deal with infinite values.

---

[2]By this figure, readers might consider the explicit method is similar to trinomial tree. Indeed, the explicit method is essentially the same as the trinomial tree. However, the implicit method is not the same as the trinomial tree, as we shall see later.

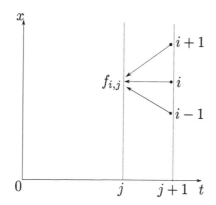

Figure 9.2: Conceptual diagram of the explicit method

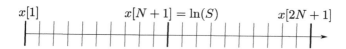

Figure 9.3: An example of the calculation grid used on the x-axis in the explicit method

Thus, we need to set a sufficiently large area and define the boundary condition on the boundary region.

In the following numerical example, let S be the price of the underlying asset, K be the strike price, r be the risk free rate, sigma be the volatility, T be the maturity of the option, M be the number of grid points on time interval, and N be the number of grid points on the price of underlying asset: these variables are input variables and the price of the option is the output variable. Note that the number of grid points on the price of underlying asset is set as 2N such that the price at present coincides with one of the grid points (see Figure 9.3). Note also that, the larger j implies *t* approaching to 0 in the following script for efficient calculation, although the direction might be opposite to our intuition.

Numerical example of explicit method

```
> PDEex_call <- function(S,K,r,sigma,T,M,N){
+   # The region of possible prices of the underlying asset is given
+   # by 20 times of the present price of underlying asset.
+   Smax <- 20*S
+   # calculation of x_max corresponding to Smax
+   xmax <- log(Smax)
+
+   # time interval [0,T] divided by M
+   dt <- T/M
```

```
+  # length from x=log(S) to xmax divided by N
+  dx <- (xmax-log(S))/N
+  # xmin is given such that the interval from xmin to x=log(S)
+  # is divided by N.
+  xmin <- log(S)-N*dx
+  x <- seq(xmin,xmax,by=dx)  # 2N+1 dimensional vector
+  # such that x[1] and x[2N+1] correspond to boundaries.
+
+  # NN=2*N is set for x=log(S) to be on the grid
+  NN <- 2*N
+
+  dd <- dt/(dx^2) # delta
+
+  # Initial Condition
+  f <- pmax(exp(x)-K,0) # pay-off at t=T
+  # pmax() is a function to calculate the maximum value of
+  # each factor
+
+  # store the information at the previous step in g
+  g <- f
+
+  # Boundary Condition
+  g[1] <- 0
+  a <- (dd/2)*(sigma^2-dx*(r-sigma^2/2))
+  b <- (1-dd*sigma^2)
+  c <- (dd/2)*(sigma^2+dx*(r-sigma^2/2))
+  # iteration in the direction of t->0(j->M)
+  for(j in 1:M){
+    g[NN+1] <- exp(r*j*dt)*(Smax-K) # the boundary condition
+    for(i in 2:NN){
+      f[i] <- a*g[i-1]+b*g[i]+c*g[i+1]
+    }
+    g <- f# the data for the next step
+  }
+
+  # the price of the derivative
+  C0 <- exp(-r*T)*f[N+1]
+
+  # analytical solution
+  d1 <- (log(S/K) + (r+sigma^2/2)*T)/(sigma*sqrt(T))
+  d2 <- d1 - sigma*sqrt(T)
+
+  C0_A <- S*pnorm(d1) - exp(-r*T)*K*pnorm(d2)
+
+  # results by finite difference method and
```

```
+   # analytical solution
+   return(c(CO,CO_A))
+ }
```

We run the above script, then we get the following results.

```
> PDEex_call(100,110,0.01,0.2,5,50,20)
[1] 15.90431  15.87741
> PDEex_call(100,110,0.01,0.2,5,300,100)
[1] 15.87972  15.87741
```

Minimizing the grid spacing (increasing M,N) usually makes the solution converge to the analytical solution. However, we must note that the stability of the
numerical solution is dependent on the relationship between Δt and Δx. The following example shows such an instability.

```
> PDEex_call(100,110,0.01,0.2,5,50,50)
[1] -430.95516   15.87741
```

The reason this phenomenon appears is intuitive. When Δt is much larger
than Δx, information about x in between x and $x + \Delta x$ is missed after a time step
of Δt. This generates an instability in the finite differencing. It is well known
that the numerical calculation is stable if $\delta = \Delta t / (\Delta x)^2 < 1/2$, according to the
knowledge of numerical solutions to the heat equation. This is the von Neumann
stability condition [CFvN50].

9.2   The implicit method

The implicit method is a good candidate to overcome the instability problem
of the explicit method, because the implicit method unconditionally satisfies the
von Neuman stability condition.[3] The big difference between the two methods
is that the implicit method describes the difference on the space (x) by unknown
$f_{i-1,j}, f_{i,j}, f_{i+1,j}$, choosing the value at j, not at $j+1$, as follows,

$$
\begin{cases}
\dfrac{\partial f}{\partial t} = \dfrac{f_{i,j+1} - f_{i,j}}{\Delta t} \\[2ex]
\dfrac{\partial f}{\partial x} = \dfrac{f_{i+1,j} - f_{i-1,j}}{2\Delta x} \\[2ex]
\dfrac{\partial^2 f}{\partial x^2} = \dfrac{f_{i+1,j} - 2f_{i,j} + f_{i-1,j}}{\Delta x^2}
\end{cases}
.
$$

---

[3]The Crank-Nicolson scheme [CN50] is also a good candidate which has unconditional stability
[TR00]. However, this book focuses only on the implicit method.

Substituting them into the partial differential equation (9.1) and we get the following

$$f_{i,j+1} = -\frac{\delta}{2}\left[\sigma^2 - \Delta x\left(r - \frac{\sigma^2}{2}\right)\right]f_{i-1,j} + (1+\delta\sigma^2)f_{i,j} - \frac{\delta}{2}\left[\sigma^2 + \Delta x\left(r - \frac{\sigma^2}{2}\right)\right]f_{i+1,j}$$

$$= af_{i-1,j} + bf_{i,j} + cf_{i+1,j}, \tag{9.2}$$

where we denote each coefficients as a, b, c. Note that the left hand side is a known variable and the right hand side has unknown variables, which is opposite to what we have with the explicit method. For $i = 0, 1, \cdots, N$, we define the following matrix,

$$\boldsymbol{f}_j = \begin{pmatrix} f_{1,j} \\ f_{2,j} \\ \vdots \\ f_{N-1,j} \end{pmatrix}, \quad D = \begin{pmatrix} b & c & 0 & \cdots & & 0 \\ a & b & c & 0 & \cdots & 0 \\ & & & \ddots & & \\ 0 & & \cdots & 0 & a & b \end{pmatrix}, \quad \boldsymbol{g} = \begin{pmatrix} af_{0,j} \\ 0 \\ \vdots \\ cf_{N,j} \end{pmatrix}.$$

Since (9.2) is written as $\boldsymbol{f}_{j+1} = D\boldsymbol{f}_j + \boldsymbol{g}$, it holds that

$$\boldsymbol{f}_j = D^{-1}\left(\boldsymbol{f}_{j+1} - \boldsymbol{g}\right), \tag{9.3}$$

where D^{-1} is inverse matrix of D. Similarly to the explicit method, we can solve (9.3) backward by $j \to 0$ to calculate the price of the derivative at time 0 (see Figure 9.4). Compared with the explicit method, the implicit method calculates the value of $f_{i,j}$ by implicitly using the information at time j.

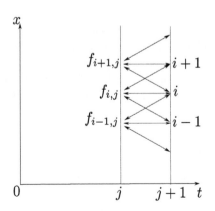

Figure 9.4: Conceptual diagram of the implicit method

We show a numerical example to calculate the price of a call option by the implicit method. As in the explicit method, we divide the time interval of t-axis

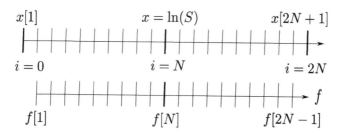

Figure 9.5: An example of the calculation grid on the x-axis with the implicit method

into a grid of size M and the space of the x-axis into a grid of size $2N$, where $2N$ is defined such that the current underlying asset price will fall on the grid (see Figure 9.5). Notice also that j in the following script is defined to approach $t = 0$ when j is increased.

Numerical example of the implicit method using R

```
> PDEim_call <- function(S,K,r,sigma,T,M,N){
+   # The region of the possible prices of the underlying asset
+   # is given by 20 times as the present underlying asset price
+   Smax <- 20*S
+   # calculation xmax corresponding to Smax
+   xmax <- log(Smax)
+
+   # time interval [0,T] divided by M
+   dt <- T/M
+   # length from x=log(S) to xmax divided by N
+   dx <- (xmax-log(S))/N
+   # xmin is given such that the interval from xmin to x=log(S)
+   # is divided by N
+   xmin <- log(S)-N*dx
+   x <- seq(xmin,xmax,by=dx)   # 2N+1 dimensional vector
+   # such that x[1] and x[2N+1] correspond to boundaries
+
+   # NN=2*N is set for x=log(S) to fall on the grid
+   NN <- 2*N
+
+   dd <- dt/(dx^2) # delta
+
+   a <- -dd*(sigma^2-dx*(r-sigma^2/2))/2
+   b <- (1+dd*sigma^2)
+   c <- -dd*(sigma^2+dx*(r-sigma^2/2))/2
+
+   Da <- cbind(rbind(0,a*diag(NN-2)),0)
```

```
+  Db <- b*diag(NN-1)
+  Dc <- cbind(0,rbind(c*diag(NN-2),0))
+
+  D <- Da + Db + Dc  # the matrix D
+
+  # Calculate D^(-1)
+  library(MASS) # MASS package is used to
+  # calculate the inverse of the matrix D using ginv().
+  Dinv <- ginv(D)
+
+  # Initial Condition
+  f0 <- pmax(exp(x)-K,0) # pay-off at t=T
+  # 2N-1 dimensional vector of which the points at
+  # boundary f0[1](i=0) and f0[NN+1](i=2N) are removed.
+
+  f <- f0[2:NN]
+
+  # Boundary Condition
+  g <- seq(0,0,l=NN-1) # a sequence from 0 to l=NN-1
+  g[1] <- a*0  # the boundary condition at i=0
+
+  # iteration in the direction of t->0(j->M)
+  for(j in 1:M){
+   # the boundary condition at i=2N
+   g[NN-1] <- c*exp(r*j*dt)*(Smax-K)
+   f <- Dinv%*%(f-g)
+  }
+  # the price of the derivative
+  C0 <- exp(-r*T)*f[N]
+
+  # analytical solution
+  d1 <- (log(S/K) + (r+sigma^2/2)*T)/(sigma*sqrt(T))
+  d2 <- d1 - sigma*sqrt(T)
+
+  C0_A <- S*pnorm(d1) - exp(-r*T)*K*pnorm(d2)
+
+  # results by finite difference method and analytical solution
+  return(c(C0,C0_A))
+ }
```

By the following calculations, we can confirm that the solution by implicit method approaches the analytical solution by increasing the number of grid points (M,N).[4]

```
> PDEim_call(100,110,0.01,0.2,5,10,10)
[1] 15.56797 15.87741
> PDEim_call(100,110,0.01,0.2,5,50,50)
[1] 15.84162 15.87741
> PDEim_call(100,110,0.01,0.2,5,100,100)
[1] 15.85572 15.87741
> PDEim_call(100,110,0.01,0.2,5,500,500)
[1] 15.87356 15.87741
```

We can calculate the price of a call option as a function of the initial underlying asset price (or 'spot') by changing the output of the function as follows

```
return(list(exp(x[2:NN]),exp(-r*T)*f))
```

and setting the following

```
> z <- PDEim_call(100,110,0.01,0.2,5,500,500)
> x <- z[[1]]
> y <- z[[2]]
> plot(x[1:600],y[1:600],xlab="Spot",ylab="Price",type="l")
```

The results are plotted in Figure 9.6.

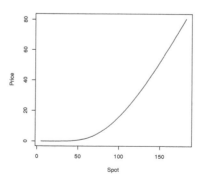

Figure 9.6: The price of a call option as a function of the underlying asset spot price.

---

[4]We have further techniques to improve the accuracy by methods of how we set the time and space grids and the setting of boundary conditions. For example, it is possible to modify the grid size corresponding to the asset price range according to the option maturity.

Since there is an analytical solution for the price of a call option, we can compare the approximated solution by the implicit method with analytical solution. However, many derivatives that we may have interest in, do not necessarily have analytical solutions in general. However, the method for solving partial differential equations applied to derivative pricing is general. We can use modified versions of the above scripts to calculate approximated values of derivative prices which do not necessarily have analytical solutions [WDH93].

In this book, we have introduced various models, methods, and programs to tackle problems in finance using R. Following along with the implementation of the R code introduced should help the understanding of methods and lead to discoveries of new ideas. At the close of this book, we hope that our introduction has been helpful for readers to solve many problems and to encourage readers to progress into more advanced stages of study.

APPENDIX

Appendix A

Optimization with R

CONTENTS

A.1   Multi variate optimization problem

In Section 7.4, we used `optimize()` in the example of an optimization problem for calculating the implied volatility. In this example, there was only 1 unknown variable (the implied volatility). However, more complicated models often require us to determine several variables. Thus, we consider the following problem which might not necessarily be practical if we are focused on implied volatility, but demonstrate a good example of multiple unknown variables in optimization problem. Here, we consider a problem to derive the most appropriate candidates of volatility σ and risk free rate r to the market prices given in Section 7.4. We often consider the factor in such a model that the risk free rate r is known and apply the Black-Scholes formula. However, to show the method of a multi-variable optimization problem, we tackle the problem in which r is also unknown. R has a function `optim()` for this type of optimization. The idea is similar to the 1 dimensional case (of course, `optim()` can be applied to the 1 dimensional case). Note that the function `optim()` will do minimization by default.

First, we define the function to derive the Black-Scholes formula.

```
> black_scholes <- function(S,K,r,sigma,T)
+ {
+   d1 <- (log(S/K) + (r+sigma^2/2)*T)/(sigma*sqrt(T))
```

```
+   d2 <- d1 - sigma*sqrt(T)
+
+   C0 <- S*pnorm(d1) - exp(-r*T)*K*pnorm(d2)
+   return(C0)
+ }
```

We rewrite the error function err1() given in Section 7.4 as err2() for multi-variable optimization as follows:

```
> err2 <- function(S,K,var,T,MktPrice)
+ {
+   # var is to include (r,sigma)
+   tmp <- (MktPrice-black_scholes(S,K,var[1],var[2],T))^2
+
+   return(sum(tmp))
+ }
```

We run the above script by giving option prices for each strike.

```
> K_sample <- c(80,90,100,110,120)
> Mkt_sample <- c(22.75,15.1,8.43,4.72,3.28)
> # to calculate risk free rate and volatility as optimizers,
> # we set their initial value as 0.01 and 0.1, respectively.
> optim(c(0.01,0.1),err2,MktPrice=Mkt_sample,S=100,
+ K=K_sample,T=1)
$par
[1] 0.02190933 0.19890999

$value
[1] 0.9296892

$counts
function gradient
      65       NA

$convergence
[1] 0

$message
NULL
```

This result shows that the optimal risk free rate is 2.2% and the optimal volatility is 19.9%. The error is given by 0.93. We give initial values of unknown variables in the argument of the error function. However, if we choose the initial values inappropriately (too large, or too small, for example), then the solution of the optimization might be a local solution, which is different from the true, global solution. We need to have a good guess of the initial values, and can do this by trial and error.

Next, we discuss the usage of the function `constrOptim()` which is used for the constrained optimization problem. Unlike `optim()` which does not put the constraint for optimization on risk free rate and volatility, we try to put constraints on these variables to have positive values.

```
constrOptim(c(0.01,0.1),err2,ui=rbind(c(1,0),c(0,1)),ci=c(0,0),
method="Nelder-Mead",MktPrice=Mkt_sample,S=100,K=K_sample,T=1)
```

Here, we set the method of optimization to Nelder-Mead method by denoting `method="Nelder-Mead"` (note that the function `optim()` chooses Nelder-Mead method by default). We can choose other methods for optimization, such as `BFGS`, `CG`, `L-BFGS-B`, `SANN`. In practice, we can arbitrarily choose any one of them, because if we inappropriately choose a method, then R gives us a warning. Further, we can set the range of constraints by `ui` and `ci` in `constrOptim()`. By `ui` and `ci`, we can define the following constraint,

$$\text{ui} \times \text{unknowns} - \text{ci} \geq 0$$

In the above example, $\text{ui} = \begin{pmatrix} 1 & 0 \\ 0 & 1 \end{pmatrix}$ and $\text{ci} = (0,0)$. Thus, the solution (r^*, σ^*) by `constrOptim()` satisfies that

$$\begin{pmatrix} 1 & 0 \\ 0 & 1 \end{pmatrix} \begin{pmatrix} r^* \\ \sigma^* \end{pmatrix} - \begin{pmatrix} 0 \\ 0 \end{pmatrix} \geq 0.$$

From this, we can add the constraint that the risk free rate and volatility take positive values. The result of numerical calculation of the above example is given by

```
$par
[1] 0.02191454 0.19889573

$value
[1] 0.9296888

$counts
function gradient
      55       NA

$convergence
[1] 0
```

```
$message
NULL

$outer.iterations
[1] 4

$barrier.value
[1] 6.257486e-05
```

Even if we did not give any constraint, we could get non-negative solutions of risk free rate and volatility. Thus, we can confirm that the solutions with constraints are almost the same to the case without constraints.

A.2   The efficient frontier by optimization problem

In this section, we consider the efficient frontier with a short selling constraint. Let 3 assets exist such that their expected return, volatilities and covariances are given by $\mu_1 = 0.1$, $\mu_2 = 0.05$, $\mu_3 = 0.15$, $\sigma_1 = 0.2$, $\sigma_2 = 0.1$, $\sigma_3 = 0.3$, $\sigma_{1,2} = -0.015$, $\sigma_{13} = 0.01$ and $\sigma_{2,3} = -0.02$.

Denoting the weight of investment as w, the vector of expected returns as μ and variance covariance matrix as V, our problem is described by the minimization problem such that

$$\sigma_p^2 = w'Vw,$$

subject to the short selling constraint, in addition to constraints of the optimization problem introduced in Section 4.5; i.e.,

$$w'1 = 1, \quad w'\mu = \mu_p, \quad w_i \geq 0.$$

Decomposing the equality condition $w'1 = 1$ into 2 inequality conditions $w'1 \geq 1$ and $-w'1 \geq -1$, we can apply the above problem for constrOptim() which only allows inequality conditions. However, constrOptim() requires complicated initial conditions. For such problems, it is suggested to use the function solve.QP(D, d, A, b_0, meq=x) which comes with the package quadprog for Quadratic Programming Problem.[1] The function solve.QP() derives the solution b minimizing $(-d'b + 1/2b'Db)$ with the constraints $A'b \geq b_0$. This function solves the optimization problem with x as an equality condition and the rest as inequality conditions by denoting meq=x (without explicit denotion, it is interpreted as x=0).

---

[1] For this classic problem, see [Dor60][Dor61] and [FW56]. [Lue69] gives us more comprehensive guidance for optimization, including the quadratic programming problem.

Here, let us use the function `solve.QP()`. First, we load and install the package quadprog (see Section 1.9).

```
> library(quadprog)
```

Next, we define the expected return and variance covariance matrix.

```
> # expected returns
> mu <- c(0.1,0.05,0.15)
> # variance covariance matrix
> V <- rbind(c(0.2^2,-0.015,0.01),c(-0.015,0.1^2,-0.02),
+ c(0.01,-0.02,0.3^2))
```

In this example, the argument D is interpreted as the variance-covariance matrix and the argument d is interpreted as 0 vector. We define A in the following script such that the first two columns correspond to equality conditions and the other three columns are inequality conditions.

```
> d <- rep(0,3)
> d
[1] 0 0 0
> tmp <- matrix(0,nrow=3,ncol=3)
> diag(tmp) <- 1
> A <- cbind(rep(1,3),mu,tmp)
> A
        mu
[1,] 1 0.10 1 0 0
[2,] 1 0.05 0 1 0
[3,] 1 0.15 0 0 1
```

Here, we calculate weights of a portfolio minimizing the risk under the constraint that the return is 0.1. In this case, we need to set b_0 as follows:

```
> b0 <- c(1, 0.1, rep(0,3))
> b0
[1] 1.0 0.1 0.0 0.0 0.0
```

The first argument is denoted 1 which means that the sum of weights be 1, the second argument is denoted 0.1 meaning that the return be 0.1, the other three arguments are set 0 meaning each weight is larger than 0. Under these constraints, we solve the optimization problem using `solve.QP()`.

```
> solve.QP(V,d,A,b0,meq=2)
$solution
[1] 0.2916667 0.3541667 0.3541667
```

```
$value
[1] 0.004947917

$unconstrained.solution
[1] 0 0 0

$iterations
[1] 3 0

$Lagrangian
[1] -0.02572917  0.35625000  0.00000000  0.00000000  0.00000000

$iact
[1] 1 2
```

The result shows that each weight should be given around $0.3, 0.35, 0.35$, then the minimum value of $\frac{1}{2}\sigma_p^2$ will be 0.005. Further, we can confirm that the sum of the weights is 1 and the return of the portfolio is 0.1. To plot the efficient frontier, we write the following script and run it and plot the results in Figure A.1 (see also Figure 4.2 to compare with it).

```
> Frontier <- function(n,mu,V){
+   library(quadprog)
+   # mu_p by the increment of 0.001
+   mu_p <- seq(min(mu) + 0.001,max(mu) - 0.001,by=0.001)
+   m <- length(mu_p)
+   sigma_p <- rep(0,m)
+   weight <- matrix(0,nrow=m,ncol=n)
+
+   # d is set as zero vector in this case
+   d <- rep(0,n)
+   tmp <- matrix(0,nrow=n,ncol=n)
+   diag(tmp) <- 1
+   # first two columns of A vector are equality conditions,
+   # the rest three columns are short selling constraints
+   A <- cbind(rep(1,n),mu,tmp)
+
+
+   for(i in 1:m){
+     b0 <- c(1, mu_p[i], rep(0,n))
+     Z <- solve.QP(V,d,A,b0,meq=2)
```

```
+    sigma_p[i] <- sqrt(2*Z$value)
+    weight[i,] <- Z$solution
+  }
+
+  plot(sigma_p,mu_p,xlim=c(0,max(sqrt(diag(V)))),"l")
+
+ }
```

We run the script.

```
> Frontier(3,mu,V)
```

By rewriting the last part of the above script as follows, we can show the weights of each asset which construct the minimum variance for the target return in Figure A.2.

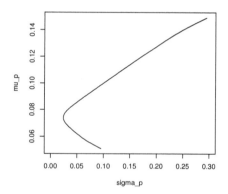

Figure A.1: The efficient frontier with short selling constraint

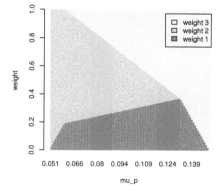

Figure A.2: Weights of each asset

```
list<-paste("weight", 1:n)
barplot(t(weight),names.arg=mu_p,xlab="mu_p",ylab="weight",
border=0,legend=list)
# We delete the frame border by denoting border=0.
# By denoting col=1:3, we can depict coloured plot.
```

In addition, we can also use the function portfolio.optim() which utilizes the function solve.QP() and is included in tseries package. Another type of optimization function in R is uniroot() which searches a root of a function in given interval. Further, the nleqslv package is used for solving non-linear simultaneous equation. Readers should use them as necessary.

Appendix B

Noise Reduction via Kalman Filter

CONTENTS

We have learned about various models; e.g., AR, GARCH, Tree model, Black-Scholes model, etc. Based on a model, we can do different things, for example forecast values of stock prices, construct trading strategies, and so on. Whatever we do, we must start from observation of the data. However, although it may seem intuitive, simple, and straightforward, observation is not so simple. That is because the data observed by us might be distorted with various sources of noise. Even if there exists a law which consistently drives a process of financial instruments, the real-world observed data will likely be contaminated with sources of noises such as climate, disaster, results of elections, wars or something like that. In our life, we can hardly observe any data without noises. Thus, it is important how we remove such noise so that one can estimate the true laws driving processes of financial instruments.

Filtering is a method for removing (ideally) or reducing (practially) the noise present in various data. Filtering is the technology not originally for finance, but rather for engineering like rocket engineering. Imagine a case in which we need to observe the velocity and position of an object with physical laws, but we can only observe the position of the object with noise. How can we remove noise and estimate the true state regarding the velocity and position? This is a typical type of filtering problem. If we replace the position of the object into prices of financial instruments, the technology of filtering can easily be applicable to finance.

In this chapter, we briefly introduce the method called the Kalman filter [KB61] which is one of the most widely applied methods for various fields. The wide applicability of the Kalman filter is partially due to the property based on serial processing. Here, we use the term of serial processing as follows: Let observations be $S_1, \cdots, S_N$. Then, we can calculate the mean m_N by

$$m_N = \frac{S_1 + \cdots + S_N}{N}.$$

When we get a new observation S_{N+1}, the mean m_{N+1} is given by $m_{N+1} = (S_1 + \cdots + S_N + S_{N+1})/(N+1)$, but it is also described by the following form,

$$
\begin{aligned}
m_{N+1} &= \frac{S_1 + \cdots + S_N + S_{N+1}}{N+1} \\
&= \frac{S_1 + \cdots + S_N}{N+1} + \frac{S_{N+1}}{N+1} \\
&= \frac{S_1 + \cdots + S_N}{N} \frac{N}{N+1} + \frac{S_{N+1}}{N+1} \\
&= \frac{N}{N+1} m_N + \frac{1}{N+1} S_{N+1}.
\end{aligned}
$$

This means that we do not need to re-sample all observations $S_1, \cdots, S_N$ and S_{N+1}, but we just need to memorize m_N and calculate the weighted sum of m_N and S_{N+1}. This is a very simple example of serial processing, but the estimation based on the Kalman filter is essentially like this.

By a wide applicability of the Kalman filter, it is used in various fields as one of the most significant technologies for estimation. In addition to the wide applicability, filtering theory, including the Kalman filter, has a deep mathematical background, and many excellent textbooks have been published on the subject (see for example, [BC09, Kal80, LS01a, LS01b] and [Xio08]).

B.1   Introduction to Kalman filter

Let y be the observation and a be the unobserved signal. Our problem is to estimate the signal a_t for any time t. In order to estimate the signal at for any time t, let us calculate expected value conditioned on the observation y_t; i.e.,

$$\hat{a}_{t|t} = \mathbb{E}[a_t|y_t]. \tag{B.1}$$

We also calculate one-step ahead predictor for updating estimation;

$$\hat{a}_{t+1} = \mathbb{E}[a_{t+1}|y_t], \tag{B.2}$$

by using $\hat{a}_{t|t}$ and estimated variance $P_{t|t} = Var(a_t|y_t)$. The filtered estimator at the following period, $\hat{a}_{t+1|t+1} = \mathbb{E}[a_{t+1}|y_{t+1}]$ is calculated by $\hat{a}_{t+1}$ and estimated variance $P_{t+1} = Var(a_{t+1})$. Such serial processing is called the Kalman filter.

More precisely, we consider the following system: Let the signal a be m-dimensional vector and the observation y be d-dimensional vector such that

$$a_{t+1} = d_t + T_t a_t + H_t \eta_t \tag{B.3}$$

$$y_t = c_t + Z_t a_t + G_t \varepsilon_t, \tag{B.4}$$

where η, ε are i.i.d. with $\mathcal{N}(0, I_m)$ and $\mathcal{N}(0, I_d)$ for m and d dimensional identity matrix I_m and I_d, respectively. Further, let parameters be $d_t \in \mathbb{R}^m$, $T_t \in \mathbb{R}^{m \times m}$, $H_t \in \mathbb{R}^{m \times m}$, $c_t \in \mathbb{R}^d$, $Z_t \in \mathbb{R}^{d \times m}$ and $G_t \in \mathbb{R}^{d \times d}$.

We assume that the initial estimates $\hat{a}_0$ and P_0 are given. Using them, we estimate $\hat{a}_{0|0}$ and $P_{0|0}$. For a given $\hat{a}_0$, we can estimate y_0. Indeed, $\hat{y}_0$ is given by $\hat{y}_0 = c_0 + Z_0 \hat{a}_0 + G_0 \varepsilon_0$. The mean and variance of the error $v_0 = y_0 - \hat{y}_0$ is given by

$$\mathbb{E}[v_0] = \mathbb{E}[y_0 - \hat{y}_0] = \mathbb{E}[y_0 - c_0 - Z_0 \hat{a}_0 - G_0 \varepsilon_0] = y_0 - c_0 - Z_0 \hat{a}_0$$

$$F_0 := Var(v_0) = Var(y_0 - c_0 - Z_0 \hat{a}_0 - G_0 \varepsilon_0) = Z_0 P_0 Z_0' + G_0 G_0'$$

$$Cov(a_0, v_0) = Cov(a_0, y_0 - c_0 - Z_0 \hat{a}_0 - G_0 \varepsilon_0) = P_0 Z_0',$$

where we used law of total expectation and independence between a_0 and ε_0.

Using the above, we can calculate $\hat{a}_{0|0}$ and $P_{0|0}$. Note that v_0 is the observation y_0 subtracting the constant $\hat{y}_0$. This means that $\mathbb{E}[\cdot|y_0] = \mathbb{E}[\cdot|v_0]$. Then it follows that

$$\hat{a}_{0|0} = \mathbb{E}[a_0|y_0] = \mathbb{E}[a_0|v_0] = \mathbb{E}[a_0] + Cov(a_0, v_0)Var(v_0)^{-1}v_0$$

$$= \hat{a}_0 + P_0 Z_0' F_0^{-1} v_0 = \hat{a}_0 + K_0 v_0,$$

where $K_0 = P_0 Z_0' F_0^{-1}$.

We also calculate $P_{0|0}$,

$$P_{0|0} = Var(a_0|y_0) = Var(a_0|v_0) = Var(a_0) - Cov(a_0, v_0)^2 Var(v_0)^{-1}$$

$$= P_0 - Z_0 P_0' P_0 Z_0' F_0^{-1} = P_0 - Z_0 P_0' K_0.$$

Using $\hat{a}_{0|0}$ and $P_{0|0}$, we calculate $\hat{a}_1$ and P_1. This is easy because we just use the given system to calculate them; i.e.,

$$\hat{a}_1 = \mathbb{E}[a_1|y_0] = \mathbb{E}[d_0 + T_0 a_0 + H_0 \eta_0|y_0]$$

$$= d_0 + T_0 \mathbb{E}[a_0|y_0] = d_0 + T_0 \hat{a}_{0|0} = d_0 + T_0(\hat{a}_0 + K_0 v_0),$$

and

$$P_{1|0} = Var(a_1|y_0) = Var(d_0 + T_0 a_0 + H_0 \eta_0|y_0)$$

$$= Var(T_0 a_0|y_0) + Var(H_0 \eta_0|y_0)$$

$$= T_0 Var(a_0|y_0) T_0' + H_0 Var(\eta_0|y_0) H_0'$$

$$= T_0 P_{0|0} T_0' + H_0 H_0'.$$

These procedures can be generalized. For a given $\hat{a}_t$ and P_t, we can calculate $\hat{a}_{t|t}$ and $P_{t|t}$ as follows

$$\hat{a}_{t|t} = \hat{a}_t + K_t v_t.$$
$$P_{t|t} = P_t - Z_t P_t' K_t.$$

From them we can also calculate

$$\hat{a}_{t+1} = d_t + T_t \hat{a}_{t|t}$$
$$P_{t+1} = T_t P_{t|t} T_t' + H_t H_t',$$

and we can update the estimate.

Application of Kalman filter

Let us apply the Kalman filter for a system described below

$$a_{t+1} = 0.1 + 0.5 a_t + 0.4 \eta_t,$$
$$y_t = a_t + 0.6 \varepsilon_t,$$

where a_t is the signal and our observation y_t is a_t with noise $0.6 \varepsilon_t$. Here, we try to remove noise from the observation. The system is $d_t = 0.1$, $T_t = 0.5$, $H_t = 0.4$, $c_t = 0$, $Z_t = 1$, $G_t = 0.6$ in (B.3) and (B.4).

We can estimate the signal a by using the Kalman filter according to the procedure discussed above. However, R is equipped with various packages for the Kalman filter. Thus, we will try one of them. Here, we use the FKF package which is very easy for implementation.

After the installation of FKF, we introduce the package.

```
> library(FKF)
```

Further, we set sample numbers, observations and parameters of the Kalman filter.

```
> # parameters
> dt_ <- matrix(0.1) # a matrix corresponding to d_t
> Tt_ <- matrix(0.5) # an array corresponding to T_t
> H_ <- matrix(0.4) # factors of H_t
> HHt_ <- H_%*%t(H_)# an array corresponding to H_t*H_t'
>
> ct_ <- matrix(0) # a matrix corresponding to c_t
> Zt_ <- matrix(1) # an array corresponding to Z_t
> G_ <- matrix(0.6) # factors of G_t
> GGt_ <- G_%*%t(G_) # an array corresponding to G_t*G_t'
>
```

```
> a0_ <- c(0) # a vector giving the initial value
> # of the signal
> P0_ <- matrix(0.001) # a matrix giving the variance of a0
>
> # create data sample
> n_ <- 100 # number of sample (observations)
>
> eta <- rnorm(n_,0,1)
> eps <- rnorm(n_,0,1)
>
> a <- rep(0,n_)
> y <- rep(0,n_)
> a[1] <- dt_[1,1]+H_[1,1]*eta[1]
> y[1] <- a[1]+G_[1,1]*eps[1]
> for(i in 2:n_){
+   a[i] <- dt_[1,1]+Tt_[1,1]*a[i-1]+H_[1,1]*eta[i]
+   y[i] <- a[i]+G_[1,1]*eps[i]
+ }
> yt_ <- rbind(y) # observations
```

Finally, we calculate the Kalman filter using the function `fkf()`.

```
> kalman.obj <- fkf(a0 = a0_,P0 = P0_,dt = dt_, ct = ct_, Tt = Tt_,
+        Zt = Zt_, HHt = HHt_,GGt = GGt_,yt=yt_)
```

Figure B.1 plots the result (see the following script).

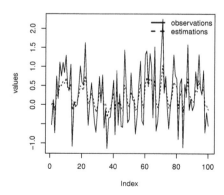

Figure B.1: Original data and smoothing data by the Kalman filter

```
> plot(y,type="l",ylab="values",)
> lines(ts(kalman.obj$att[1,],start=start(y),
+ frequency=frequency(y)),lty=2)
```

```
> legend("topright", c("observations","estimations"),
+ lty=c(1,2),lwd=c(2.5,2.5),bty="n")
```

We can see the signal appear by removing noise from observations.

In the above example, we assume that all parameters of a system are known. However, in general such parameters may not be expected to be given since signal a is unobservable. While, of course, we need to assume parameters or models more or less to analyze a system, the Kalman filter is also useful not only to remove noise but also to find these parameters. In order to do that, we need to use an optimization tool. While we show how to use optimization function optim() in Appendix A, we give an example code with optim() here too.

Let us assume that we do not know H_t and G_t in the above system, and try to estimate these parameters from observable data.

```
> # parameters
> dt_ <- matrix(0.1)
> Tt_ <- matrix(0.5)
> ct_ <- matrix(0)
> Zt_ <- matrix(1)
> a0_ <- c(0)
> P0_ <- matrix(0.001)
>
> # create data sample
> n_ <- 100 # number of sample (observations)
>
> eta <-rnorm(n_,0,1)
> eps <-rnorm(n_,0,1)
>
> a <- rep(0,n_)
> y <- rep(0,n_)
> a[1] <- dt_[1,1]+0.4*eta[1]
> y[1] <- a[1]+0.6*eps[1]
> for(i in 2:n_){
+   a[i] <- dt_[1,1]+Tt_[1,1]*a[i-1]+0.4*eta[i] # set H_=0.4
+   y[i] <- a[i]+0.6*eps[i] # set G_=0.6
+ }
> yt_ <- rbind(y) # observations
>
> # use logLik to calculate log-likelihood
> # use -fkf() to find max log-likelihood since optim() finds
> # minimum.
> maxlog <- function(a0,P0,dt,ct,Tt,Zt,para,yt){
+   -fkf(a0,P0,dt,ct,Tt,Zt,HHt=matrix(para[1]),
+   GGt=matrix(para[2]),
```

```
+   yt)$logLik
+ }
> # use optim to find max log-likelihood (see also Appendix A)
> # we set initial values HHt=0.16,GGt=0.36 since we
> # know the answers
> parafit <- optim(c(HHt=0.16,GGt=0.36),maxlog,a0=a0_,P0=P0_,
+   dt=dt_,ct=ct_,Tt=Tt_,Zt=Zt_,yt=yt_)
> parafit$par
       HHt          GGt
0.1683014 0.3208311
```

B.2   Nonlinear Kalman filter

Systems do not necessarily have a linear form like (B.3) and (B.4). Let's consider a system in a more general form;

$$a_{t+1} = f(a_t, \eta_t), \tag{B.5}$$
$$y_t = g(a_t, \varepsilon_t). \tag{B.6}$$

If functions f, g are linear, we can straightforwardly apply the Kalman filter. However, when the functions have a non-linear form, how do we estimate the signal by the Kalman filter? The following three methods are used: first, the extended Kalman filter (EKF). Second is the unscented Kalman filter (UKF). Third is the particle filter.

The EKF is the method using first order Taylor approximation for f, g. The unscented Kalman filter is also approximation but the approximation is applied for the conditional distribution of the signal, since the filtering theory including the Kalman filter is essentially the estimation of the conditional distribution of the signal on observations. The particle filter is the application of Monte Carlo simulation for filtering.

In this book, we focus on the EKF. Since the EKF adapts Taylor series expansion to linearize a model, first order continuous differentiability of f and g is required. In EKF, model parameters are evaluated with current predicted states at each time step. This process essentially linearizes the non-linear function applying the first order Taylor expansion around the current estimate, i.e., $\hat{a}_t$ and $\eta_t = \varepsilon_t = 0$.

Thus, we calculate the following Jacobian matrix:

$$\tilde{T}_t := \frac{\partial f}{\partial a}(\hat{a}_t, 0), \ \tilde{H}_t := \frac{\partial f}{\partial \eta}(\hat{a}_t, 0),$$
$$\tilde{Z}_t := \frac{\partial g}{\partial a}(\hat{a}_t, 0), \ \tilde{G}_t := \frac{\partial f}{\partial \varepsilon}(\hat{a}_t, 0).$$

Hence, functions f, g are approximated as

$$f(a_t, \eta_t) \approx \tilde{d}_t + \tilde{T}_t a_t + \tilde{H}_t \eta_t,$$
$$g(a_t, \varepsilon_t) \approx \tilde{c}_t + \tilde{Z}_t a_t + \tilde{G}_t \varepsilon_t,$$

where $\tilde{d}_t := f(\hat{a}_t, 0) - \tilde{T}_t \hat{a}_t$ and $\tilde{c}_t := g(\hat{a}_t, 0) - \tilde{Z}_t \hat{a}_t$. Then, the system (B.5) and (B.6) can be written in linear form

$$a_{t+1} \approx \tilde{d}_t + \tilde{T}_t a_t + \tilde{H}_t \eta_t,$$
$$y_t \approx \tilde{c}_t + \tilde{Z}_t a_t + \tilde{G}_t \varepsilon_t.$$

And then, we can apply the Kalman filter to the above model.

Application of EKF

Let us apply the EKF to the following non-linear time series model.

$$a_{t+1} = 0.1 + 0.5 a_t + 0.5 \cos(a_t/5) + 0.4 \eta_t,$$
$$y_t = a_t + 0.1 a_t^2 + 0.6 \varepsilon_t.$$

And then, Jacobian matrix is calculated as

$$\tilde{T}_t = 0.5 - 0.1 \sin(\hat{a}_t/5), \quad \hat{H}_t = 0.4,$$
$$\tilde{Z}_t = 1 + 0.2 \hat{a}_t, \quad \hat{G}_t = 0.6.$$

We can also define $\tilde{d}_t = 0.1 + 0.5 \hat{a}_t + 0.5 \cos(\hat{a}_t/5) - (0.5 - 0.1 \sin(\hat{a}_t/5)) \hat{a}_t$ and $\tilde{c}_t = \hat{a}_t + 0.1 \hat{a}_t^2 - (1 + 0.2 \hat{a}_t) \hat{a}_t$.

We will apply the extended Kalman filter for the above model. The basic idea is simple, because once approximations like $\tilde{T}, \tilde{Z}$ are derived at each step, the other procedures are the same as the ordinary Kalman filter; i.e., we just use FKF.

```
> library(FKF)
> # function f
> f <- function(state_,eta_){
+   0.1 + 0.5*state_ + 0.5*cos(state_/5) + 0.4*eta_
+ }
>
> # Jacobian of f
> T <- function(state_){
+   0.5 - 0.1*sin(state_/5)
+ }
>
> H <- function(state_){
+   0.4
+ }
```

```
>
> func_d <- function(state_){
+   f(state_,0) - matrix(T(state_)*state_)
+ }
>
> # function g
> g <- function(state_,eps_){
+   state_ + 0.1*state_^2 + 0.6*eps_
+ }
>
> # Jacobian of g
> Z <- function(state_){
+   1 + 0.2*state_
+ }
>
> G <- function(state_){
+   0.6
+ }
>
> func_c <- function(state_){
+   g(state_,0) - matrix(Z(state_)*state_)
+ }
>
> # create data sample
> n_ <- 100 # number of sample
> eta <- rnorm(n_,0,1) # n_ random numbers
> eps <- rnorm(n_,0,1) # n_ random numbers
>
> # initial values
> a0 <- c(0) # a vector giving the initial value
> # of the signal
> P0_ <- matrix(0.001) # a matrix giving the variance of a0
>
>
> # signals and observations
> state <- rep(0,n_)
> obs.obj <- rep(0,n_)
>
> state[1] <- f(a0,eta[1])
> obs.obj[1] <- g(state[1],eps[1])
>
> for(i in 2:n_)
+ {
```

```
+   state[i] <- f(state[i-1],eta[i-1])
+   obs.obj[i] <- g(state[i],eps[i])
+ }
>
> at_ <- rep(0,n_) # a priori estimate
> att_ <- rep(0,n_) # a posteriori estimate
>
> at_[1] <- state[1]
> att_[1] <- state[1]
>
> # the object of Kalman filter
> for(i in 2:n_)
+ {
+     # observations
+     yt_ <- matrix(obs.obj[i])
+     tmp.kalman.obj <- fkf(
+       a0 = at_[i-1],
+       P0 = P0_,
+       dt = matrix(func_d(at_[i-1])),
+       ct = matrix(func_c(at_[i-1])),
+       Tt = matrix(T(at_[i-1])),
+       Zt = matrix(Z(at_[i-1])),
+       HHt = H(at_[i-1])%*%H(at_[i-1]),
+       GGt = G(at_[i-1])%*%G(at_[i-1]),
+       yt=yt_)
+
+     # updates of at_, P0_
+     at_[i] <- tmp.kalman.obj$at[1,2]
+     P0_ <- matrix(tmp.kalman.obj$Pt[1,1,2])
+     att_[i] <- tmp.kalman.obj$att[1,1]
+ }
>
>
> plot(obs.obj,ylab="values",type="l")
> lines(ts(g(att_,0),start=start(obs.obj),
+ frequency=frequency(obs.obj)),lty=2)
> legend("topright", c("observations","estimations"),
+ lty=c(1,2), bty="n")
```

Figure B.2 plots the result that represents filtered signals of non-linear model. However, note that the EKF is just first order approximation.

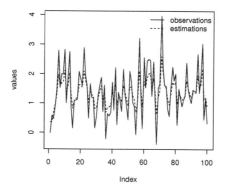

Figure B.2: Extended Kalman filter

We have shown a brief introduction of the Kalman filter in this section. Filtering is a method to eliminate noise from observations. While there are many filtering methods, *the Kalman filter is not just a filter but also a predictor and is applicable to find model parameters too.* Further, the Kalman filter can also be used for nonparametric statistics [CKL97].

Appendix C

The Other References on R

CONTENTS

C.1 Information sources on R

In the final appendix, we mention references on R. Especially in topics on finance, the largest resource for R may be the R-sig-finance mailing list (`https://stat.ethz.ch/pipermail/r-sig-finance/`). The easiest way to find what we are looking for is to google search by `targeted terms + R-sig-finance`. However, this may give us too many search results to find specific information. In such a case, we often use Rseek (`http://www.rseek.org/`) where we can easily find information related to R.

If a reader wants more organized information, he or she should refer to CRAN Task View (`http://cran.r-project.org/web/views/`), where we may find the required information in categories, like "Finance", "Time Series", or "Optimization" and so on.

Further, we can join a famous conference on R; Applied Finance with R where we may see the latest studies on R programming. We can also join a workshop and summer school held by a project called Rmetrics which issues a textbook (`https://www.rmetrics.org/ebooks`) and distributes packages related to finance.

For getting news on R, you may check R-Bloggers (`http://www.r-bloggers.com/`). This source is a blog, and there is a wide variety of information, but it includes a lot of useful information and we often refer to it. Other sources of useful information are the websites Revolutions (`http:/blog.revolutionanalytics.com/`) and Microsoft R Application Network (`https:/mran.microsoft.com/`).

C.2 R package on finance

In this book, we have used only the basic R packages to introduce finance theory. However, there are many R packages available that focus on finance theory. Some good examples are `RquantLib` and `quantmod`.

We have also discussed the estimation of model parameters by using an optimization technique. However, estimation may be difficult in expanded models. For more sophisticated models, the package `yuima` offers us good solutions using R. Indeed, with this package we can calculate even asymptotic expansions and parameter estimation for a jump diffusion model. However, note that this advanced package may not be compatible with older versions of R.

If you are an academic person focused on purely theoretical things, you might be indifferent to the many country-specific holiday calendars. However, it is crucial for practitioners when working with financial data, especially if dealing with different assets traded in different regional markets. The package `timeData` gives us functions in R to extract information on holidays. For example, we can get information on holidays of the New York stock exchange by the function `holidayNYSE()` in this package.

If you have access to a Bloomberg workstation, you can use `RBloomberg` which is a package designed to use data from Bloomberg on R. Note that we need to install the package `RDCOMClient` or `rcom` on your Bloomberg workstation for it to work.

References

[ABR97]   L. Andersen and R. Brotherton-Ratcliffe. The equity option volatility smile: An implicit finite-difference approach. *Journal of Computational Finance*, 1:5–37, 1997.

[Aka74]   H. Akaike. A new look at the statistical model identification. *IEEE Transactions on Automatic Control*, 19:716–723, 1974.

[AL10]   M. Avellaneda and J. Lee. Statistical arbitrage in the US equities market. *Quantitative Finance*, 10:761–782, 2010.

[And98]   J. Andreasen. The pricing of discretely sampled Asian and lookback options: A change of numéraire approach. *Journal of Computational Finance*, 2:5–30, 1998.

[Arr64]   K. Arrow. The role of securities in the optimal allocation of risk bearing. *Review of Financial Studies*, 31:91–96, 1964.

[Bac00]   L. Bachelier. Théorie de la speculation. *Annales scientifiques de l'Ecole Normale Supérieure*, 3:21–86, 1900.

[Bar95]   J. Barraquand. Numerical valuation of high dimensional multivariate european securities. *Management Science*, 41:1882–1891, 1995.

[BBC94]   L. Bouaziz, E. Briys, and M. Crouhy. The pricing of forward-starting Asian options. *Journal of Banking & Finance*, 18:823–839, 1994.

[BBG97]   P. Boyle, M. Broadie, and P. Glasserman. Monte Carlo methods for security pricing. *Journal of Economics Dynamics and Control*, 21:1267–1321, 1997.

[BC09]   A. Bain and D. Crisan. *Fundamentals of Stochastic Filtering.* Springer, New York, 2009.

[BEG89]   P. Boyle, J. Evnine, and S. Gibbs. Numerical evaluation of multivariate contingent claims. *Review of Financial Studies*, 2:241–250, 1989.

[BF06]   D. Brigo and F. Mercurio. *Interest Rate Models - Theory and Practice: With Smile, Inflation and Credit (2nd edition).* Springer, Berlin, 2006.

[Bil86]   P. Billingsley. *Probability and Measure (2nd edition).* John Wiley & Sons, Inc., New York, 1986.

[BJRL15]   G.E.P. Box, G. Jenkins, G.C. Reinsel, and G.M. Ljung. *Time Series Analysis: Forecasting and Control (5th edition).* John Wiley & Sons, Inc., Hoboken, New Jersey, 2015.

[Bla72]   F. Black. Capital market equilibrium with restricted borrowing. *Journal of Business*, 45:444–454, 1972.

[BO10]   M. Bouzoubaa and A. Osseiran. *Exotic Options and Hybrids: A Guide to Structuring, Pricing and Trading.* John Wiley & Sons, Inc., New Delhi, 2010.

[Bol86]   T. Bollerslev. Generalized autoregressive conditional heteroscedasticity. *Journal of Econometrics*, 31:307–327, 1986.

[Boy77]   P. Boyle. Options: a Monte-Carlo approach. *Journal of Financial Economics*, 4:323–338, 1977.

[Boy90]   P. Boyle. Valuation of derivative securities involving several assets using discrete time methods. *Insurance: Mathematics and Economics*, 9:131–139, 1990.

[Bre79]   D. Breeden. An intertemporal asset pricing model with stochastic consumption and investment opportunities. *Journal of Financial Economics*, 7:265–296, 1979.

[BS73]   F. Black and M. Scholes. The pricing of options and corporate liabilities. *Journal of Political Economy*, 81:637–659, 1973.

[BS78]   M.J. Brennan and E.S. Schwartz. Finite difference methods and jump processes arising in the pricing of contingent claims: A synthesis. *Journal of Financial and Quantitative Analysis*, 13:461–474, 1978.

[Car97]   M. Carhart. On persistence in mutual fund performance. *The Journal of Finance*, 52:57–82, 1997.

[CC90]   A. Carverhill and L. Clewlow. Average-rate options. *Risk*, 3:25–29, 1990.

[CFvN50]   J.G. Charney, R. Fjörtoft, and J. von Neumann. Numerical integration of the barotropic vorticity equation. *Tellus*, 2:237–254, 1950.

[CK05]   M. Capiński and E. Kopp. *Measure, Integral and Probability (2nd edition)*. Springer, London, 2005.

[CKL97]   C.S. Chow, R.Z. Khasminskii, and R.S. Liptser. Tracking of a signal and its derivatives in Gaussian white noise. *Stochastic Processes and their Applications*, 69:259–273, 1997.

[CLM97]   J.Y. Campbell, A.W. Lo, and A.C. MacKinlay. *The Econometrics of Financial Markets*. Princeton University Press, Princeton, New Jersey, 1997.

[CN50]   J. Crank and P. Nicolson. A practical method for numerical evaluation of solutions of partial differential equations of the heat-conduction type. *Mathematical Proceedings of the Cambridge Philosophical Society*, 43:50–67, 1950.

[Cou82]   G. Courtadon. A more accurate finite difference approximation for the valuation of options. *Journal of Financial and Quantitative Analysis*, 17:697–703, 1982.

[CRR79]   J. Cox, S. Ross, and M. Rubinstein. Option pricing: A simplified approach. *Journal of Financial Economics*, 7:229–263, 1979.

[CRR86]   N. Chen, R. Roll, and S. Ross. Economic forces and the stock market. *Journal of Business*, 59:383–403, 1986.

[CS87]   J. Campbell and R. Shiller. Cointegration and tests of present value models. *Journal of Political Economy*, 95:1062–1087, 1987.

[CS97]   L. Clewlow and C. Strickland. *Exotic Options: The State of the Art*. Thomson Business Press, London, 1997.

[CV91]   A. Conze and R. Viswanathan. European path-dependent options: The case of geometric averages. *The Journal of Finance*, 46:1893–1907, 1991.

[Deb59]   G. Debreu. *Theory of Value*. John Wiley & Sons, Inc., New York, 1959.

[DF79]   D.A. Dickey and W.A. Fuller. Distribution of the estimators for autoregressive time series with a unit root. *Journal of the American Statistical Association*, 74:427–431, 1979.

[DG95]   D. Duffie and P. Glynn. Efficient monte carlo simulation of security prices. *Annals of Applied Probability*, 5:897–905, 1995.

[DH96]   D. Duffie and M. Huang. Swap rates and credit quality. *Journal of Finance*, 51:921–949, 1996.

[DK94]   E. Derman and I. Kani. Riding on a smile. *Risk*, 7:32–39, 1994.

[DK98]   E. Derman and I. Kani. Stochastic implied trees: Arbitrage pricing with stochastic term and strike structure of volatility. *International Journal of Theoretical and Applied Finance*, 1:61–110, 1998.

[DKC96]   E. Derman, I. Kani, and N. Chriss. Implied trinomial trees of the volatility smile. *Journal of Derivatives*, 3:7–22, 1996.

[Doo42]   J. Doob. *Stochastic Processes*. John Wiley & Sons, Inc., New York, 1942.

[Dor60]   W.S. Dorn. Duality in quadratic programming. *Quarterly Journal of Applied Mathematics*, 18:155–162, 1960.

[Dor61]   W.S. Dorn. Self-dual quadratic programs. *Journal of Society for Industrial and Applied Mathematics*, 9:51–54, 1961.

[DT85]   W. DeBondt and R. Thaler. Does the stock market overreact? *Journal of Finance*, 40:793–805, 1985.

[Dup94]   B. Dupire. Pricing with a smile. *Risk*, 7:18–20, 1994.

[Dur05]   R. Durret. *Probability: Theory and Examples (3rd edition)*. Duxbury Press, Belmont, Canada, 2005.

[EG87]   R.F. Engle and C. Granger. Cointegration and error-correction: Representation, estimation, and testing. *Econometrica*, 55:251–276, 1987.

[Ein05]   A. Einstein. On the movement of small particles suspended in a stationary liquid demanded by the molecular-kinetic theory of heat. *Annalen der Physik*, 17:549–560, 1905.

[ELT11]   E. Ekström, C. Lindberg, and J. Tysk. Optimal liquidation of a pairs trade. In G.D. Nunno and B. Øksendal, editors, *Advanced Mathematical Methods for Finance*, pages 247–255. Springer, Berlin, 2011.

[Eng82]   R.F. Engle. Autoregressive conditional heteroscedasticity with estimates of the variance of U.K. inflation. *Econometrica*, 50:987–1008, 1982.

[EVDHM05] R.J. Elliott, J.M. Van Der Hoek, and W.P. Malcolm. Pairs trading. *Quantitative Finance*, 5:271–276, 2005.

[Fam65] E. Fama. The behavior of stock-market prices. *Journal of Business*, 38:34–105, 1965.

[Fam91] E. Fama. Efficient capital market: II. *Journal of Finance*, 46:1575–1618, 1991.

[FF93] E. Fama and K. French. Common risk factors in the returns on stocks and bonds. *Journal of Financial Economics*, 33:3–56, 1993.

[FF14] E. Fama and K. French. A five-factor asset pricing model. *Journal of Financial Economics*, 116:1–22, 2014.

[Fis96] G. Fishman. *Monte Carlo: Concepts, Algorithms, and Applications*. Springer, New York, 1996.

[Fri00] M. Frittelli. The minimal entropy martingale measure and the valuation problem in incomplete markets. *Mathematical Finance*, 10:39–52, 2000.

[Fri07] C. Fries. *Mathematical Finance: Theory, Modelling and Implementation*. John Wiley & Sons, Inc., Hoboken, New Jersey, 2007.

[FW56] M. Frank and P. Wolfe. An algorithm for quadratic programming. *Naval Research Logistics*, 3:95–110, 1956.

[FY05] J. Fan and Q. Yao. *Nonlinear Time Series*. Springer, New York, 2005.

[Gat06] J. Gatheral. *The Volatility Surface*. John Wiley & Sons, Inc., Hoboken, New Jersey, 2006.

[GL91] C. Gilles and S. LeRoy. On the arbitrage pricing theory. *Economic Theory*, 1:213–230, 1991.

[Gla04] P. Glasserman. *Monte Carlo Methods in Financial Engineering*. Springer, New York, 2004.

[GRS99] S. Gurmu, P. Rilstone, and S. Stern. Semiparametric estimation of count regression models. *Journal of Econometrics*, 88:123–150, 1999.

[GY93] H. Geman and M. Yor. Bessel processes, Asian options and perpetuities. *Mathematical Finance*, 3:349–375, 1993.

[Hes93]   S. Heston. A closed-form solution for options with stochastic volatility, with application to bond and currency options. *Review of Financial Studies*, 6:327–343, 1993.

[HH64]   J. Hammersley and D. Handscomb. *Monte Carlo Methods*. Chapman and Hall, London, 1964.

[HH80]   P. Hall and C.C. Heyde. *Martingale Limit Theory and its Application*. Academic Press, New York, 1980.

[HK79]   J.M. Harrison and D. Kreps. Martingales and arbitrage in multiperiod securities markets. *Journal of Economic Theory*, 20:381–408, 1979.

[HKLW02]   P. Hagan, D. Kumar, A. Lesniewski, and D. Woodward. Managing smile risk. *Wilmott Magazine*, (September):84–108, 2002.

[HP81]   J.M. Harrison and S.R. Pliska. Martingales and stochastic integrals in the theory of continuous trading. *Stochastic Processes and their Applications*, 11:215–260, 1981.

[Hul12]   J. Hull. *Options, Futures, and other Derivatives (8th edition)*. Pearson, Harlow, U.K., 2012.

[HW88]   J. Hull and A. White. The use of the control variate technique in option pricing. *Journal of Financial and Quantitative Analysis*, 23:237–252, 1988.

[HW90]   J. Hull and A. White. Valuing derivative securities using the explicit finite difference method. *Journal of Financial and Quantitative Analysis*, 25:87–100, 1990.

[HW93]   J. Hull and A. White. One-factor interest-rate models and the valuation of interest-rate derivative securities. *Journal of Financial and Quantitative Analysis*, 28:235–254, 1993.

[Itô44]   K. Itô. Stochastic integral. *Proceedings of the Imperial Academy*, 20:519–524, 1944.

[Itô51]   K. Itô. On stochastic differential equations. *Memoirs of the American Mathematical Society*, 4:1–51, 1951.

[JB78]   C.M. Jarque and A.K. Bera. A test for normality of observations and regression residuals. *International Statistical Review*, 55:163–172, 1978.

[Joh88]   S. Johansen. Statistical analysis of cointegration vectors. *Journal of Economic Dynamics and Control*, 12:231–254, 1988.

[Joh91]   S. Johansen. Estimation and hypothesis testing of cointegrated vectors in gaussian VAR models. *Econometrica*, 59:1551–1580, 1991.

[JP04]   J. Jacod and P. Protter. *Probability Essentials*. Springer, Berlin Heidelberg, 2004.

[JT95]   N. Jagadeesh and S. Titman. Overreaction, delayed reaction, and contrarian profits. *Review of Financial Studies*, 8:973–993, 1995.

[JW00]   J. James and N. Webber. *Interest Rates Modelling: Financial Engineering*. John Wiley & Sons, Inc., Chichester, U.K., 2000.

[JW07]   R. Johnson and D. Wichern. *Applied Multivariate Statistical Analysis (5th edition)*. Pearson, Upper Saddle River, New Jersey, 2007.

[Kal80]   G. Kallianpur. *Stochastic Filtering Theory*. Springer, New York, 1980.

[KB61]   R.E. Kalman and R.S. Bucy. New results in linear filtering and prediction theory. *Transaction of the ASME, Series D., Journal of Basic Engineering*, 83:95–108, 1961.

[KS98]   I. Karatzas and S.E. Shreve. *Methods of Mathematical Finance*. Springer, New York, 1998.

[KV90]   A.G.Z. Kemna and C.F. Vorst. A pricing method for options based on average asset-values. *Journal of Banking & Finance*, 14:113–129, 1990.

[KW86]   M. Kalos and P. Whitlock. *Monte Carlo Methods, Volume I: Basics*. John Wiley & Sons, Inc., New York, 1986.

[LB78]   G.M. Ljung and G.E.P. Box. On a measure of a lack of fit in time series models. *Biometrika*, 65:297–303, 1978.

[Leh97]   J. Lehoczky. Simulation methods for option pricing. In M. Dempster and S. Pliska, editors, *Mathematics of Derivative Securities*, pages 133–149. Cambridge University Press, Cambridge, U.K., 1997.

[Lin65a]   J. Lintner. Security prices, risk and maximal gains from diversification. *Journal of Finance*, 20:587–615, 1965.

[Lin65b]   J. Lintner. The valuation of risky assets and the selection of risky investment in stock portfolios and capital budgets. *Review of Economics and Statistics*, 47:13–37, 1965.

[Lit92]   R. Litzenberger. Swaps: Plain and fanciful. *Journal of Finance*, 47:831–850, 1992.

[LLW13]   S. Larsson, C. Lindberg, and M. Warfheimer. Optimal closing of a pair trade with a model containing jumps. *Applications of Mathematics*, 58:249–268, 2013.

[LS01a]   R.S. Liptser and A.N. Shiryaev. *Statistics of Random Processes I (General theory)*. Springer, Berlin, 2001.

[LS01b]   R.S. Liptser and A.N. Shiryaev. *Statistics of Random Processes II (Applications)*. Springer, Berlin, 2001.

[Lue69]   D. Luenberger. *Optimization by Vector Space Methods*. John Wiley & Sons, Inc., New York, 1969.

[LX08]   T.L. Lai and H. Xing. *Statistical Models and Methods for Financial Markets*. Springer, New York, 2008.

[Man63]   B. Mandelbrot. The variation of certain speculative prices. *Journal of Business*, 36:394–419, 1963.

[Mar52]   H.M. Markowitz. Portfolio selection. *Journal of Finance*, 7:77–91, 1952.

[Mer73a]   R. Merton. An intertempral capital asset pricing model. *Econometrica*, 41:867–887, 1973.

[Mer73b]   R. Merton. The theory of rational option pricing. *Bell Journal of Economics and Management Science*, 4:141–183, 1973.

[Mer77]   R. Merton. On the pricing of contingent claims and the Modigliani-Miller theorem. *Journal of Financial Economics*, 5:241–250, 1977.

[MN98]   M. Matsumoto and T. Nishimura. Mersenne Twister: A 623-dimensionally equidistributed uniform pseudorandom number generator. *ACM Transactions on Modeling and Computer Simulation*, 8:3–30, 1998.

[Mos66]   J. Mossin. Equilibrium in a capital asset market. *Econometrica*, 34:768–783, 1966.

[MPV12]   D.C. Mongomery, E.A. Peck, and G.G. Vining. *Introduction to Linear Regression Analysis (5th edition)*. John Wiley & Sons, Inc., Hoboken, New Jersey, 2012.

[MR05]   M. Musiela and M. Rutkowski. *Martingale Methods in Financial Modelling (2nd edition)*. Springer, New York, 2005.

[Nel90]   D.B. Nelson.   Stationarity and persistence in the GARCH(1,1) model. *Econometric Theory*, 6:318–334, 1990.

[NP33]   J. Neyman and E.S. Pearson. On the problem of the most efficient tests of statistical hypotheses. *Philosophical Transactions of the Royal Society A*, 231:694–706, 1933.

[Phi87]   P. Phillips. Time series regression with a unit root. *Econometrica*, 55:277–301, 1987.

[PO90]   P. Phillips and S. Ouliaris. Asymptotic properties of residual based tests for cointegration. *Econometrica*, 58:165–193, 1990.

[PP88]   P. Phillips and P. Perron.   Testing for a unit root in time series regression. *Biometrika*, 75:335–346, 1988.

[PT95]   S. Paskov and J. Traub.   Faster valuation of financial derivatives. *Journal of Portfolio Management*, 22:113–120, 1995.

[PTVF92]   W. Press, S. Teukolsky, W. Vetterling, and B. Flannery. *Numerical recipes in C*. Cambridge University Press, Cambridge, U.K., 1992.

[RB79]   J. Rendleman and B. Bartter. Two-state option pricing. *Journal of Finance*, 34:1093–1110, 1979.

[RM67]   R. Richtmeyer and K. Morton.   *Difference Methods for Initial-Value Problems*. Interscience, New York, 1967.

[Ros76]   S. Ross. The arbitrage theory of capital asset pricing. *The Journal of Economic Theory*, 13:341–360, 1976.

[RS95]   C. Rogers and Z. Shi. The value of an Asian option. *Journal of Applied Probability*, 32:1077–1088, 1995.

[Sha64]   W. F. Sharpe. Capital asset prices: A theory of market equilibrium under conditions of risk. *The Journal of Finance*, 19:425–442, 1964.

[Shr04]   S. Shreve. *Stochastic Calculus for Finance II*.   Springer, New York, 2004.

[Smi85]   G.D. Smith. *Numerical Solution of Partial Differential Equations: Finite Difference Methods (3rd edition)*. Clarendon Press, Oxford, U.K., 1985.

[Tay86]   S.J. Taylor. *Modelling Financial Time Series*. John Wiley & Sons, Inc., New York, 1986.

[TR00]   D. Tavella and C. Randall. *Pricing Financial Instrument: The Finite Difference Method.* John Wiley & Sons, Inc., New York, 2000.

[TW91]   S.M. Turnbull and L.M. Wakeman. A quick algorithm for pricing European average options. *Journal of Financial and Quantitative Analysis*, 26:377–389, 1991.

[Vec1]   J. Večeř. A new PDE approach for pricing arithmetic average Asian options. *Journal of Computational Finance*, 4:105–113, 2001.

[Vec2]   J. Večeř. Unified Asian pricing. *Risk*, 15:113–116, 2002.

[Vor92]   T. Vorst. Prices and hedge ratios of average exchange rate options. *International Review of Financial Analysis*, 1:179–193, 1992.

[VX04]   J. Večeř and M. Xu. Pricing Asian options in a semimartingale model. *Quantitative Finance*, 4:170–175, 2004.

[WDH93]   P. Wilmott, J.N. Dewynne, and S. Howison. *Option Pricing: Mathematical Models and Computations.* Oxford Financial Press, Oxford, U.K., 1993.

[Wie23]   N. Wiener. Differential spaces. *Journal of Mathematical Physics*, 2:131–174, 1923.

[Wil91]   D. Williams. *Probability with Martingales.* Cambridge University Press, Cambridge, U.K., 1991.

[Wil97]   G. Willard. Calculating prices and sensitivities for path-independent derivative securities in multifactor models. *Journal of Derivatives*, 5:45–61, 1997.

[Xio08]   J. Xiong. *An Introduction to Stochastic Filtering Theory.* Oxford University Press, New York, 2008.

[Yos17]   D. Yoshikawa. An entropic approach for pair trading. *Entropy*, 19:320, 2017.

Index

For Product Safety Concerns and Information please contact our EU
representative GPSR@taylorandfrancis.com
Taylor & Francis Verlag GmbH, Kaufingerstraße 24, 80331 München, Germany

www.ingramcontent.com/pod-product-compliance
Ingram Content Group UK Ltd.
Pitfield, Milton Keynes, MK11 3LW, UK
UKHW021616240425
457818UK00018B/590

* 9 7 8 0 3 6 7 7 8 1 4 7 7 *